THE BIRTH OF ROMANCE IN ENGLAND:

THE *ROMANCE OF HORN*
THE *FOLIE TRISTAN*
THE *LAI OF HAVELOC*
AND *AMIS AND AMILUN*

FOUR TWELFTH-CENTURY ROMANCES
IN THE FRENCH OF ENGLAND

MEDIEVAL AND RENAISSANCE
TEXTS AND STUDIES
VOLUME 344

THE FRENCH OF ENGLAND TRANSLATION SERIES
(FRETS)
VOLUME 4

The Birth of Romance in England:

The *Romance of Horn*
The *Folie Tristan*
The *Lai of Haveloc*
and *Amis and Amilun*

Four Twelfth-Century Romances in the French of England

Translated and Introduced by
Judith Weiss

Robinson College Cambridge

FRETS Series Editors
Thelma Fenster and
Jocelyn Wogan-Browne

ACMRS
(Arizona Center for Medieval and Renaissance Studies)
Tempe, Arizona
2009

Published with the assistance of Fordham University.

Library of Congress Cataloging-in-Publication Data
The birth of Romance in England : four twelfth-century romances in the French of England / translated and introduced by Judith Weiss.
    p. cm. -- (Medieval and Renaissance texts and studies ; v. 344) (French of England translation series ; v. 4)
  Includes bibliographical references and index.
  ISBN 978-0-86698-392-1 (alk. paper)
  1. Romances, English. 2. English literature--Middle English, 1100–1500.
I. Weiss, Judith (Judith Elizabeth)
  PR2064.B57 2009
  821'.1--dc22
                                                                    2009052278

∞
This book is made to last.
It is set in Adobe Caslon Pro,
smyth-sewn and printed on acid-free paper
to library specifications.
Printed in the United States of America

For Ursula, Leslie, and Derek

CONTENTS

SERIES EDITORS' PREFACE

The French of England Translation Series (FRETS) has been designed to make available works composed in French in medieval England over the twelfth to fifteenth centuries. Many such texts have been given excellent editions by the Anglo-Norman Text Society, but more general awareness of the large French literary corpus of England (nearly a thousand works) has often fallen between continental French scholarship and scholarship in medieval English. Not only do the works composed in the French of England include many texts that deserve more attention in their own right, but medieval English and Latin literature and historiography need to be studied together with them in the multilingual culture of medieval Britain.

FRETS translations into modern English are offered partly in the hope of encouraging readers to return to the original French texts. The romances composed in French in England in the late twelfth and thirteenth centuries have contributed certain narratives, such as that of Tristan and Isolde, to the enduring canon of Western literature and they also constitute richly varied accounts of insular identities and concerns. But many remain better known through their later medieval English adaptations than in their own first forms. Dr. Judith Weiss has kindly offered to re-issue with FRETS her translations of four twelfth-century romances (*The Romance of Horn, The Folie Tristan, The Lai of Haveloc,* and *Amis and Amilun*), revised for the series and with the new title, *The Birth of Romance in England.* Her pioneering anthology of romances, which first appeared in Everyman's Library in 1992, has lost none of its interest and appeal since, and has indeed become still more important to the informed understanding of insular medieval culture. For its literary distinction, the *Romance of Horn* in particular begs comparison with *Beowulf* and Chrétien de Troyes in the eleventh and twelfth centuries and with *Sir Gawain and the Green Knight* in the fourteenth. Other texts in the anthology include a fascinating shorter narrative concerning the madness of the supreme medieval lover Tristan; an early version in the French of England of *Amis e Amilun,* the famous medieval romance celebrating male friendship; and the *Lai d'Haveloc,* the origin story of a displaced prince and of the Lincolnshire town of Grimsby, separately reworked from Geffrei Gaimar's history of the Danelaw, the *Estoire des Engleis* (itself an early response by French inhabitants of England to its Anglo-Danish past). We are needless to say very grateful to Dr. Weiss for giving FRETS the opportunity of reprinting this essential treasure trove of insular romance.

Dr. Weiss has also made other French narratives from medieval England available under the FRETS/MRTS imprint. She is the first modern English translator of the thirteenth-century romances *Boeve de Hamtoune* and *Gui de Warewic*, which have appeared as FRETS 3. She has also translated Wace's influential twelfth-century *Roman de Brut* into modern English (as *A History of the Britons* [Exeter: Exeter University Press, 1999, 2nd ed. 2002]).

For their support of the French of England Project we are grateful to the National Endowment for the Humanities, USA; to Fordham University, New York; and to the University of York, UK. We thank Dr. Nancy Busch, Associate Vice President for Academic Affairs at Fordham, and Professor Maryanne Kowaleski, Director of the Center for Medieval Studies at Fordham, for their continuing support. We thank Professor Ian Short and the Anglo-Norman Text Society for graciously permitting the reproduction of passages from its editions. We are indebted as always to Professor Robert Bjork, who saw the merit of the FRETS project and placed his confidence in us; and to Roy Rukkila, Todd Halvorsen, and Leslie MacCoull for their care, efficiency, and hard work in producing FRETS volumes.

Thelma Fenster
Professor Emerita,
Department of Modern Languages and Literatures
Fordham University, New York

Jocelyn Wogan-Browne
Professor of Medieval Literature,
Centre for Medieval Studies,
University of York UK

Translator's Preface

The first version of this book grew out of my thesis in 1968 on medieval English romance. In the course of my research, I realised how much English romances owed to their Anglo-Norman predecessors, how fascinating some of those were, and also how little known. There have been many studies on the English *Havelok* and *King Horn* over the last fifty years, but few of them are thoroughly familiar with what is probably the source-material for them in Anglo-Norman. The *Romance of Horn* in particular deserves wider recognition, but the other three romances presented here are also lively and entertaining narratives. With the exception of the Oxford *Folie Tristan*, which has hitherto been translated only into modern French, this is the first time these texts have appeared in translation.

The book was first published by Everyman in 1992, as *The Birth of Romance: An Anthology*. Orion Press has kindly allowed me to re-issue it in the French of England Translation Series, Medieval and Renaissance Texts and Studies, at Arizona State University. MRTS and the FRETS have given me the opportunity to bring translations, introduction, and footnotes up to date, to make corrections where needed, and to refer to more recent scholarly work; for all this I am most grateful to them. I have benefited enormously from the advice and suggestions of the series' editors, Jocelyn Wogan-Browne and Thelma Fenster, who have introduced me to up-to-the-minute research and opened my eyes to new ideas.

My dedication expresses my gratitude to my thesis supervisors, Ursula Dronke, Derek Brewer, and Leslie Topsfield (the latter two are no longer alive). I owe warm thanks to all of the following for their help: Martin Brett, Robin Cormack, Anne Darvall, Jenny Fellows, Richard Gameson, Christopher Page, Erich Poppe, James Simpson, and the Bodleian Library, Oxford, for its permission to reproduce the manuscript illustration on the cover. My greatest debt is, as always, to my husband, for his unstinting help and encouragement.

Abbreviations

ANTS	Anglo-Norman Text Society
CCM	*Cahiers de Civilisation Médiévale*
CFMA	Classiques Français du Moyen Age
EETS	Early English Text Society
ODS	*The Oxford Dictionary of Saints*
SATF	Société des Anciens Textes Français

INTRODUCTION

Romances, long narratives of adventure that combine the real and the improbable, appeared in Britain only a few years after they originated in France. The *romans antiques*, versions of classical stories and texts such as Virgil's *Aeneid*, were written around the 1150s-60s in the Northern French territories belonging to Henry II, king of England.[1] They first ran parallel to, then gradually replaced, the older epic and martial literature of the *chansons de geste* with narratives catering to a newer interest in the individual and his personal fulfilment.[2] Insular romance followed hard on the heels of the *romans antiques*, with Thomas's superb *Romance of Horn*, around 1170. It was written in Anglo-Norman, the insular dialect of French, for the descendants of those barons who had landed with William the Conqueror. These patrons, though they spoke French and had estates the other side of the Channel, often had connections with native English families through intermarriage, and seem to have become increasingly interested in stories of their adopted country.[3]

---

[1] Continental scholars have long claimed that romance's origins lie unequivocally in France, but the situation seems more nuanced than this: it seems that geographically all early romance arises in the territories belonging to the Plantagenet rulers of England and Wales. Indeed, if we take into account the story of Haveloc which begins Gaimar's *Estoire des Engleis*, romance arises in Lincolnshire as early as the late 1130s.

[2] Recent scholarship has sought to challenge older views on the anteriority of epics to romances. Sarah Kay (*The Chansons de Geste in the Age of Romance: Political Fictions* [Oxford: Clarendon Press, 1995], 4–5) and Robert M. Stein (*Reality Fictions: Romance, History, and Governmental Authority 1025–1180* [Notre Dame: University of Notre Dame Press, 2006], 8, 167) have both pointed to the simultaneous composition of many *chansons de geste* and romances in the long twelfth century, and urged a re-evaluation of attitudes towards the two genres. Such a re-evaluation is most welcome, though there is still a significant number of early *chansons de geste* which—until their dating is completely revised—precede the *romans antiques* (*Gormont et Isembard*, *Le Couronnement Louis*, *La Prise d'Orange*, *Mainet*). The wide variation in dating the earliest extant manuscript of *La Chanson de Roland* (between 1130 and 1170) complicates our sense of the date of the original text: see Ian Short, "Literary Culture at the Court of Henry II," in *Henry II: New Interpretations*, ed.Christopher Harper-Bill and Nicholas Vincent (Woodbridge: Boydell Press, 2007), 335–61, at 350.

[3] See Susan Crane, "Anglo-Norman Cultures in England, 1066–1460," in *The Cambridge History of Medieval English Literature*, ed. David Wallace (Cambridge: Cambridge

Three such stories appear in the romances presented here. Only *Amis e Amilun* is linked to the Continent, whereas native traditions have provided us with the tales of Horn, Haveloc, and Tristan. These have unmistakeable connections with insular history, topography, and folk-tale, although these may be difficult to make precise.[4] All of them also show, even at this early date, features characteristic of insular romance, whether in French or English: relatively few marvels, monsters, or signs of the supernatural and relatively little interest in chivalry, *courtoisie,* or passionate love (the *Folie Tristan* is the honourable exception to this last). The four texts fall into two contrasting pairs. *Haveloc* and *Horn* are tales of wrongful dispossession and rightful reinstatement, where the destiny of the hero is linked with that of his land: in that sense, they are political poems.[5] *Tristan* and *Amis e Amilun* are intensely personal tales of love triumphing over every other social bond: in a way, they are socially subversive poems. The genre of romance has from its inception been used to convey political and social attitudes.[6]

The authors of these romances are anonymous, except for Thomas, the poet of *Horn* (not to be confused with the Thomas who wrote one of the Tristan romances, or the Thomas who wrote a romance about Alexander). This earliest of the insular romance poets is also the most sophisticated, using the long Alexandrine line of French epic, divided into units of varying lengths, *laisses,* to create at leisure a rich, elaborate world. His successors employ the more characteristic metre of early romance, octosyllabic couplets, and tell their tales more briskly, but not without subtlety.[7]

University Press, 1999), 35–60, at 40–42, and Rosalind Field, "Romance in England, 1066–1400," in *Cambridge History of Medieval English Literature,* ed. Wallace, 152–76, at 161.

[4] On the historicity and "geographical specificity" of insular romance, in both French and English, see Rosalind Field, "Romance as History, History as Romance," in *Romance in Medieval England,* ed. Maldwyn Mills, Jennifer Fellows, and Carol Meale (Cambridge: D.S. Brewer, 1991), 149–61, at 163, and Laura Ashe, "The Hero and his Realm in Medieval English Romance," in *Boundaries in Medieval Romance,* ed. Neil Cartlidge (Cambridge: D. S. Brewer, 2008), 129–47, at 135. See also Beate Schmolke-Hasselmann, *The Evolution of Arthurian Romance: The Verse Tradition from Chrétien to Froissart,* trans. Margaret and Roger Middleton (Cambridge: Cambridge University Press, 1998), 228–32.

[5] See Susan Crane, *Insular Romance* (Berkeley: University of California Press, 1986), esp. chap. 1.

[6] See Stein, *Reality Fictions*: "even when they are most overtly fantastic, romances are immersed in the contemporary secular world" (8).

[7] Three other Anglo-Norman romances besides *Horn* use *laisses* and either decasyllabics or alexandrines: *Boeve de Haumtone* (c. 1190), *Otinel* (thirteenth century), and Thomas of Kent's *Geste d'Alisaundre* (or *Roman de Toute Chevalerie*) (c. 1175–85). For a general survey of insular romance, see Crane, *Insular Romance*; Field, "Romance in England,

By 1200, the impulse or demand that produced these romances, and seven others, had died away, and by the mid-thirteenth century there were few new productions. It was, however, a time in which English writers were picking up where the francophone writers of England left off, and the same stories emerge reinvigorated in a new language, directed at a new audience with a broader social base. The French romances of England are not only of interest in their own right, however, but they are also essential reading for those studying Middle English romance. Any assessment of medieval English romances is incomplete without a knowledge of the achievements of their Anglo-Norman predecessors.

The *Romance of Horn*

The *Romance of Horn* was written around 1170 by a clerk known only as Thomas. A neglected masterpiece, and incontestably the finest of the romances in the French of England, its underlying folk-tale content received literary shaping at the hands of a sophisticated and erudite poet. We know nothing about where Thomas found this story of an exiled prince who finally regains his lands, except that it is probably one native to Britain: the principal names in it are Scandinavian/Germanic,[8] and in its depiction of repeated raids by heathen invaders on Ireland and the south coast of England, it probably reflects the Viking raids on Britain in the eighth to tenth centuries,[9] even though in the poem these raiders are said to come from Africa.

1066–1400"; and Judith Weiss, "Insular Beginnings: Anglo-Norman Romance," in *A Companion to Romance: From Classical to Contemporary*, ed. Corinne Saunders (Oxford: Blackwell, 2004), 26–44.

[8] See W. H. French, *Essays on King Horn,* Cornell Studies in English 30 (Ithaca and London: Humphrey Milford, 1940), 120 f.; Ernest Langlois, *Table des noms propres dans les romans du Moyen Age* (Poitiers: C.E.S.C.M. Publications, 1962); G. Fellows Jensen, *Scandinavian Names in Lincolnshire and Yorkshire* (Copenhagen: Akademisk Forlag, D.B.K, 1968), xxxvi-vii, 143, 213. No trace of either Horn or Rigmel/Rimenhild/Ragnhildr is found in Scandinavian personal names in Normandy, so they could not have come over with the Conquest: see J. Adigard des Gautries, *Les Noms de Personnes Scandinaves en Normandie, 911–1066* (Lund: C. Bloms boktr., 1954). On the names in the Irish episode being of Germanic, Scandinavian or Old English origin, see J. E. Martin [Weiss], "Studies in Some Early Middle English Romances" (Ph.D. diss., Cambridge University, 1967), 12–14.

[9] For different views on who the Saracens of the story are, see Diane Speed, "The Saracens of *King Horn*," *Speculum* 65 (1990): 564–95; she does not, however, discuss the names in *The Romance of Horn.*

The Poem

Though the *Romance of Horn* owes much to the French *chanson de geste*, and employs its form with skill, it marks rather a transitional stage of writing, containing elements characteristic both of epic and of the romance genre, that developed in England from the mid-twelfth century.[10] Women play a far more important role in romance than in *chanson de geste*, and in the *Romance of Horn* the love of the Breton and Irish princesses for the hero, and the fidelity to Rigmel that causes his two "returns" to Brittany and Suddene to rescue her, are an intrinsic part of the plot. Though Thomas frequently adopts the moralising and misogynistic rhetoric so often used of women by medieval clerks,[11] he also describes women with sympathy and humour. Two episodes stand out here. First, the chess-game between Horn and Lenburc, where the reactions of the Irish princess are portrayed with shrewd psychological insight: Lenburc, whose overtures to Horn have previously been rejected, longs to play chess with him as a move towards greater intimacy, and (with some pathos) does not mind losing to him (*laisses* 133–34). The second impressive episode is when the imperious and passionate Rigmel realises she has been duped by the steward into making love to the wrong man and flies into a rage (*laisse* 45). The scene leading up to this moment, when Rigmel bribes the steward with rich gifts to constrain him to grant her request to see Horn (*laisses* 28–33), is second to none in medieval literature in its lovingly comic portrayal of a man manipulated by a woman into a tight spot through his love of fine possessions. The meticulous attention to the material details of clothes, jewels, and animals here is characteristic of romance narrative[12] but surpasses the achievements of most romances, and appears again in the descriptions of social

---

[10] For further discussion of vernacular literature in twelfth-century Britain, see Short, "Literary Culture," 350–55.

[11] Throughout the poem, the tendency of women to fall in love instantly with the hero is remarked upon as illustrating their hasty succumbing to sexual temptation (see *laisses* 35 and 118). Perhaps the most disturbing occasion, for a modern reader, is when Rigmel's waiting-woman Herselot says she would like to be raped by Horn (*laisse* 49). Though more explicit than the words of many women in romance, this wish is not far from, say, that of Felice's waiting women in *Gui de Warewic* or the advances made by Josiane to the hero in *Boeve de Haumtone* (see *Boeve de Hamtoune and Gui de Warewic: Two Anglo-Norman Romances*, trans. Judith Weiss, FRETS 3 [Tempe: ACMRS, 2008], 99, 103 [*Gui*, vv. 205–46, 568–82], 37–39 [*Boeve*, vv. 450–794], and Judith Weiss, "The Wooing Woman in Anglo-Norman Romance," in *Romance in Medieval England*, ed. Mills, Fellows, and Meale, 149–61). Herselot is perhaps as outspoken as she is because the poet wants to emphasise Horn's beauty and seductive potential, which is nevertheless kept tightly controlled (see *laisse* 63).

[12] On luxurious clothing and what it might say about its wearers, see E. Jane Burns, *Courtly Love Undressed: Reading through Clothes in Medieval French Culture* (Philadelphia: University of Pennsylvania Press, 2002).

activities at the Irish court: games of throwing the stone, chess, and, above all, an astonishingly technical account of harping, "possibly the finest account of accompanied vocal performance anywhere in medieval literature."[13]

While showing such skill in the creation of vivid characters and settings, Thomas also evinces a strong desire for parallelism and interconnection among the incidents and personages of his text,[14] which may detract from verisimilitude but offers a stylized representation of social relations. Not only does he give Aalof a career which replicates that of his son,[15] but he also relates everyone to everybody, amongst Christians and Saracens alike. Horn is a relation of Modin, the bridegroom imposed on Rigmel; the pilgrim who brings news of this is the son of Herland, brought up with Horn; the first Saracen Horn kills is a companion of Rodmund who killed Aalof; the two Saracen princes who attack Ireland are Rodmund's brothers; their champion and nephew Rollac is also the nephew of Rodlac, killed by Aalof. The Christian interconnections may well reflect twelfth-century realities: strong ties were created between young noblemen who were fostered together in royal or baronial households, leading to lasting friendships and military help in later life.[16]

None of these connections, or the previously mentioned episodes, occur in the two other principal English versions of the Horn story,[17] the thirteenth-century *King Horn* and the fourteenth-century *Horn Childe*, both of which appear ultimately to depend on the *Romance of Horn*, though in ways impossible to unravel totally.[18] The bones of the Horn story survive intact, but clad in sparer and simpler dress, which does not (as was once assumed) derive from a more "primitive" form of the tale, but from very different conceptions of it. Beside them, Thomas's version looks ornate: its events carefully plotted and prepared, its actions motivated and explained. The strongly patterned narrative and its intricate detail combine to present us with a vividly realised, complex world and dramatically plausible characters and situations. There is no British narrative of the period in

---

[13] Christopher Page, *Voices and Instruments of the Middle Ages* (London: J. M. Dent, 1987), 4.

[14] On parallelism and symmetry as frequent features of medieval narrative, see William W. Ryding, *Structure in Medieval Narrative* (The Hague: Mouton, 1971), 91–110.

[15] Aalof, born in Suddene, is "found" there, along with Hardré, father of Horn's friend Haderof, by King Silauf, who brings him up. Aalof fights pagans for Silauf, and is accused of an unspecified crime by Denerez, ancestor of Wikele the accuser of Horn.

[16] See chapter 5 of Rebecca Slitt, "Military Friendship: Fostering and Aid in Battle" (Ph.D. diss., Fordham University, 2008). I am grateful to Dr. Slitt for allowing me to use her unpublished work.

[17] There are several versions of a ballad, *Hind Horn*, printed in *The English and Scottish Popular Ballads*, ed. F. J. Child (New York: Dover Publications, 1965), 187–208. There is also a later French version, *Ponthus et la Belle Sidoyne*.

[18] See *Horn Childe and Maiden Rimnild*, ed. Maldwyn Mills (Heidelberg: C. Winter, 1988), 44, 49, 77–78.

English or Anglo-Norman to compare with it, and it is a worthy rival to the con-temporary French *romans antiques*.

Sources and Influences

We know nothing of Thomas's sources. The shorter and simpler form of the late thirteenth-century English *King Horn*, in comparison with the longer and more elaborate Anglo-Norman romance, has been used in the past to construct an "original" Horn story, but this approach is no longer adopted.[19] Thomas himself makes numerous references to sources, some of them written (e.g., *escrit, letre, parchemin*), and gives Horn's father's name as Aalof. This name may, in Thomas's *escrit*, have been taken from the Cornish prince Alef in the *Gesta Herwardi* (end eleventh or early twelfth century),[20] a Latin prose text much influenced by ro-mance material, with close parallels to the first wedding-feast episode in the *Ro-mance of Horn*; it may go even further back, to the kernel of the Horn story. It is certainly probable that the Hereward and Horn stories borrowed from each other over some fifty years.[21]

But Thomas does not make it easy for us to ascertain where his story came from. While suggesting his unquestioned access to both written and oral sourc-es—he remarks on several occasions that he listened to certain narrative de-tails[22]—his account of the previous story of Aalof suggests it is a tale of his own construction rather than an independently-existing, earlier, one. His version of the Horn story has also been elaborated in a way which suggests a poet given to parallelism and duplication (see above). If we bring together the pieces of Aalof's supposed life which Thomas scatters through the first part of the poem, they are

---

[19] See *King Horn*, ed. Rosamund Allen (New York and London: Garland Publish-ing, 1984), 3–8, and R. Allen, "The Date and Provenance of *King Horn*: Some Interim Reassessments," in *Medieval English Studies Presented to George Kane*, ed. E. D. Kennedy, R. Waldron, and J. P. Wittig (Woodbridge: D. S. Brewer, 1988), 99–125, at 122–23. In the light of recent, fuller attention to medieval manuscript culture, copies of texts have ceased to be treated as degenerations from the original text and are treated with more re-spect as contexts for medieval texts, as witnesses to their reception, and as expressions of a textual culture very different from our own (where identical reproduction is assumed as a basic value in a print-based culture).

[20] *De Gestis Herwardi Saxonis*, transcr. and trans. S. H. Miller and W. D. Sweeting, *Fenland Notes and Queries* 3 (1895–1897): 7–72, at 12.

[21] For a full account of these arguments, see Judith Weiss, "Thomas and the Earl: Literary and Historical Contexts for the *Romance of Horn*," in *Tradition and Transforma-tion in Medieval Romance*, ed. Rosalind Field (Cambridge: D. S. Brewer, 1999), 1–13, at 7–13. An *Aelof li bons reis* is referred to by the author of the early thirteenth-century *Waldef*.

[22] For example, *Herlant l'oï nomer* (I heard he was called Herland, 127); *cum l'oï re-cunter* (as I heard tell, 2579).

inconsistent and raise more questions than they answer; they are explicable only as making Aalof's career a duplication of his son's.[23] Thomas, however, is hardly the only twelfth-century poet to invent fake sources while trying to persuade us of his truthfulness and reliability.[24]

Thomas's family may well have come from France,[25] where experience of Viking invasions, and later of encounters with Muslims, was transmuted into battles between Christians and "Saracens" in *chansons de geste*. Thomas was obviously well acquainted with this epic form of narrative: not only does he divide his poem into its characteristic *laisses*, but the masculine and martial ethos of the *chansons de geste* was also congenial to him: the poem has three lengthy battles with the Saracens, which are carefully differentiated to mark stages in Horn's career. Thomas's enthusiasm for the crusading spirit of the *chansons de geste* is such that he imagines his hero as one of a family of dedicated pagan-killers: Horn is the father of Hadermod (who will conquer Africa) and son of Aalof (who died in action against Saracen invaders). The rather abrupt opening of the poem indicates audience knowledge not just of Aalof but of what has happened to Horn and his fifteen companions, presented as hiding from Saracens in a garden, but neither this material nor any narrative about Hadermod, to be composed by Thomas's son "Wilmot" (*Gilemot*), survive. Nor do we know anything about where Thomas got his hero's name, except that its rarity suggests that it goes back to the very beginning of the story. It is inseparably tied to a crucial element in it: the moment when the disguised Horn, at the wedding feast of his sweetheart, makes riddles linking his name with the horn from which he drinks. The name is thus invented to fit the plot and shows that that plot depends on a knowledge of English.[26]

[23] For the details, see Weiss, "Thomas and the Earl," 7. Maldwyn Mills is also sceptical about Thomas's version of the Aalof story: "some of the detail . . . may not actually have been in [the lost] *Aalof at all, but was created, off-the-cuff, to give weight and backing to events in [the Romance of Horn]": *Horn Childe and Maiden Rimnild*, ed. Mills, 61. On Horn, Aalof and "the past endowing the present with its legitimacy," see Laura Ashe, *Fiction and History in England* (Cambridge: Cambridge University Press, 2007), 146.

[24] Compare the other Thomas: *Les Fragments du Roman de Tristan*, ed. Bartina H. Wind (Geneva: Droz, 1960), Douce Fragment, vv. 835–84.

[25] See *The Romance of Horn*, ed. M. K. Pope, Anglo-Norman Texts 9–10, 12–13, 2 vols. (Oxford: Basil Blackwell for ANTS, 1955–1964), 2:122–23 and Alexander Bell's review of vol. 1, *Medium Aevum* 25 (1957): 26–30: "Thomas was perhaps better acquainted with the Continent than with England" (27).

[26] See Morgan Dickson, "Twelfth-Century Insular Narrative: *The Romance of Horn* and Related Texts" (Ph.D. diss., Cambridge University, 1996), chap. 3, and Weiss, "Thomas and the Earl," 9, n. 34: "Dickson assembles evidence to show that in insular texts horns could be used as symbols of aristocratic or royal power."

Style

Thomas's style shows him ably working within the conventions of *chanson de geste* while bringing to it the characteristics of romance. The three long battles with Horn's Saracen enemies are often described in terms of a series of single combats between two opponents, in a formulaic way which can be repetitive and dull in the hands of a lesser poet, but Thomas, like the author of the *Chanson de Roland*, knows how to vary familiar patterns skilfully.[27] The *laisse* form often gives rise to a paratactic style of narrative (that is, the ranging of clauses or phrases one after another without subordination) where actions or speeches are apparently described twice; this enhances the lyrical intensity of certain emotional moments in the poem, notably the death of Egfer (*laisses* 167–68) and Rodmund's recognition of betrayal (*laisses* 223–24). Both these scenes share the heroic ethos of French epic, the first reminiscent of devoted male friendship on the battlefield, the second recalling reluctant Christian admiration and sympathy for a brave Saracen foe. Parataxis is not confined to martial moments, however.[28] Thomas also makes use of a topos familiar in *chanson de geste*, the so-called "epic prayer."[29]

The romance is written in monorhymed alexandrines of varying length with a consistent caesura mid-line.[30] This proves a good vehicle for dialogue. Conversations in martial scenes are well handled and conventional; those in domestic situations are livelier and more entertaining, as in Rigmel's interchanges with her waiting-women (*laisse* 52) and above all at the first wedding feast, in the build-up to Rigmel's recognition of Horn (*laisses* 198–203). This latter episode, and Rigmel's exchanges with Herland, also show Thomas's ability to sustain suspense over a long period.

Author and Date

The little we know of Thomas comes from within his poem and has been admirably investigated by M. K. Pope in her two-volume edition of the poem.[31] From a study of his language, she deduced that the correctness of his French, the

---

[27] See J. Rychner, *La Chanson de Geste: Essai sur l'art épique des jongleurs* (Geneva: Droz, 1955).

[28] It is used to good effect in the scenes in Rigmel's chamber, in *laisses* 43–44, 45–46 and 60–61.

[29] See G. Raynaud de Lage, "L'Inspiration de la prière 'Du plus Grand Péril'," *Romania* 93 (1972): 568–70.

[30] For a full discussion of this, see Pope, *Horn*, 2: 21–27. The alexandrine, so-called because of its association with texts about Alexander, is notionally twelve syllables long but in practice can vary between ten and fourteen syllables. See also T. D. Hemming's discussion of *chanson de geste* versification in his introduction to Frederick Whitehead's edition of *La Chanson de Roland* (London: Bristol Classical Press, 1993), x-xi.

[31] Pope, *Horn*.

patchy Anglo-Norman element in it, and a strong link between its usage and that of both Poitou and the Loire valley identified him as an offspring of immigrant stock from France.[32]

He obviously knew some English, judging by his use of two runic letters in spelling the name *Godswith* (Rigmel's nurse, *laisses* 43–44), his pun on the name Horn (*laisse* 199) and his contemptuous reference to the English oath (*witegod*, "as God is my witness," *laisse* 191) which Anglo-Norman barons would let slip when in their cups. His knowledge of English topography, however, seems slight and general, that of France more specific, and there is some acquaintance with the region round Dublin;[33] he also refers to a former name for Ireland, *Westir* (*laisses* 103, 106), which seems the same as the Norse name (*Vestr*) for the British Isles and Ireland in particular.[34] It is possible Thomas travelled widely; indeed, he may have composed and delivered his poem in Dublin, at Christmas 1171–72, to an audience including Henry II, Richard FitzGilbert, Earl of Clare (known as Strongbow), and other Anglo-Norman barons who had come to Ireland at the request of the king of Leinster.[35] Certainly the addresses to an audience of *seignurs*, and the aristocratic tone of the poem, indicates "a frequenter of baronial and royal halls," as Pope puts it. She dates the work between the mid-twelfth century and "not much later than 1170" (*Horn*, 2: 3, 123–24).

Thomas figures prominently in his own work. Like other insular writers, authors of historiography as well as romance, he is eager to persuade us of his learning and his reliability.[36] Little phrases such as "Herland, I believe" (*laisse* 55), "I know for sure that . . ." (*laisse* 149), and "as the text says" (*laisse* 81) combine to assure us that he is in possession of the facts, whether learned aurally or from reading; "now you shall hear the truth; who says differently is lying" (*laisse* 173) remind us of the other Thomas who wrote about Tristan, who insists on his version of the tale as the correct one—which only makes us more aware of its constructed nature.[37] He frequently admonishes his audience to pay attention, to listen and to be quiet, usually in martial contexts, which reminds us of similar addresses to the *seignurs* in *chansons de geste*.

---

[32] Pope, *Horn*, 2: 122–23; see also her "Notes" and "Titles."

[33] Pope, *Horn*, 2: 4–6; M. Dominica Legge's review of vols. 1 and 2, in *Modern Language Review* 61 (1966): 309–13, at 310.

[34] H. L. D. Ward, *A Catalogue of Romances in the Department of Manuscripts in the British Museum*, 2 vols. (London: Printed by the Trustees of the British Museum, 1883–1893).

[35] Legge first advanced this theory, which seems persuasive. See M. Dominica Legge, "The Influence of Patronage on Form in Medieval French Literature," in *Stil- und Formprobleme in der Literatur*, ed. Paul Böckmann (Heidelberg: C. Winter, 1959), 136–41, at 140, and Weiss, "Thomas and the Earl," 1–7.

[36] See Weiss, "Insular Beginnings," 31.

[37] See above, n. 24.

We know that Thomas represents himself as elderly: he does not want to die without telling the story of Horn, and he hopes his son Willemot, whose abilities he advertises, will continue his work. He is clearly well-educated, with an extensive knowledge of the Bible, and he imbues his version of the Horn story with a strong religious colouring.[38] He appears to have been a fully trained harpist, and his wide range of vocabulary includes musical terms used as figures of speech.[39] His detailed acquaintance with, in particular, the terminology of architecture, war, and games is demonstrated in a section of Pope's introduction to vol. 2 of her edition (110–18).

The Text and Its Translation

The poem survives in substantial length in three manuscripts: "O," Oxford, Bodleian Library, MS Douce 132; "C," Cambridge, University Library, MS. Ff.6.17; "H," London, British Library, MS Harleian 527; and in the fragments of two more (F1 and F2, Cambridge, University Library MSS Addit. 4407 and 4470 respectively).

The thirteenth-century C, which lacks beginning and ending, contains 4519 lines of *Horn*; it also contains a Latin treatise on temperance in a fifteenth-century hand. O, also thirteenth-century, contains the beginning and ending but has a large gap between 2391 and 4586; it numbers 3042 lines. It contains, besides *Horn*, Grosseteste's *Le Chasteau d'Amour*, Marie de France's *Fables*, and an illustrated Bestiary in French, but it was once bound with a larger manuscript, now Oxford, Bodleian Library, MS Douce 137, mostly a collection of legal documents assembled in the mid-thirteenth century. The list of contents of Douce 132 supplies a title for *Horn*: *De Horn bono milite* (about Horn the good soldier), which words are also written just above the first line of the poem, with *Horn le bon cheualer* (Horn the good knight) written higher up on the page. H, from three manuscripts bound together, has 2761 lines of *Horn*, and lacks beginning and ending; it begins at 1455 and ends at 4234. Besides *Horn* it contains *Gui de Bourgogne* and a *Historia Alexandri Regis Macedonum*, a collection of Latin moral precepts, and two works by Isidore of Seville. It too has been dated to the thirteenth century. Of the two Cambridge fragments, Additional 4407 (F1) contains only 21 lines; it dates from the end of the thirteenth century. Additional 4470 (F2) dates from the early fourteenth and has 238 lines. F2 and O are the only manuscripts to preserve the end of the poem. In all the manuscripts *Horn* is in Anglo-Norman.[40]

---

[38] On *Horn*'s "Christian narrative," see Ashe, *Fiction and History*, 147–50.

[39] Pope, *Horn*, 2: 2, 12. Page thinks the *lai* perfomed by Lenburc and Horn is "an important witness to performing techniques"; see *Voices and Instruments*, 92–107.

[40] See Pope, *Horn*, 1: ix–xii; Rudolf Brede, "Ueber die Handschriften der Chanson de Horn," *Ausgaben und Abhandlungen aus dem Gebiete der Romanischen Philologie* 4 (1883):

Pope established that O, H, and the fragments all went back to Y, a hypothetical source which was based on a versifier's memory of the poem. The unusually careful copyist of C had slightly remodelled the poem at the start of the thirteenth century, correcting and updating it.[41] C is the longest and the best manuscript so it is this that Pope edits, supplying its missing beginning and end from O. I have used her version in almost all cases and am immensely indebted to her scrupulous and learned edition, a model of its kind, without which this translation would hardly have been possible. But occasionally I have ventured to select manuscript readings of a passage other than hers when I thought they fitted the context and tone better,[42] and several times I prefer to translate differently from the suggestions in her Glossary or Notes,[43] helped by information in the Anglo-Norman Dictionary. Any inadvertent mistakes in such translations are, of course, entirely my responsibility.

The language and style of the romance offer a translator of today particular problems, and in resolving them I have had occasionally to depart from fidelity to the text. Medieval narrative changed from past to present tense and back more frequently than we are used to, and I have thus set the whole poem in the past tense (as I have also done with the three other romances in this volume), no doubt sometimes sacrificing dramatic immediacy in the process. It is, again, common to find in both French and English medieval literature a certain redundancy of description—two similar words instead of one (*dit e mustrez; pris e los;* etc.) and ubiquitous superlatives (*mult, bien, grant, forment*)—which I have not always faithfully reproduced. There were many more, carefully graded, modes of address than there are today,[44] and these, if exactly rendered, risk sounding strange: *beaus*

175–254; Cyril Ernest Wright, *Fontes Harleiani* (London: Trustees of the British Museum, 1972), 76; Ward, *Catalogue of Romances*, 468; *Gui de Bourgogne*, ed. F. Guessard and H. Michelant (Paris: A. Franck, 1859), who date the Harley manuscript; and E. G. W. Braunholtz, "Cambridge Fragments of the Anglo-Norman 'Roman de Horn'," *Modern Language Review* 16 (1921): 23–33.

[41] See Pope, *Horn,*1: ix–xvii, xlv, lv–lvii.

[42] E.g., *laisse* 45, v. 877: O manuscript *jaial* (prostitute: Pope, *Horn*, 1: xxxix, notes interestingly that manuscript C tends to tone down crudities of expression for "a more refined audience"; *laisse* 135, v. 2789): H manuscript, *Se nus le peussum oir cum sereit escuté* (if we could only hear it, how we should listen to it!); *laisse* 171, v. 3558: H manuscript, *Ki eurent receu icel damage mortal* (who had received their fatal injuries).

[43] E.g., *laisse* 135, v. 2782, *bien noté*: I have translated this as "highly regarded" instead of "well played/accompanied"; 158, v. 3309: *si.t parras em praele*: I have regarded this as a scribal slip for *paieras*, "you will pay for it"; 152, v. 3165: *forment hastez*, an ambiguous phrase which Pope prefers to translate as "overhasty"; I prefer her first suggestion, "hard pressed" (Pope, *Horn*, 2: 159).

[44] See M. K. Pope, "Titles of Respect in the *Romance of Horn*," in *Studies in Romance Philology and French Literature Presented to John Orr* (Manchester: Manchester University Press, 1953), 226–32.

amis ("fair friend") and *bele* ("lovely one") are the commonest. I have taken a few liberties with these. *Witegod* and the pun on *corn*/Horn posed real problems: the latter because a pun is lost in translation, the former because it is impossible to find a modern oath that adequately renders both the religious reference and the change into a language obviously regarded as inferior. Finally, descriptive epithets, applied constantly to the main protagonists — Horn, *le meschin/l'enperial/ od la face loée;* Rigmel, *l'onurée/od le vis coluré/la bele od le cler vis* — tend to sound odd, however translated and positioned. They are too notable a feature of the style, however, to be jettisoned, especially when they are used to fine ironical effect: the unwitting palmer describes Rigmel, about to be forcibly wed to Modin, as *al vis riaunt* ("with a smiling face").

 In her edition of *Horn* Pope has sequentially numbered the *laisses* into which the poem is divided. I have retained this numbering, and also supplied line references (as in my translation of the other three romances).

The *Folie Tristan*

The story of Tristan has always enjoyed huge popularity, from its earliest appearances in twelfth-century literature, when it was the object of constant allusions, rebuttals, and imitations, to the nineteenth century, when it was celebrated in the music of Wagner, and even to the present day, when it has given rise to many recastings and a veritable industry of criticism.[45] Its success lies in its combination of certain potent factors: it is a story of love and death, sex and suffering, where the adulterous lovers are innocent, because they are compelled to love each other, yet responsible, in that they choose constantly to confront the accepted social norms. The Celtic origins and locations of the tale have provided an extra attraction from the outset, purveying the twelfth, no less than the nineteenth, century with an irresistible image of a wilder, stranger, and more mysterious civilization.

 On precisely what these Celtic origins were, much ink has flowed from the nineteenth century on, but the current opinion seems to be that the story comes from Cornwall. Cornwall is the setting for most of the action in all literary versions of Tristan's tale, Tintagel is the seat for Mark's court, and Mark is said to be king of Cornwall.[46] Beroul's twelfth-century poem has close and detailed reference to place-names in Cornwall, and there are also Cornish references in Eil-

---

 [45] See the introduction and various articles in Joan Grimbert, ed., *Tristan and Isolde: A Casebook*, Arthurian Characters and Themes 2, Garland Reference Library of the Humanities 1514 (New York and London: Garland Publishing, 1995).

 [46] In the poems of Beroul and Eilhart. In the poems of Gottfried and the *Saga*, Mark is king of both Cornwall and England, information probably also once contained in Thomas's fragmentary poem.

hart's *Tristrant* and one of the two poems called *Folies Tristan*. Moreover, there appear to be some early (sixth- and tenth-century) topographical references to Tristan and Iseut in Cornwall.[47] Later episodes and motifs accrued to the tale from the "Celtic commonwealth"[48] of Brittany, Ireland, and Wales.

Seignurs, cest cunte est mult divers ("My lords, this tale is very varied") wrote Thomas in his account of Tristan, which has unfortunately survived only in fragments, but was much imitated in his day and notably (for our purposes) by the poet of the Anglo-Norman *Folie* (the *Folie Oxford*). His words point to a problem which has exercised Tristan scholarship for a hundred years: that of finding the "original" Tristan story, of guessing, through the remaining, divergent, versions of it, at the supposedly perfect and unspoilt whole it must once have been.[49] Nowadays, we are more inclined to accept that if the earliest poets to use

---

The following are the principal twelfth- and thirteenth-century texts (and their editions) of the Tristan story to which I shall refer, in addition to the two *Folies Tristan*:

Beroul, *The Romance of Tristran*, ed. A. Ewert, vol. 1 (Oxford: Basil Blackwell, 1939). Continental French, probably Norman. Dated c. 1175–1200. Incomplete.

Eilhart von Oberg, *Tristrant und Isalde*, ed. Danielle Buschinger and Wolfgang Spiewok (Greifswald: Reineke-Verlag, 1993). German. Dated second half of the twelfth century. Complete.

Thomas, *Les Fragments du Roman de Tristan*, ed. Bartina H. Wind (Geneva: Droz, 1960). Anglo-Norman. Dated between 1150 and c. 1175. Incomplete.

Gottfried von Strassburg, *Tristan*, ed. Peter Ganz (Wiesbaden: Brockhaus, 1978). German. Dated 1200–20. Incomplete.

Friar Robert, *Tristramssaga*, ed. Gisli Brynjulfson (Copenhagen: Thieles bogtr., 1878). Norwegian. Dated 1226. Complete.

Sir Tristrem, ed. C. P. McNeill, Scottish Text Society Publications 8 (Edinburgh: Printed for the Scottish Text Society by W. Blackwood and Sons, 1886). English. Late thirteenth century. Incomplete.

[47] O. J. Padel, "The Cornish Background of the Tristan Stories," *Cambridge Medieval Celtic Studies* 1 (1981): 53–80, and André de Mandach, "Le Berceau des amours splendides de Tristan et Iseut," in *La Légende de Tristan au Moyen Âge*, ed. Danielle Buschinger, Göppinger Arbeiten zur Germanistik 355 (Göppingen: Kümmerle, 1982), 7–25. Padel also points to what he sees as an "historical aspect" of the Tristan story, namely Cornwall raided from, and paying tribute to, Ireland, a situation common in western Britain from the third to the fourth centuries. See, for Welsh evidence of this, L. Alcock, *Dinas Powys* (Cardiff: University of Wales Press, 1963), 57 and W. Davies, *Wales in the Early Middle Ages* (Leicester: Leicester University Press, 1982), 87–88. Rachel Bromwich now shares many, if not all, of Padel's views on origins: "Tristan of the Welsh," in *The Arthur of the Welsh*, ed. eadem, A. O. H. Jarman, and Brynley F. Roberts (Cardiff: University of Wales Press, 1991), 209–28.

[48] De Mandach, "Berceau," 25.

[49] The most famous scholar to attempt this was Joseph Bédier, who reconstructed the rest of Thomas's poem by adding to it episodes from those poems (like those of

it—Thomas, Beroul, Eilhart—differ markedly from each other, it is not only because they adapted rather than merely transmitted it, but because, almost from its inception, it existed in many different and competing forms, both oral and written.[50] These allowed writers to adopt, reject, or invent whatever episodes and motifs suited their own conception of the story: in this they possessed considerable narrative freedom,[51] which they applied in particular to the second half of the story, when Iseut arrives in Cornwall as the bride of King Mark.

The two *Folies Tristan,* one Continental, the other in the French of England,[52] belong to this second half, and in particular to the period when, exiled from court because of his love for the queen, Tristan makes clandestine visits under numerous disguises, to see her and, if possible, sleep with her. The tradition of

---

Gottfried and Friar Robert) which had derived their material from him. He then deduced the substance of the original *estoire* or archetype by comparing this reconstruction with the poems of Eilhart, Beroul, and the thirteenth-century *Prose Tristan.* See Joseph Bédier, *Le Roman de Tristan par Thomas,* 2 vols. (Paris: Firmin Didot, 1902–1905). Though influential for more than fifty years, this method always seemed risky, shaped as it was by Bédier's own tastes and the use of some dubious material. See Renée L. Curtis, *Tristan Studies* (Munich: William Fink, 1969), 51–65; Beroul, *Tristran,* ed. Ewert, 2:40–42; Rosemary Picozzi, *A History of Tristan Scholarship,* Canadian Studies in German Language and Literature 5 (Berne and Frankfurt: Herbert Lang, 1971), 40–49; Jean-Charles Huchet, "Le Mythe du Tristan primitif et les *Folies Tristan,*" in *Tristan et Iseut, mythe européen et mondial,* ed. Danielle Buschinger, Göppinger Arbeiten zur Germanistik 474 (Göppingen: Kümmerle, 1987), 139–50. The risks inherent in Bédier's method appeared when new Tristan material came to light, as in the discovery reported by Michael Benskin, Tony Hunt, and Ian Short, "Un nouveau fragment du *Tristan* de Thomas," *Romania* 113 (1992–1995): 289–319.

[50] Eilhart, *Tristrant,* xii–xiv; Merritt R. Blakeslee, *Love's Masks,* Arthurian Studies 15 (Cambridge: D. S. Brewer, 1989), 9; Huchet, "Mythe," 143. All these critics recall the numerous allusions in Thomas, Beroul, Eilhart, and Gottfried to various Tristan stories in circulation; Huchet also usefully reminds us of the twelfth- and thirteenth-century habit of citing *fictional* sources!

[51] Thomas, *Tristan,* vv. 1835–84 (Douce Fragment); Bédier, *Roman de Tristan,* 1:377, n. to vv. 2125–56; 2:301–4; Douglas Kelly, "La vérité tristanienne: quelques points de repère dans les romans," in *Tristan et Iseut, mythe européen,* 168–80, at 172–74.

[52] *La Folie Tristan de Berne* is usually dated to the end of the twelfth or beginning of the thirteenth century, *La Folie Tristan d'Oxford* to c. 1175–1200. For editions, see *Les Deux Poèmes de la Folie Tristan,* ed. J. Bedier (Paris: Firmin-Didot, 1907); *La Folie Tristan d'Oxford,* ed. E. Hoepffner (Paris: Les Belles Lettres, 1943); *La Folie Tristan de Berne,* ed. E. Hoepffner (Paris: Les Belles Lettres, 1949); *Le Tristan en Vers,* ed. J.-C. Payen (Paris: Garnier, 1974); *Les Deux Poèmes de la Folie Tristan,* ed. Félix Lecoy, CFMA (Paris: Champion, 1994); *The Anglo-Norman Folie Tristan,* ed. Ian Short, ANTS Plain Texts Series 10 (London: ANTS, 1993); and *Le Roman de Tristan par Thomas suivi de La Folie Tristan de Berne et La Folie Tristan d'Oxford,* trans. and intro. Emmanuèle Baumgartner and Ian Short (Paris: Champion, 2003).

these "returns," couched in episodic poems, seems to be a very old one,[53] and in the twelfth century it appears in two other short texts in the French of England, beside the *Folies*: the *Donnei des Amants* and the much better known lay of *Chevrefoil* by Marie de France. The "returns" occur within the romances too: in Beroul, Tristan appears as a leper, to carry the queen over a ford; in Thomas he comes back as a leper and as a penitent, in Eilhart and in the later Prose *Tristan* (in Paris, Bibliothèque Nationale, MS fr. 103) as a fool. The return of the disguised hero to see his mistress or wife is, of course, a theme going back to the story of Odysseus (of which we are especially reminded, in the *Folie Oxford*, by the dog Husdent and his rapturous recognition of his master), and it seems to have been popular in twelfth-century romance: the two returns of Horn to Rigmel are another example of it.[54] It is difficult to ascertain whether the oldest form of the Tristan story circulated in episodic form, or if poets like Marie and the writers of the *Folies* detached the "returns" from an already existing whole text.[55]

Hunters for origins and archetypes have found the *Folies* useful for their brief recapitulation of most of the important episodes in the story. Recollecting these aloud is the way the disguised Tristan attempts to reveal his identity to a sceptical Iseut. The structure of both *Folies* is that of a *mise en abyme*: tales within a tale.[56] The poems contain a range of previous incidents, originally widely scattered in time and space, now recalled within the confines of Mark's palace and the space of a single day: they are simultaneously episodic and concentrated. Each *Folie* exercises the narrative freedom to order and select incidents differently, but both successfully exploit certain key themes in the Tristan story, which are sometimes only embryonic in the romances. The lovers suffer, physically and morally, as much in each other's presence as apart, from a passion viewed as a kind of madness (*folie*);[57] Tristan, in adopting the disguise of a fool or madman

---

[53] Blakeslee, *Masks*, 9, citing Bromwich, "Tristan of the Welsh," 33–35, on the (perhaps) eleventh-century Welsh triad of the "Three Mighty Swineherds"; the tryst arranged between Drystan and Essylt, however, need not rank as a "return" from anywhere but could resemble the meeting in the orchard at court in the Tristan romances.

[54] Tristan's return as a leper in Thomas' *Tristan* has similarities with the first return of Horn, as a penitent (the disguise Tristan adopts for his second return). In Thomas this return doesn't "work" because Brengain prevents the lovers communicating, in particular by stopping Iseut from throwing her gold ring into the *hanap* (goblet) Tristan has brought as a token of recognition (vv. 547–48, Douce); compare the ring and drinking-horn scene in *Horn (laisses* 198–201). *Amis e Amilun* has an interesting variant on the theme: one friend, a real, not disguised, leper, reveals himself to the beloved other by a *hanap*.

[55] Baumgartner and Short, *Roman de Tristan*, 285–86.

[56] See Jacqueline T. Schaefer, "Specularity in the Mediaeval *Folie Tristan* Poems or Madness as Metadiscourse," *Neophilologus* 77 (1993): 355–68, at 356.

[57] Love which makes the lover go mad is a recurrent theme in twelfth-century romance. See J.-C. Payen, "Tristan, l'*Amans-Amens* et le masque dans les *Folies*," in *La Légende de Tristan*, 61–68; Mary Frances Wack, *Lovesickness in the Middle Ages* (Philadelphia:

(*fol* means both), is thus, like Hamlet, only in part feigning a role he finds easy to play. The degradation to which love subjects the lovers is evoked, not just by recalled incidents like the flour and the bloody bed, but much more powerfully by the rough, coarse appearance and manners of the fool as social outcast. Yet the *Folies* also draw upon the paradoxical truth of the fool possessing more wisdom than the sane and being privileged to utter this, however obscurely, in the highest company.[58] The fool may be the real wise man, purveying truths which are hidden to the eyes and ears of the sane — an idea proverbially expressed in the *Folie Oxford: Tels me tendra pur asoté / Ke plus de lu serai sené* ("I'll be wiser than the man who considers me stupid," vv. 185–86).

The Poem

The *Folie Oxford* (like the shorter *Folie Berne)* assumes an audience already fully acquainted with the Tristan story and so begins *in medias res*: it does not need to explain its hero, his "land," or the reasons for his suffering. The love-suffering itself, because of its intrinsic importance in romance, is the most weighty of these reasons and is extended for twenty-four lines. The opening section, with its mixture of brevity and amplitude, characterises the poem as a whole: it proceeds mostly at a brisk pace, recalling many incidents but pausing over very few of them, lingering over their emotional impact rather than their details. And even before these recollections in the central court scene get under way, the poem pauses over three entirely fanciful creations: the beautiful, magical castle of Tintagel which, twice a year, "so the peasants say," disappears — a setting of mystery and unreality for Tristan's meeting with Iseut; the fantastic birth and upbringing of Tristan-as-fool, child of a whale, suckled by a tigress;[59] and the sky-palace of glass and crystal to which the fool proposes to take the queen.[60] The lyrical expansiveness of these flights of imagination[61] contrasts shockingly with the rapid and brutal

---

University of Pennsylvania Press, 1990); and Sylvia Huot, *Madness in Medieval French Literature* (Oxford: Oxford University Press, 2003), chap. 5; see also Huot's remarks on lovers like Tristan and Lancelot being both "sublime and abject," 38–39.

[58] See P. Ménard, "Les Fous dans la société médiévale," *Romania* 98 (1977): 433–59.

[59] Payen sees in this account of Tristan's origin a symbolic reference to his precarious childhood. See Payen, "L'Amans-Amens," 62 and also Schaefer, "Specularity," 358. The tigress allusion is to Virgil, *Aeneid*, 4.367.

[60] A fantasy expanded from vv. 166–69 in the *Folie Berne.*

[61] See also the bizarre "hunting" of the fool which, departing from a truth (Tristan as skilled hunter), expands into a fictional and absurd world where goshawks catch wolves and falcons, deer and wildcat (vv. 505–14). Blakeslee thinks the series of references to hunting in the *Folie Oxford* is an extended metaphor for the lovers' attempts to be reconciled in love (*Masks*, 45).

transformation of Tristan into a persecuted madman, hooted at, belaboured, returning with a vengeance the violence to which he is subjected.

The briskness of the narrative also enhances the brief, but arresting, glimpses into the three main characters. The figure of Tristan in twelfth-century literature is a most uncourtly one.[62] Though he is accomplished in all aristocratic pursuits, his knightly prowess or moral nobility receive less attention than his daring and cunning. In this poem there is a multiplicity of terms emphasising these qualities,[63] and there is also a certain savagery about his determination to inflict as much suffering on Iseut, through his "playing the fool," as she has caused him. The licence traditionally accorded the fool permits Tristan to alternate his lyrical flights of fancy with barbed remarks and crude allusions, as when he recalls that the mission of his second voyage to Ireland was to acquire Iseut "for the king's use" (v. 401). Nor is Tristan the only figure capable of cruelty. Mark's character is ambivalently drawn as either stupidly unaware of the identity of the fool and amused, when he should be alarmed, at his remarks, or aware of Iseut's suffering from the "folly" and happy to encourage and prolong it (vv. 381–86).[64]

Iseut herself is in agony which she betrays by abrupt movements, sweating, changes of colour, and abusive speech, but she gives as good as she gets when she humiliates the fool by shrinking from his embrace in disgust (vv. 679–86). One of the master strokes of the *Folie Oxford* is to prolong the tension and suspense of her failure to recognise Tristan until the moment when she believes him dead.[65] At last she is forced to express her love for him—the desired climax of the whole episode. But that love is inextricably connected with death, as indeed the opening of the poem made clear.

The complicity of the audience is an important part of the *Folie Oxford*. We supply the background and missing information in this summary account of the Tristan story and, unlike the fictional audience of Mark and his courtiers, we are in the know, alert to the truths the fool purveys, wise when they are *foles*. This complicity also characterises the *Folie Berne*. Both poems provided the medieval

---

[62] On the "courtly" and "popular" versions of the Tristan story, see J. Frappier, "Structure et sens du Tristan: version commune, version courtoise," *Cahiers de Civilisation Médiévale* 6 (1963): 255–80; he saw Thomas's version as adapting the story to fit conceptions of *fine amor* (259).

[63] Rosanna Brusegan, "La Folie de Tristan: de la loge du Morrois au palais de verre," in *La Légende de Tristan*, 49–59, at 50.

[64] In the *Folie Berne*, he has a moment of distinct unease: *Lai or huimais ester tes gas* (now stop your jokes, v. 191).

[65] In the *Folie Berne*, the ring produced by Tristan at last enables Iseut to identify him; in the *Folie Oxford*, it convinces her of her lover's death, even though the dog Husdent has recognized him. On the importance of Tristan changing his voice to persuade Iseut of his true identity, see Matilda Tomaryn Bruckner, *Shaping Romance: Interpretation, Truth and Closure in Twelfth-Century French Fictions* (Philadelphia: University of Pennsylvania Press, 1993), chap. 1.

audience (as they provide the deaf ears of king and court) with a kind of *aide-mémoire* to all the Tristan material, a tool, perhaps, enabling future narratives on the subject to be constructed.[66]

The Poet and His Audience

We have no information on the poet of the *Folie Oxford* nor, indeed, on that of the *Folie Berne*. Unlike Thomas, he left no names or verses on the subject of selecting or rejecting episodes in the Tristan material. He does, however, write very much in the manner of Thomas, as both Bédier and Hoepffner demonstrated. If we accept Bédier's reconstruction of Thomas's romance, then the *Folie Oxford* poet mostly (but not always)[67] follows Thomas in his ordering of episodes.[68] Tristan's tortured and highly rhetorical lament at the start of the poem (vv. 1–24) reads like an imitation of Thomas's style, as does the habitual use of axiomatic and proverbial sayings.[69] The linguistic characteristics of the *Folie* are very close indeed to those of Thomas.[70] These similarities, coupled with the interesting, but perhaps fortuitous, fact that the only text of the poem, in Bodleian Library MS Douce d.6, follows the longest surviving fragment of Thomas's poem, made Hoepffner wonder whether the *Folie* poet was in fact Thomas. This seems unlikely in view of the many similarities in subject matter and wording which also link the poem to the *Folie Berne*. There is, moreover, an unexplained connection with the *folie* episode in Eilhart. Attempts at detecting origins here seem doomed to failure. It seems more fruitful to suppose that the *Folie Oxford* poet, like most of those using the Tristan material, drew on a wide variety of sources, perhaps including oral traditions,[71] and probably added his own original contributions too. We no longer consider, as Bédier did, that departure from a hypothetical "archetype" constitutes a deterioration in a poem's quality.

This poet, as Hoepffner demonstrated, was well-read in the vernacular literature of his time: he seems to have known Wace's chronicle, the *Roman de Brut*, Marie de France's *Lais* (from his text's similarities with *Chevrefoil* and his reference to the *lais bretuns* which Tristan teaches Iseut), and the romances of *Troie*, *Enéas*, and *Thebes*.[72] He writes in an Anglo-Norman which, like Thomas's, is not

---

[66] Suggested by Huchet, "Mythe," 146–47.

[67] For example, he uses the "Irish Harper" episode in a different order from Thomas, placing it after the plots of seneschal and dwarf, instead of before the birth of Mark's suspicion.

[68] An order which, as Baumgartner and Short point out (*Roman de Tristan*, 289–90), follows the chronology of the romances, whereas that of the *Folie Berne* is more "affective."

[69] Hoepffner, *Folie d'Oxford*, 10, 31–33.

[70] Bédier, *Folie Tristan*, 3–12; Hoepffner, *Folie d'Oxford*, 21–30.

[71] Hoepffner, *Folie d'Oxford*, 20.

[72] Hoepffner, *Folie d'Oxford*, 16–19.

far removed from Continental French. Like Thomas too, his approach to his material is somewhat less coarse than that of the *Folie Berne,* Eilhart, or Beroul,[73] but we cannot assume from it that his audience is an aristocratic one (from beginning to end there is no address or reference to it), only that they are fully conversant with the details of the Tristan story.

The Text and Its Translation

The *Folie Oxford* is preserved in a single, thirteenth-century manuscript, Douce d. 6. Its Anglo-Norman scribe rendered it with reasonable care, and there is only one serious lacuna, after line 101; however, a considerable number of lines have either an extra or a missing syllable.[74] The text is divided into units of irregular length, marked by blue or red ornamented letters, which may just follow an aesthetic impulse of the scribe or correspond to pauses in delivery.[75] I share the latter view and think the "paragraphs" may even originate with the poet, so I have retained them in my translation. These units become shorter once the court scenes are under way, corresponding carefully to changes of scene, interlocutor, or recalled episodes, and are notably at their shortest once Iseut has recognised Tristan, where the pauses seem to highlight the emotional climax of the poem.

A single manuscript means there is no helpful check on obscure lines, of which there are several. Earlier editions of the poem, by Hoepffner and Bédier, have attempted to deal with this problem by "extensively and heavily" emending the text; the more recent editions by Lecoy and Short emend less, trying to "respect the integrity of the text."[76] I have accepted many of Hoepffner's suggestions on problematic readings with occasional help also from Payen's, and Baumgartner and Short's, modern French translations. Though the names in the *Folie* are usually abbreviated, the anagram *Trantris* is spelt in full, indicating that the hero's name here is Tristran, as in the original title. I have thus kept it in this

---

[73] Hoepffner, *Folie d'Oxford,* 5, citing the "coarse proposals and violent words" of Iseut and Brenguain in the *Folie Berne.* I have avoided labelling versions of the Tristan story as "courtly" and "popular," a favourite way of categorising them earlier in the twentieth century (see n. 62) but less used now. Payen, for example, prefers the terms "lyric" and "epic": *Tristan en vers,* 1–2.

[74] Metrical irregularity is not unusual in Anglo-Norman versification from the mid-twelfth century onwards and cannot necessarily be attributed to careless scribal copying; on this see Johan Vising, *Anglo-Norman Language and Literature* (London: Oxford University Press, 1923), 79–88. A desire for metrical regularity should not serve as a reason for replacing *Engleterre,* in vv. 70 and 78, with *Bretaine,* as Hoepffner does. According to Thomas, Mark's kingdom is England (as well as Cornwall), so it is logical to retain it here, as do Short and Lecoy in their recent editions.

[75] Payen, *Tristan en vers,* xix. The fragment of Thomas's poem in the Douce manuscript is also broken up into units of irregular length.

[76] Short, *Anglo-Norman "Folie,"* 1.

form in the text although, since editors and critics invariably "normalize" his name to Tristan, for the sake of simplicity I have followed their practice in my commentary and notes.

The *Lai d'Haveloc*

Like *Horn*, the *Lai d'Haveloc*, written between 1190 and 1220,[77] presents a story of a prince's exile and return, though in a simpler form. Unlike *Horn*, the *Lai*, its immediate source, and its better-known successor, the English *Havelok*, are all firmly located in one area of England: East Anglia and, more particularly, Lincolnshire. So specific is its topography, and so tantalising are the connections with history it has seemed to possess, that the Haveloc story has attracted all kinds of scholarly attention. But it is equally a product of legend and folk-tale, and gives us the earliest English example of a "male Cinderella" hero: the scullion who becomes king.[78]

The Poem

The *Lai* is not the first time the Haveloc story was put into verse. It draws very closely upon the chronicle of an earlier twelfth-century writer, Geffrei Gaimar's *Estoire des Engleis* (1136–37).[79] At the time, audiences in England were eager for histories of the various peoples which had inhabited their country. Geoffrey of Monmouth supplied one in Latin around 1135, the *Historia Regum Britanniae;* soon afterwards, Gaimar was working on an ambitious scheme to chronicle the history of the British and the English in the vernacular. His *Estoire des Bretuns* is lost, perhaps supplanted by Wace's *Brut* (1155), but his history of the English, down to the death of William Rufus, survives.[80]

---

[77] *Le Lai d'Haveloc*, ed. Alexander Bell (Manchester: Manchester University Press and Longmans, Green, 1925), 25.

[78] Harald E. Heyman, *Studies on the Havelok Tale* (Uppsala: Wretman Trycken, 1903), 97, compares him with Rainouart in the *chansons de geste* about Guillaume. The story of Gareth in Malory's *Morte D'Arthur* is the best-known English example of the "male Cinderella."

[79] On Gaimar as vernacular historian, see Peter Damian-Grint, *The New Historians of the Twelfth-Century Renaissance* (Woodbridge: Boydell Press, 1999), 49–53.

[80] Geffrei Gaimar, *Estoire des Engleis*, ed. Alexander Bell, Anglo-Norman Texts 14–16 (Oxford: Basil Blackwell, 1960), xi-xii, li-liii, and also Bell, "Gaimar's Early 'Danish' Kings," *Publications of the Modern Language Association* 65 (1950): 601–40, at 639. For this dating of the *Estoire*, see Ian Short, "Gaimar's Epilogue and Geoffrey of Monmouth's *Liber vetustissimus*," *Speculum* 69 (1994): 323–43, at 337–38.

Gaimar had a patroness, Constance, from Hampshire, who married Ralf FitzGilbert, a Lincolnshire landowner.[81] The *Estoire* shows familiarity with stories from both counties, but those from Lincolnshire, like the Haveloc tale, appear to have been inserted late in the process of composition. We can conclude that Gaimar, already engaged on his task, moved to Lincolnshire and, hearing the stories, decided to insert them in his chronicle as further evidence of Cnut's claim (*Estoire*, vv. 4309–18) that the Danes had rights of sovereignty in England long before the Saxons arrived.[82] In placing the Haveloc story at the beginning of the Chronicle, Gaimar gave a local tale a political importance and a chronological placing—linked to the supposed time of King Arthur, around 500 CE—it could not originally have possessed.[83]

Yet, while one feature of the story—the sobriquet "Cuaran" for the hero—links it to the tenth century and a Danish king of Dublin and York,[84] other features, however blurred, do connect it with an earlier period, not so far from that of the mythical Arthur. Gaimar and the poet of the *Lai* after him both set Haveloc's upbringing and marriage in an East Anglia divided into two kingdoms: Lindsey and "Norfolk," as Gaimar calls it (though it runs from southeast Lincolnshire to Colchester). A British king rules Lindsey, which reaches from the Humber down to Stamford and the county of Rutland, whilst a Danish king,

---

[81] *Estoire* v. 6430 ff. See Alexander Bell, "Gaimar's Patron, Raul le Fiz Gilebert," *Notes and Queries* 8 (1921): 104–5; D. M. Williamson, "Ralf son of Gilbert and Ralf son of Ralf," *Lincolnshire Architectural and Archaeological Society: Reports and Papers* 5 (1953): 19–26; Short, "Gaimar's Epilogue," 327; Judith Weiss, "The Power and the Weakness of Women in Anglo-Norman Romance," in *Women and Literature in Britain 1150–1500*, ed. Carol Meale (Cambridge: Cambridge University Press, 1993), 7–23; and Jean Blacker, "'Dame Custance la gentil': Gaimar's Portrait of a Lady and her Books," in *The Court and Cultural Diversity*, ed. Evelyn Mullally and John Thompson (Cambridge: D.S. Brewer, 1997), 109–19.

[82] On the importance of the Danes as "historical agents in the Arthurian, pre-English past" and the penetration of Lincolnshire by Scandinavian cultural influence, see Henry Bainton, "Translating the 'English' Past: Cultural Identity in the *Estoire des Engleis*," in *Language and Culture in Medieval Britain: The French of England c. 1100–c. 1500*, ed. Jocelyn Wogan-Browne et al. (Woodbridge and York: York Medieval Press and Boydell Press, forthcoming). I am most grateful to Mr Bainton and Professor Wogan-Browne for their permission to cite this article.

[83] See Bell, *Estoire*, lvii–lviii and *Lai*, 1–10.

[84] The Irish name "Cuaran," meaning "[with] the leggings," was the nickname of the tenth-century Dane Olaf Sihtricson, sometime king in both York and Dublin, who died in 981. It must have been transferred to the Haveloc story some time after this. According to Smithers, "not enough is known of [Anlaf Cwaran] to make him a model for the story of *Haveloc*. All that seems clear is that a form of the story was known among the Welsh of Cumberland and passed from them to the Anglo-Danish inhabitants of Lincoln" (*Havelok*, ed. G. V. Smithers [Oxford: Clarendon Press, 1987], lv–lvi).

his brother-in-law, rules Norfolk. This reflects historical fact. There were immigrants to East Anglia from Denmark around 500 or even earlier; their royal dynasty, the Wuffings, eventually produced the powerful Raedwald, overlord of southern England in the first quarter of the seventh century.[85] The separate kingdom of Lindsey dates from the end of the fifth century; its name is Celtic, and the half-British name of one of its kings, Caedbaed, points to intermarriage between British and Angles at a peaceful period, most likely in the first years after the Anglian settlements.[86]

The Haveloc story was certainly taken seriously as history for centuries, as extended references to it in fourteenth-century chronicles, like those of Peter Langtoft and Robert Mannyng, and by sixteenth-century historians like Camden and Leland, bear witness.[87] It was still going as a street ballad in the eighteenth century.[88] Local traditions, independent of the literary versions of the tale, continued to flourish and are reported in histories of Grimsby at the end of the nineteenth century.[89]

Gaimar places this story at the start of his chronicle, surrounding it with an "historical" context—Constantine, Arthur's nephew, is supposedly overlord in Britain—and references to his *Estoire des Bretuns*. Because he is telling us the history of the English, he begins the tale in England, with the dispossession of the heroine, Argentille, by her wicked uncle. Only gradually are the names and origin of Haveloc disclosed. There is suspense and mystery in this, but in other ways the narrative ordering is clumsy and full of small obscurities. But viewed in their proper perspective, in a tale forming only one part of a long history, these defects are less important. The *Lai*, however, is composed to stand alone, and its author seems to have thought Gaimar's account needed improvement and elaboration for, while not itself devoid of all inconsistency and obscurity, his poem clarifies elements of the story, changes its narrative structure, and expands upon

[85] Rainbird Clarke, *East Anglia* (London: Thames and Hudson, 1960), 138–40; John Hines, *The Scandinavian Character of Anglian England in the Pre-Viking Period*, B.A.R. British Series 124 (Oxford: B.A.R., 1984), 300.

[86] F. M. Stenton, "Lindsey and its Kings," in *Essays in History Presented to R. L. Poole*, ed. H. W. C. Davis (Oxford: Clarendon Press, 1927) 136–50; C. Brooke, *The Saxon and Norman Kings* (London: B. T. Batsford, 1963), 90–98. Lindsey's artistic richness is gradually being revealed through the discoveries of archaeologists, as the exhibits from the Scunthorpe Museum on view in the British Museum exhibition "The Making of England" demonstrated (see its catalogue, *The Making of England: Anglo-Saxon Art and Culture, A.D. 600–900*, ed. Leslie Webster and Janet Backhouse [London: British Museum Press, 1991], 94–101).

[87] For details of all references to the Haveloc story in chronicles and historians, see *The Lay of Havelok the Dane*, ed. W. W. Skeat (Oxford: Clarendon Press, 1902), xliii-lii; Heyman, *Studies*, 108–38; and *Havelok*, ed. Smithers, xxii-xxx.

[88] Heyman, *Studies*, 138.

[89] See note to v. 144 in translation of *Haveloc*, and Heyman, *Studies*, 129–34.

certain scenes, reshaping its material into a polished and easy poem. Above all, it introduces an improbable courtliness: Haveloc is knighted (v. 928), Argentille has a "chamberlain" to advise her (v. 493), and Grim the fisherman is transformed into a "baron" (v. 57), worrying lest Horn is not receiving the right kind of education. The courtly colouring is consistent with the author's moulding of the tale into a Breton lay, a form which under Marie de France had also acquired distinct conventions of introduction and conclusion.[90]

The author of the *Lai* inherited from Gaimar a hero and heroine who form an interesting pair. Argentille, disinherited and humiliated, is nevertheless not a helpless, passive woman but a forceful character who uses her husband to help her regain her land.[91] The *Lai* poet enhances her role still further by taking every opportunity to mention her presence and her qualities, noting her beauty, her courtly manners, her resource and initiative. It is she who takes prompt action after her dream—and who is granted the dream;[92] she who persuades her husband to win the battle against Edelsi, when he would prefer to go home, by using a trick. In contrast, Haveloc resembles the "dümmling" in folk-tale, a sexual innocent in Gaimar's portrayal of him (vv. 175–88), naive, if not simple-minded, despite his beauty, strength, and generosity. Though the *Lai* tries to render the story more courtly and refined, its picture of Haveloc remains very much the same as in Gaimar: Haveloc shows affection for his wife and concern for the *gent menue* (humble folk) in the battle with Odulf, yet his position in Edelsi's court—despised, humiliated, and forced to fight, like a bear or cock, for the entertainment of the courtiers,—is even more menial than in the *Estoire*. The *Lai* author's creative (mis)understanding of Haveloc's other name, Cuaran, contributes to this degraded picture: he explains it as meaning "scullion," bestowed on the kitchen-boy in contempt. The disparity between hero and heroine is thus further heightened. The strong-minded and energetic Argentille is not unusual in Anglo-Norman romance: there are other women with similar force of character (Josiane in *Boeve de Haumtone*, Ydoine in *Amadas et Ydoine*, La Pucele in

---

[90] For detailed discussion of the changes made by the *Lai* to Gaimar, see M. Kupferschmidt, "Die Haveloksage bei Gaimar und ihr Verhältnis zum Lai d'Havelok," *Romanische Studien* 4 (1880): 411–30, and E. Fahnestock, *A Study of the Sources and Composition of the Old French "Lai d'Haveloc"* (New York: Marion Press, 1915).

[91] See Weiss, "The Power and the Weakness," 8–9, 13, 15.

[92] Heyman, *Studies*, 108, points out an interesting parallel with a dream in the *chanson de geste*, *Aiol*, v. 359 ff. The hero's father, Elie, dreams that the forests bow down to his son, as in Gaimar's *Estoire* (vv. 21–22) and the *Lai* (vv. 421–22) (based on Genesis 37:6–7). There are also other interesting similarities between the Haveloc story and this, the earlier section, of *Aiol*: the hero travels to France to regain his father's lands, of which he has been unjustly dispossessed, and is sheltered by a former *seneschal* of Elie's, who is struck by his resemblance to his father.

Protheselaus).[93] But Haveloc is exceptional, ashamed of the flame which marks him out as royal, unwilling to sound the horn which will confirm that royalty, and thoroughly submerged in his base disguise because he has never known it *is* a disguise.

The Poet and His Audience

The *Lai*'s poet resembles Thomas, the poet of *Horn*, in that his language is not far removed from Continental French. As his knowledge of local topography seems fairly precise, but that of general English geography rather more vague,[94] it is likely he had only recently travelled from the Continent to Lincolnshire. There he must have come across Gaimar's version of the Haveloc story and reshaped it. But he also, probably orally, found other elements of the tale, like the require-ment that Argentille should marry the strongest man available, and he inserted these too into his poem. From the threefold repetition of the story of Grim's landing and the foundation of Grimsby, we may suspect the poet lived there, or had some other strong reason for celebrating the town[95] (which in medieval times was an important port).

So a story that was originally used as a piece of pro-Danish propaganda was modified and polished for an audience with different interests. Its style neverthe-less has not moved very far from Gaimar's: it is still straightforward, almost pro-saic, its syntax relatively uncomplicated. It is markedly succinct, one verb often being used for two objects, and ruthlessly omits inessential particulars. On the other hand, like Marie de France, whose *Lais* may well be an influence, within a fast narrative pace it can pause to emphasise an important scene or a telling detail. Of the audience which received this poem, and preferred it to Gaimar's version, we know nothing except that it presumably shared the author's taste for Breton lays and a more courtly ambience. From its "language of homage, herit-age, fief and feudal law" it has been assumed to be baronial.[96]

---

[93] See Weiss, trans., *Boeve de Haumtone and Gui de Warewic*, 7, and eadem, "The Power and the Weakness," 13–16.

[94] He adds Stamford to Gaimar's description of Edelsi's kingdom: five out of six of its wards are recorded in the Domesday Book as belonging to Lincolnshire. On the other hand, Grim's instruction to Haveloc *(Va t'en, bel fiz, en Engleterre,* "Go to England, my fair son," v. 175), sounds as if the poet did not know that Grimsby and Lincoln were both in Lindsey.

[95] Bell, *Lai*, 25–28, 40–41, 59–60.

[96] Crane, *Insular Romance*, 50.

The Text and Its Translation

The *Lai d'Haveloc* survives in two manuscripts: Cologny-Geneva, Bibliotheca Bodmeriana, MS 82 (formerly Phillips 3713), a late thirteenth- or early fourteenth-century collection of *lais* and short romances, and London, College of Arms, MS Arundel XIV, later fourteenth century. The latter is also one of the four manuscripts of Gaimar's *Estoire des Engleis:* his account of Haveloc has been omitted and the *Lai* substituted. Bell prints the text from the Bodmer manuscript but substitutes words or names from Arundel where he thinks fit.[97] I have translated his text and thus kept the proper names used in Bodmer, but I think Arundel's alternative forms of the names of the two East Anglian kings are worth a mention: "Edelsi" appears as "Alsi" and "Achebrit" as "Ekenbright/Echebrit/Ethebrut/Ethebrit."

The text as it stands is not broken into units. I have inserted paragraphs for easier reading.

Amis e Amilun

Amis e Amilun, the medieval story par excellence of friendship between two men, was written in the late twelfth century. A great deal of attention has been paid to the versions of the narrative found on the Continent (where it was very popular and widespread), but the versions that were composed and circulated in the French of England have yet to be given the notice they deserve. Similar in appearance and also in names—which, derived from *amicus,* friend, announce their essence and demand the appropriate behaviour—Amis and Amilun help each other in actions which involve them in ordeals, self-sacrifice, and perversion of the course of justice. Finally they die in the odour of sanctity and miracles are performed at their graves.

The story exists in many versions and several languages,[98] but is thought to derive ultimately from a lost southern French poem, possibly a *chanson de geste*,[99] which may have been based on an actual historical friendship between the elev-

---

[97] *Lai*, ed. Bell, 93–135, 140.

[98] These are set out in *Amis and Amiloun*, ed. MacEdward Leach, EETS, o.s. 203 (London: Oxford University Press, 1937), who tries to divide the versions into "romantic" and "hagiographic", a distinction not always possible to maintain: see O. Kratins, "The Middle English *Amis and Amiloun*: Chivalric Romance or Secular Hagiography?" *Publications of the Modern Language Association* 81 (1966): 347–54, at 348–49.

[99] William Calin, *The Epic Quest* (Baltimore: Johns Hopkins University Press, 1966), 116; J. Bédier, *Les Légendes Épiques* (Paris: Champion, 1908), 171 ff; Leach, *Amis and Amiloun*, xix-xx. Southern French because of the localities mentioned in most of the versions; *chanson de geste* because of the Charlemagne connections and perhaps because of the friendship theme characteristic of many *chansons*: see Calin, *Epic Quest,* 70. On the

enth-century counts of Poitou and Angoulême, both called Guillaume.[100] The Anglo-Norman romance is one of the earliest versions: the other important early accounts are those contained in a Latin verse epistle c. 1090 by a monk at Fleury, Raoul le Tourtier; a French *chanson de geste, Ami et Amile*, c. 1200; and a twelfth-century Latin prose *Vita Amici et Amelii*.[101] All these mention that their heroes are buried at Mortara in Lombardy, and it would seem that there was an early and successful attempt to make Amis and Amilun into saintly figures whose tombs and relics could be venerated by pilgrims on their way to Rome.[102]

The folkloric elements of the story have attracted much attention. It is clear that the author of the lost original skilfully wove into his tale popular motifs such as the Sword of Chastity and the substitution of one friend (or twin) for another in an ordeal.[103] But the depiction of leprosy, the disease that is Amilun's fate, has excited almost as much interest, because it provides yet more evidence of medieval ideas about the origin and nature of the disease, though the ancient and horrifying suggestion that children's blood might provide a cure was apparently never widely suggested or adopted.[104]

---

chanson de geste Ami et Amile, see Sarah Kay, "Seduction and Suppression in *Ami et Amile*," *French Studies* 44 (1990): 129–42.

[100] Leach, *Amis and Amiloun*, xxxiv, quoting John Koch, *Über Jourdain de Blaives* (Königsberg, 1875).

[101] Leach, *Amis and Amiloun*, ix-xiv; Leach prints a translation of Raoul in an Appendix. In his letter, *Ad Bernardum*, Raoul summarises the story, saying "both Gauls and Saxons know the song." See John Ford, "From *Poésie* to Poetry: *Remaniement* and Medieval Techniques of French-to-English Verse Romance" (Ph.D. diss., Glasgow University, 2000), 3. I am grateful to Dr. Ford for allowing me to quote from his thesis. The *chanson de geste* is edited by P. Dembowski, CFMA (Paris: Champion, 1969); the *Vita* is found in E. Kölbing, *Amis and Amiloun* (Heilbronn: Henninger, 1884), xcvii-cx.

[102] Bédier, *Légendes*, 170–81.

[103] For a long discussion of these, see Leach, *Amis*, xxxii-lxxxviii. For the correlation of motifs with Stith Thompson's *Motif Index of Folk Literature* and Aarne-Thompson's (see bibliography) see Calin, *Epic Quest*, 60–67.

[104] See S. N. Brody, *The Disease of the Soul* (Ithaca and London: Cornell University Press, 1974), 72, 152 n. 5; P. Rémy, "La lèpre, thème littéraire au moyen âge," *Le Moyen Age* 42 (1946): 195–242, at 211–27; L. Demaitre, *Leprosy in Premodern Medicine* (Baltimore: Johns Hopkins University Press, 2007). The legend was even told of Constantine the Great; see, e.g., S. Lieu, "From History to Legend and Legend to History: The Medieval and Byzantine Transformation of Constantine's *Vita*," in *Constantine: History, Historiography, and Legend*, ed. idem and D. Montserrat (London: Routledge, 1998), 136–76, at 144.

The Poem

When the Anglo-Norman poet chose to use this tale, he was thus faced with the task of making his own mark on an already well-known story. By comparing his version with others we can see that he thought carefully about a key element in the tale, that of substitution. Amilun can stand in for Amis (and *vice versa*) because to a large extent they are identical, the two halves of a split protagonist. The poet describes them acting as one — in plural verbs and the same phrases[105] — and omits to describe their different *enfances*, a feature of the other versions, to concentrate only on their inseparability.

The parallels in their lives' actions are also stressed,[106] and the poet added another, unique to him: both Amis and Amilun refuse to sleep with each other's wife (though Amilun gives Amis permission to do so, v. 512). In this most private of relationships, substitution is not possible, because it involves an unacceptable betrayal of friendship, as Amilun recognises when in bed with Florie (vv. 731–56). It is acceptable to deceive the court and to kill the steward, who actually tells the truth; it is, however, a betrayal of one's own integrity to give a false name for one's own. This substitution is avoided by Amilun as long as he can, but when the priest requests it at the church door (v. 708) he cannot escape it, despite the mysterious warning voice. Leprosy punishes him for perjury as much as for bigamy.[107]

Amilun is punished for betraying his integrity in concealing his identity: leprosy "conceals" him, indeed, by making him unrecognisable, and his non-recognition by Amis is the emotional climax of the romance.[108] The Anglo-Norman poet plays with ideas of appearance and reality, of *semblant e fet* ("appearance and fact," v. 512): the one is, and is not, a guide to the other. The beauty of Amis, Amilun, and Owain is an index to their souls; the beauty of Amilun's wife, and the affectionate behaviour of the steward, are only skin-deep — there is no *quer* ("heart") beneath (vv. 114–16). When the former reveals her true self, then she is a mirror image of her leprous husband: she is beautiful sin, he virtuous ugliness. The count, father of Florie, is cynically portrayed as a man going entirely by appearances, changing his attitude abruptly according to what he sees.[109] He — and Florie — are *paié*, "satisfied" with appearances (vv. 577, 723); Amilun's unnamed

---

[105] *Leaus furent vers lur seingnur, / Fei li porterent. . .lung tens servirent / E partut tresbien le firent* (31–32, 45–46); *Amis estroit se purpensa* (287), [Amilun] *si se purpensa mut estreit* (709). (They were faithful to their lord, bore him loyalty . . . served him for a long time, and everywhere did it well . . . Amis thought hard . . . Amilun thought very hard.)

[106] For a discussion along some of the same lines, see Susan Dannenbaum [Crane], "Insular Tradition in the Story of Amis and Amiloun," *Neophilologus* 67 (1983): 611–22, at 612–13, and Weiss, "The Wooing Woman," 158–59.

[107] On leprosy as punishment for both of these, see Brody, *Disease*, 118, 129, 142.

[108] As Dannenbaum, "Insular Tradition," has finely demonstrated (616–17).

[109] See Weiss, "The Power and the Weakness," 11–12.

wife, however, is dissatisfied, because she senses deception when her supposed
husband places a sword between them. This is the only version of the story to
suggest that her later treatment of the leper may have something to do with the
way he first deceived her. If she was not *tele com dussez estre* ("what you should
have been," v. 1199), neither was he.

This hint of motivation for the wife's behaviour is one of a number of signs
that this poet was trying to be more sympathetic to the women in his story. It
was not an easy task, because the very structure of the tale places relationships
with women in a second-best category and encourages misogynistic reflections
on their sensuality and treachery. Raoul's epistle, the *Vita,* and above all the
chanson de geste warn of the dangers of women and depict them as lying, lecher-
ous, and violent.[110] The Anglo-Norman poet still portrays Florie as unscrupulous
in her courtship of Amis, but softens her portrait in other ways[111] and renames
her: instead of Belissant/Beliardis, the name she has in all other versions, he
gives her the attractive nickname of Florie, "flowering," and a "real" name, Mirabele—that of the resourceful and accomplished Saracen princess in *Aiol.*[112]

The Poet

We can only make deductions and assumptions about this poet from his poem
and the manuscripts in which it has survived. One of these, the Karlsruhe manuscript from the end of the fourteenth century,[113] is so free a rehandling of the
earlier text (it is some 400 lines longer) and so evidently related in some way
to the fourteenth-century English romance *Amis and Amiloun,* that it deserves
separate discussion as a different poem and I shall not do that here. The other
two manuscripts, Cambridge, Corpus Christi College, MS 50 (C) and London,

---

[110] *Cave tibi a filia regis* ("beware of the king's daughter," *Vita* in Kölbing, *Amis and
Amiloun,* ci). In the *chanson de geste* a woman is compared to a vixen (lines 571–74); Lubias
(Ami's wife) is *la male femme* from the outset, being related to the steward, and behaves
throughout with appropriate treachery and lust; Belissant tricks Amile into sleeping with
her. In Raoul's letter (*Epistola Ad Bernardum,* see n. 101 above), the queen's behaviour on
learning her daughter and Amelius are lovers resembles the count's in our poem.

[111] See Weiss, "Wooing Woman," 158–59: she supports Amis totally when he has
sacrificed their children, even though he doesn't tell her why.

[112] The *chanson de geste Aiol* seems to fall into two distinct halves, the first dated
to 1160–73, the second to 1205–15: *Aiol,* ed. Jacques Normand and Gaston Raynaud,
SATF (Paris: Firmin Didot, 1877), xxii-viii. Mirabele is usually a man's name in *chanson
de geste* and romance, often with Saracen connections. See Langlois, *Table*; L.-F. Flutre,
Table des noms propres de toute nature compris dans les chansons de geste imprimées (Poitiers:
C.E.S.C.M. Publications, 1962); and André Moisan, *Repertoire des noms propres de personnes et de lieux cités dans les chansons de geste françaises et les oeuvres étrangères derivées,* Publications Romanes et Françaises, 2 vols. (Geneva: Droz, 1986).

[113] Karlsruhe, Badische Landesbibliothek, MS 345 (formerly Cod. Durlac 38).

British Library, MS Royal 12 C xii (L), date from the thirteenth, and late thirteenth or early fourteenth, centuries respectively. The two almost identical texts of *Amis* in these manuscripts give us a good idea of what the original poem must have been like.

It is clear that the poet tried to play down the continental colouring of the story. Though he still has his two heroes buried at Mortara in Lombardy,[114] he omits all references to the birthplaces or fiefs of Amis and Amilun, he does not make Florie's father Charlemagne but instead an unnamed count at an unnamed court, and his steward is likewise anonymous, rather than the Adradus, or Hardré, of Ganelon's lineage, so identified in other versions.[115] Thus he severed all connections with the Charlemagne stories and removed the numerous associations with southern France. But there is no corresponding "insularisation," no British place-names, only the odd detail that two of his characters are said to possess "real" names, yet are known by nicknames: Mirabele/Florie and Owain/Amiraunt.[116] The first two, as we have seen, are unique to the Anglo-Norman romance. Owain is the Welsh form of a name frequently found in Continental and insular romance as Iwein/Yvain. It is most unlikely to be, as Leach claimed, the "primitive" name (lxxxvii), but perhaps the Anglo-Norman poet introduced it as a gesture of some kind to his insular audience: perhaps his patron was a baron from the Welsh marches? The English *Amis* uses "Belisaunt," not Mirabele/Florie, but retains Owain/Amoraunt, and in its later manuscripts keeps only the Welsh name, expunging Amoraunt altogether: the mark of insularity retained its popularity.[117]

While the figure of the wooing woman is popular in Anglo-Norman romance in general, the poet of *Amis e Amilun* seems to have been well acquainted with one particular example, that of Rigmel in Thomas's *Horn*. The parallels here are remarkably close. Both Horn and Amis bear round the cup at a feast given by their overlords; their beauty is the subject of much comment in the hall, so

---

[114] C, 1246. L removes *Morters* (Mortara), and this is the reading which Kölbing, for no good reason, prints, misleading Leach, who remarks: "The Anglo-Norman [poem] says simply that their bodies lie in Lombardy" (xxiii).

[115] On Hardré, see Langlois, *Table;* Moisan, *Repertoire;* Leach, *Amis and Amiloun,* lxxii-iii, and Calin, *Epic Quest,* 77.

[116] vv. 247–48, 888–89; the *dreit nuns* are Mirabele and Owain. The latter has no name in Raoul's Epistle, and is split into Garin, Haymme, and Girart in the *chanson de geste,* and Azones and Horatus in the *Vita Amici et Amelii.*

[117] The version of *Amis and Amiloun* in the Auchinleck Manuscript (National Library of Scotland, MS Advocates 19.2.1), 1634–37, reads: "Owaines was his name ytold . . . / When he was tvelue 3ere old, / Amoraunt than was he cald." MSS Egerton 2862 (end 14th c.) and Douce 326 (1450–1500) omit Amoraunt here and thereafter, substituting "Oweys" or "the childe." The English text also retains the Anglo-Norman switching of the heroes' names: in all other versions, Amis's role is equivalent to that of Amilun/Amiles, and *vice versa.*

that news of it finally travels to the heroine's chambers, and she falls in love with the hero by hearsay. Both heroes are reluctant to accept the proffered love; both heroines are of a violent and passionate character. We can conclude that the *Amis* poet was familiar with other insular romances.

Amis e Amilun is less richly detailed than Thomas's *Romance of Horn*, but the relative sparseness of the poet's style dramatically and emotionally conveys the high points of his romance: Amis's failure to recognise Amilun, and the sacrifice of the children. He likes to introduce an element of suspense—the behaviour of Amilun's wife is prepared for but not given away in advance, as in the *chanson de geste*. On the other hand, he omits to prepare us in any way for the recognition-tokens of the goblets, which are introduced surprisingly late. Foreshadowings of events to come, and reminders of what has happened, so characteristic of *chanson de geste* style, are signs of the epic poet's need to keep a large audience quiet and involved in a story. Their omission here may suggest a smaller, closer audience. It is certainly one of which the narration is constantly mindful: apart from a request for silence at the beginning, the text is full of references to its audience's presence.[118] It does not seem to be an aristocratic audience,[119] but the poet reassures it of the value and seriousness of his poem.[120]

The Text and Its Translation

The two early manuscripts, C and L (Cambridge, Corpus Christi College, MS 50 and London, British Library, MS Royal 12 C xii), have both been edited.[121] As C is the earlier of the two, I have chosen this as my base, using Kölbing's edition, which is sometimes confusingly composite, substituting lines from L when he feels they are more appropriate.[122] I have also sometimes chosen lines or words from L, but not necessarily in agreement with his selection, and I have kept MS

---

[118] *Je vus dirrai . . .* ; *nomer vus dei* (vv. 5, 151, 179–80, 247, 797, 799). On the epic poet "attaching the audience to the story," see Rychner, *La Chanson de Geste*, 54–67.

[119] Compare the *chanson de geste Ami et Amile* and its appeals to *seignur gentil baron* (vv. 1, 78, 853, etc.).

[120] *Ki veut oir chançoun d'amur, / De leauté et de grant douçur, / En peis se tienge pur escouter: / De trueffle ne voil mie parler* (1–4, Kölbing's numbering).

[121] The Cambridge, Corpus Christi manuscript (C) is well known, containing, among other works, the Anglo-Norman *Gui de Warewic* and Wace's *Brut. Amis* occurs between a fabliau and *L'Estorie des quatre sorurs*. The Royal manuscript (L) is a trilingual miscellany in which *Amis* occupies the sixth booklet. Manuscript C has been edited by Kölbing, *Amis and Amiloun*, 111–87, who confusingly calls it "K," because he has labelled the Karlsruhe manuscript "C"; manuscript L has been edited by Hideka Fukui, *Amys e Amillyoun*, ANTS, Plain Texts Series 7 (London: ANTS, 1990). The fourteenth-century Karlsruhe manuscript, Durlac 38, has been edited by John Ford but not published. Except for *Amis*, all its other items are in Latin prose.

[122] See Fukui, *Amys*, 1.

C's original ending. The punctuation supplied in Fukui's edition of MS L is often more sensible than Kölbing's and I have frequently adhered to it. Kölbing's line numbering is eccentric because it does not include the first five lines, preserved only in MS C; I have reluctantly preserved it only because anyone checking my translation against MS C in Kölbing might have difficulties.

In MS C, there are breaks in the text, signalled by red and blue initials, at vv. 1 (after the first 5 lines), 151, 187, 797, and 1043. I have added several more breaks, to interrupt some otherwise rather lengthy sections of narrative. As usual, I have put the whole narrative into the past tense. The text did present me with one problem: how to translate *est[e] vus* (vv. 221, 389, 710, 1140), a rather button-holing address to an audience meaning, roughly, "look here / see / lo and behold." None of these locutions fitted a modern English context very well and so I have left them out.

I have not recorded all of MS L's many variants to MS C of just a word or two, but occasionally I have given variants which amount to whole lines. The Karlsruhe manuscript introduces numerous and lengthy interpolations, seldom of great substance. I have not quoted these in my footnotes but have summarized their contents.

SUGGESTED FURTHER READING

All four romances are discussed in the following surveys of Anglo-Norman romance:

Crane, Susan. *Insular Romance.* Berkeley: University of California Press, 1986.
Field, Rosalind. "Romance in England, 1066–1400." In *The Cambridge History of Medieval English Literature* ed. David Wallace, 152–76. Cambridge: Cambridge University Press, 1999.
Legge, M. Dominica. *Anglo-Norman Literature and its Background.* Oxford: Clarendon Press, 1963.
Weiss, Judith. "Insular Beginnings: Anglo-Norman Romance." In *A Companion to Romance: from Classical to Contemporary*, ed. Corinne Saunders, 26–44. Oxford: Blackwell, 2004.

The Romance of Horn

Edition

Thomas, *The Romance of Horn*, ed. M. K. Pope. Anglo-Norman Texts 9–10, 12–13. 2 vols. Oxford: Basil Blackwell for ANTS, 1955, 1964.

Articles, chapters, or books which discuss the Anglo-Norman Horn

Ashe, Laura. *Fiction and History in England, 1066–1200.* Cambridge: Cambridge University Press, 2007.
Braunholtz, E. G. W. "Cambridge Fragments of the Anglo-Norman 'Roman de Horn'." *Modern Language Review* 16 (1921): 23–33.
Brede, Rudolf. "Ueber die Handschriften der Chanson de Horn." *Ausgaben und Abhandlungen aus dem Gebiete der Romanischen Philologie* 4 (1883): 175–254.
Burnley, J. D. "The 'Roman de Horn': Its Hero and its Ethos." *French Studies* 32 (1978): 385–97.
———. *Courtliness and Literature in Medieval England.* London: Longman, 1998.

Christmann, H. H. "Über das Verhältnis zwischen dem anglonormannischen und dem mittelenglischen 'Horn'." *Zeitschrift für französische Sprache und Literatur* 70 (1960): 166–81.

Dickson, M. "Twelfth-Century Insular Narrative: *The Romance of Horn* and Related Texts." Ph.D. diss., Cambridge University, 1996.

French, W. H. *Essays on King Horn.* Cornell Studies in English 30. Ithaca and London: Humphrey Milford, 1940.

Hofer, Stefan. "Horn et Rimel, ein Beitrag zur Diskussion über die Ursprungs-frage." *Romanische Forschungen* 70 (1958): 278–322.

Legge, M. Dominica. "The Influence of Patronage on Form in Medieval French Literature." In *Stil- und Formprobleme in der Literatur,* ed. Paul Böckmann, 136–41. Heidelberg: C. Winter, 1959.

Pope, M. K. "Notes on the Vocabulary of the Romance of Horn and Rimel." In *Mélanges de Philologie Romane et de Littérature Médiévale offerts à Ernest Hoepffner,* 63–70. Paris: Les Belles Lettres, 1949.

———. "Titles of Respect in the Romance of *Horn.*" In *Studies in Romance Philology and French Literature Presented to John Orr,* 226–32. Manchester: Manchester University Press, 1953.

———. "The *Romance of Horn* and *King Horn.*" *Medium Aevum* 25 (1957): 164–67.

Weiss, Judith. "The Wooing Woman in Anglo-Norman Romance." In *Romance in Medieval England,* ed. J. Fellows, M. Mills, and C. Meale, 149–61. Cambridge: D.S. Brewer, 1991.

———. "Thomas and the Earl: Literary and Historical Contexts for the *Romance of Horn.*" In *Tradition and Transformation in Medieval Romance,* ed. Rosalind Field, 1–13. Cambridge: D. S. Brewer, 1999.

Other Editions and Narratives of relevance for Horn

Der Anglonormannische Boeve de Haumtone, ed. Albert Stimming. Halle: Biblio-theca Normannica, 1899.

La Chanson de Roland, ed. Frederick Whitehead. London: Bristol Classical Press, 1993.

De Gestis Herwardi Saxonis, transcr. and trans. S. H. Miller and W. D. Sweet-ing. *Fenland Notes and Queries* 3 (1895–7): 7–72.

Gui de Bourgogne, ed. F. Guessard and H. Michelant. Paris: A. Franck, 1859.

Gui de Warewic: Roman du XIIIe Siècle, ed. Alfred Ewert. 2 vols. Paris: Cham-pion, 1933.

Hind Horn. In *The English and Scottish Popular Ballads,* ed. F. J. Child, 187–208. New York: Dover Publications, 1965.

Horn Childe and Maiden Rimnild, ed. Maldwyn Mills. Heidelberg: Carl Win-ter, 1988.

King Horn, ed. Joseph Hall. Oxford: Clarendon Press, 1901.

King Horn, ed. Rosamund Allen. New York and London: Garland Publishing, 1984.

Wace. *Le Roman de Brut,* ed. Ivor Arnold. 2 vols. SATF. Paris: SATF, 1938, 1940. Trans. Judith Weiss. *Wace's Roman de Brut: A History of the British.* Exeter: University of Exeter Press, 1999.

Le Roman de Waldef, ed. A. J. Holden. Cologny-Geneva: Fondation Martin Bodmer, 1984.

Background

Allen, H. Warner. *A History of Wine.* London: Faber and Faber, 1961.

Ashe, Laura. "The Hero and his Realm in Medieval English Romance." In *Boundaries in Medieval Romance,* ed. Neil Cartlidge, 129–47. Cambridge: D. S. Brewer, 2008.

Bancourt, P. *Les Musulmans dans les chansons de geste du cycle du roi.* 2 vols. Aix: Université de Provence, 1982.

Baroin, Jeanne. "Besançon dans les Chansons de Geste." In *Mélanges Roland Fiétier,* ed. François Lassus, 67–79. Annales Littéraires de l'Université de Besançon 287. Paris: Les Belles Lettres, 1984.

Blakeslee, Merritt R. "Lo dous jocx sotils: la partie d'échecs amoureuse dans la poésie des troubadours." *Cahiers de Civilisation Médiévale* 28 (1985): 213–22.

Burns, E. Jane. *Courtly Love Undressed: Reading Through Clothes in Medieval French Culture.* Philadelphia: University of Pennsylvania Press, 2002.

Corráin, D. O. *Ireland before the Normans.* Dublin: Gill and Macmillan, 1972.

Crane, Susan. "Anglo-Norman Cultures in England, 1066–1460." In *The Cambridge History of Medieval English Literature,* ed. Wallace, 35–60.

de Lage, G. Raynaud. "L'Inspiration de la prière 'Du plus Grand Péril'." *Romania* 93 (1972): 568–70.

Förster, M. "Das lateinisch-altenglische Pseudo-Danielsche Traumbuch in Tiberius A III." *Archiv für das Studium der neueren Sprachen* 125 (1910): 213–22.

Hollister, C. Warren. *Anglo-Saxon Military Institutions.* Oxford: Clarendon Press, 1962.

Hoppin, Richard H. *Medieval Music.* New York: W. W. Norton, 1978.

Kay, Sarah. *The Chansons de Geste in the Age of Romance: Political Fictions.* Oxford: Clarendon Press, 1995.

Murray, H. J. R. *A History of Chess.* Oxford: Clarendon Press, 1913.

Norton, E. Christopher. "Les carreaux de pavage en France au moyen âge." *Revue de l'Art* 63 (1984): 59–72.

Page, Christopher. *Voices and Instruments of the Middle Ages.* London: J.M. Dent, 1987.

Peirce, Ian. "The Knight, His Arms and Armour c. 1150–1250." *Anglo-Norman Studies* 15 (1992): 25–74.

Rebbert, Maria A. "The Celtic Origins of the Chess Symbolism in *Milun* and *Eliduc*." In *In Quest of Marie de France*, ed. C. A. Maréchal, 148–60. Lampeter: Edwin Mellen Press, 1992.

Reese, G. *Music in the Middle Ages*. London: J. M. Dent, 1940/41.

Rychner, J. *La Chanson de Geste: Essai sur l'art épique des jongleurs*. Geneva: Droz, 1955.

Ryding, William W. *Structure in Medieval Narrative*. The Hague: Mouton, 1971.

Short, Ian. "Literary Culture at the Court of Henry II." In *Henry II: New Interpretations*, ed. Christopher Harper-Bill and Nicholas Vincent, 335–61. Woodbridge: Boydell Press, 2007.

Speed, Diane. "The Saracens of *King Horn*." *Speculum* 65 (1990): 564–95.

Stein, Robert M. *Reality Fictions: Romance, History, and Governmental Authority 1025–1180*. Notre Dame: University of Notre Dame Press, 2006.

Stevens, J. *Words and Music in the Middle Ages*. Cambridge: Cambridge University Press, 1986.

The Oxford *Folie Tristan*

Editions

Les Deux Poèmes de la Folie Tristan, ed. J. Bédier. Paris: Firmin Didot, 1907.

La Folie Tristan d'Oxford, ed. E. Hoepffner. Paris: Les Belles Lettres, 1943.

Le Tristan en Vers, ed. J.-C. Payen. Paris: Garnier, 1974 (contains both *Folies*, Beroul and Thomas).

The Anglo-Norman Folie Tristan, ed. Ian Short. London: ANTS, 1993.

Les Deux Poèmes de la Folie Tristan, ed. Felix Lecoy. Paris: Champion, 1994.

Le Roman de Tristan par Thomas suivi de La Folie Tristan de Berne et La Folie Tristan d'Oxford. Trans. and intro. Emmanuèle Baumgartner and Ian Short. Paris: Champion, 2003.

Other Narratives Cited

The Awntyrs of Arthure, ed. Ralph Hanna. Manchester: Manchester University Press, 1974.

Beroul. *The Romance of Tristran*, ed. A. Ewert. 2 vols. Oxford: Basil Blackwell, 1939, 1970.

Eilhart von Oberg. *Tristrant und Isalde*, ed. Danielle Buschinger and Wolfgang Spiewok. Greifswald: Reineke-Verlag, 1993.

Thomas. *Les Fragments du Roman de Tristan,* ed. Bartina H. Wind. Geneva: Droz, 1960.

Gottfried von Strassburg. *Tristan,* ed. Peter Ganz. Wiesbaden: Brockhaus, 1978.

Friar Robert. *Tristramssaga,* ed. Gisli Brynjulfson. Copenhagen: Thieles bogtr., 1878

The Saga of Tristram and Isönd, trans. Paul Schach. Lincoln: University of Nebraska Press, 1973.

Sir Tristrem, ed. C. P. McNeill. Scottish Text Society Publications 8. Edinburgh: Printed for the Scottish Text Society by W. Blackwood and Sons, 1886.

On the Tristan story in general

Bédier, J. *Le Roman de Tristan par Thomas.* 2 vols. Paris: Firmin Didot, 1902–1905.

Benskin, Michael, Tony Hunt, and Ian Short. "Un nouveau fragment du *Tristan* de Thomas." *Romania* 113 (1992–1995): 289–319.

Blakeslee, Merritt R. *Love's Masks.* Arthurian Studies 15. Cambridge: D. S. Brewer, 1989.

Bromiley, G. N. "Narrative Development in the Early Tristan Poems." *Modern Language Review* 70 (1975): 743–51.

Bromwich, R. "The Tristan of the Welsh." In *The Arthur of the Welsh,* ed. eadem, A. O. H. Jarman, and Brynley F. Roberts, 209–28. Cardiff: University of Wales Press, 1991.

Curtis, Renée L. *Tristan Studies.* Munich: William Fink, 1969.

Frank, G. "Marie de France and the Tristram Legend." *Publications of the Modern Language Association* 63 (1948): 405–11.

Frappier, J. "Structure et sens du *Tristan*: version commune, version populaire." *Cahiers de Civilisation Médiévale* 6 (1963): 255–86.

Kelly, Douglas. "La vérité tristanienne: quelques points de repère dans les romans." In *Tristan et Iseut, mythe européen et mondial,* ed. Danielle Buschinger, 168–80. Göppinger Arbeiten zur Germanistik 474. Göppingen: Kümmerle, 1987.

Mandach, André de. "Le Berceau des amours splendides de Tristan et Iseut." In *La Légende de Tristan au Moyen Âge,* ed. Danielle Buschinger, 7–25. Göppinger Arbeiten zur Germanistik 355. Göppingen: Kümmerle, 1982.

Padel, O. J. "The Cornish Background of the Tristan Stories." *Cambridge Medieval Celtic Studies* 1 (1981): 53–80.

Picozzi, Rosemary. *A History of Tristan Scholarship.* Canadian Studies in German Language and Literature 5. Berne and Frankfurt: Herbert Lang, 1971.

On the *Folies Tristan* Poems in Particular

Bromiley, Geoffrey N. *Thomas' Tristan and the Folie Tristan d'Oxford.* Critical Guides to French Texts 61. London: Grant and Cutler, 1986.

Brusegan, Rosanna. "La Folie de Tristan: de la loge du Morrois an palais de verre." In *La Légende de Tristan au Moyen Age,* ed. Buschinger, 49–59.

Haidu, Peter. "Text, Pre-textuality and Myth in the *Folie Tristan d'Oxford.*" *Modern Language Notes* 88 (1973): 712–17.

Huchet, Jean-Charles. "Le mythe du Tristan primitif et les *Folies Tristan.*" In *Tristan et Iseut, mythe européen et mondial,* ed. Buschinger, 139–50.

W. Lutoslawski. "Les Folies de Tristan." *Romania* 15 (1886): 511–33.

Payen, J.-C. "Tristan, *l'Amans-Amens* et le masque dans les *Folies.*" In *La Légende de Tristan au Moyen Âge,* ed. Buschinger, 61–68.

Schaefer, Jacqueline T. "Specularity in the Mediaeval *Folie Tristan* Poems or Madness as Metadiscourse." *Neophilologus* 77 (1993): 355–68.

Background

Alcock, L. *Dinas Powys.* Cardiff: University of Wales Press, 1963.

Bruckner, Matilda Tomaryn. *Shaping Romance: Interpretation, Truth and Closure in Twelfth-Century French Fictions.* Philadelphia: University of Pennsylvania Press, 1993.

Davies, W. *Wales in the Early Middle Ages.* Leicester: Leicester University Press, 1982.

Delbouille, M. "Apollonius de Tyr et les débuts du roman français." In *Mélanges offerts à Rita Lejeune,* 2: 1171–1204. Gembloux: J. Duculot, 1969.

Frank, Grace. "Proverbs in Medieval Literature." *Modern Language Notes* 58 (1943): 508–15.

Huot, Sylvia. *Madness in Medieval French Literature.* Oxford: Oxford University Press, 2003.

Lascelles, Gerald. "Falconry." In *Coursing and Falconry,* ed. Harding Cox, 199–304. London: Longmans, Green, 1892.

Ménard, P. "Les Fous dans la société médiévale." *Romania* 98 (1977): 433–59.

Wack, Mary Frances. *Lovesickness in the Middle Ages.* Philadelphia: University of Pennsylvania Press, 1990.

The *Lai d'Haveloc*

Edition

Le Lai d'Haveloc, ed. Alexander Bell. Manchester: Manchester University
Press, Longmans, Green, 1925.

On the Havelok story in Gaimar and in general

"Adrian" (J. Hopkin). "Ancient Seals of Grimsby." *Notes and Queries,* 2nd ser.,
11 (1861): 216–17.

Bainton, Henry. "Translating the 'English' Past: Cultural Identity in the *Estoire
des Engleis.*" In *Language and Culture in Medieval Britain: The French of England 1100–1500,* ed. Jocelyn Wogan-Browne et al. Woodbridge and York:
York Medieval Press and Boydell Press, forthcoming.

Bates, Anderson. *A Gossip about Old Grimsby.* Grimsby: A. Gait, 1893.

Bell, A. "Gaimar's Patron, Raul le Fiz Gilebert." *Notes and Queries,* 12th ser., 8
(1921): 104–5.

———. "Gaimar's Early 'Danish' Kings." *Publications of the Modern Language
Association* 65 (1950): 601–40.

Blacker, Jean. "'Dame Custance la gentil': Gaimar's Portrait of a Lady and her
Books." In *The Court and Cultural Diversity,* ed. Evelyn Mullally and John
Thompson, 109–19. Cambridge: D. S. Brewer, 1997.

Cole, R. E. G., ed. *Lincolnshire Church Notes.* Lincoln Record Society. Lincoln:
W.K. Morton & Sons, 1911.

Damian-Grint, Peter. *The New Historians of the Twelfth-Century Renaissance.*
Woodbridge: Boydell Press, 1999.

d'Ardenne, S.R.T.O. "A Neglected Manuscript of British History." In *English
and Medieval Studies Presented to J. R. R. Tolkien,* ed. Norman Davis and C.
L. Wrenn, 84–93. London: Allen & Unwin, 1962.

Dunn, Charles W. "Havelok and Anlaf Cuaran." In *Medieval and Linguistic
Studies in Honor of F. P. Magoun, Jr,* ed. Jess B. Bessinger and Robert P.
Creed, 244–49. London: Allen & Unwin, 1965.

Gaimar, Geffrei. *Estoire des Engleis,* ed. A. Bell. Anglo-Norman Texts 14–16.
Oxford: Basil Blackwell for ANTS, 1960.

The Lay of Havelok the Dane, ed. W. W. Skeat. Oxford: Clarendon Press, 1902.

Havelok the Dane, ed. G.V. Smithers. Oxford: Clarendon Press, 1987.

Heyman, Harald E. *Studies on the Havelok Tale.* Upsala: Wretmans Tryckeri,
1903.

Reiss, Edmund. "*Havelok the Dane* and Norse Mythology." *Modern Language
Quarterly* 27 (1966): 115–24.

Short, Ian. "Gaimar's Epilogue and Geoffrey of Monmouth's *Liber vetustissi-mus.*" *Speculum* 69 (1994): 323–43.

Williamson, D. M. "Ralf son of Gilbert and Ralf son of Ralf." *Lincolnshire Architectural and Archaeological Society: Reports and Papers* 5 (1953): 19–26.

On the *Lai d'Haveloc* in particular

Bell, A. "The Single Combat in the *Lai d'Haveloc.*" *Modern Language Review* 18 (1923): 22–28.

Fahnestock, E. *A Study of the Sources and Composition of the Old French "Lai d'Haveloc."* New York: Marion Press, 1915.

M. Kupferschmidt. "Die Haveloksage bei Gaimar und ihr Verhältnis zum *Lai d'Havelok.*" *Romanische Studien* 4 (1880): 411–30.

Weiss, Judith. "The Power and the Weakness of Women in Anglo-Norman Romance." In *Women and Literature in Britain 1150–1500*, ed. Carol Meale, 7–23. Cambridge: Cambridge University Press, 1993.

Other Narratives Cited

Aiol, ed. Jacques Normand and Gaston Raynaud. SATF. Paris: Firmin Didot, 1877.

Le Freine, Bisclavret, and *Laustic.* In Marie de France, *Lais.* Oxford: Basil Blackwell, 1965.

Background

Brooke, C. *The Saxon and Norman Kings.* London: B. T. Batsford, 1963.

Clarke, Rainbird. *East Anglia.* London: Thames and Hudson, 1960.

Hines, John. *The Scandinavian Character of Anglian England in the Pre-Viking Period.* B.A.R. British Series 124. Oxford: B.A.R., 1984.

Stenton, F. M. "Lindsey and its Kings." In *Essays in History Presented to R. L. Poole*, ed. H. W. C. Davis, 136–50. Oxford: Clarendon Press, 1927.

———. "Personal Names in Place-Names." In *Preparatory to Anglo-Saxon England*, ed. D. M. Stenton, 84–105. Oxford: Clarendon Press, 1970.

———. *The First Century of English Feudalism 1066–1166.* Oxford: Clarendon Press, 1932.

Webster, Leslie, and Janet Backhouse, eds. *The Making of England: Anglo-Saxon Art and Culture, A.D. 600–900.* Toronto: University of Toronto Press, 1991.

Amis and Amilun

Editions

Amis and Amiloun, ed. E. Kölbing. Heilbronn: Henninger, 1884.
Amys e Amillyoun, ed. Hideka Fukui. ANTS. Plain Texts Series 7. London: ANTS, 1990.

On the Amis story in English and Anglo-Norman

Amis and Amiloun, ed. MacEdward Leach. EETS, o.s. 203. London: Oxford University Press, 1937.
Amys and Amylion, ed. Françoise Le Saux. Exeter: University of Exeter Press, 1993
Calin, William. *The Epic Quest*. Baltimore: Johns Hopkins University Press, 1966.
Dannenbaum [Crane], Susan. "Insular Tradition in the Story of Amis and Amiloun." *Neophilologus* 67 (1983): 611–22.
Delany, S. "A, A and B: Coding Same-Sex Union in *Amis and Amiloun*." In *Pulp Fictions in Medieval England: Essays in Popular Romance*, ed. N. McDonald, 63–81. Manchester: Manchester University Press, 2004.
Ford, John. "From *Poésie* to Poetry: *Remaniement* and Medieval Techniques of French-to-English Verse Romance." Ph.D. diss., Glasgow University, 2000.
Hume, Kathryn. "Structure and Perspective: Romance and Hagiographic Features in the Amicus and Amelius Story." *Journal of English and Germanic Philology* 69 (1970): 89–107.
———. "*Amis and Amiloun* and the Aesthetics of Middle English Romance." *Studies in Philology* 70 (1973): 19–41.
Kratins, O. "The Middle English *Amis and Amiloun:* Chivalric Romance or Secular Hagiography?" *Publications of the Modern Language Association* 81 (1966): 347–54.
Weiss, Judith. "The Wooing Woman in Anglo-Norman Romance." In *Romance in Medieval England*, ed. Fellows, Mills, and Meale, 149–61.

Other Narratives Cited

Aiol, ed. Jacques Normand and Gaston Raynaud. SATF. Paris: Firmin Didot, 1877.
Gui de Warewic: Roman du XIIIe Siècle, ed. Alfred Ewert. 2 vols. Paris: Champion, 1933.

Background

Ailes, M. J. "The Medieval Male Couple and the Language of Homosociality." In *Masculinity in Medieval Europe*, ed. D. M. Hadley, 214–37. London: Longman, 1999.

Bédier, J. *Les Légendes Épiques*. 4 vols. Paris: Champion, 1908–1913.

Brody, S. N. *The Disease of the Soul*. Ithaca and London: Cornell University Press, 1974.

Duby, G. *The Knight, the Lady and the Priest*, trans. B. Bray. Harmondsworth: Penguin, 1983.

Harcourt, L. W. Vernon. *His Grace the Steward*. London: Longmans, Green, 1907.

Jones, G. F. *The Ethos of the Song of Roland*. Baltimore: Johns Hopkins University Press, 1963.

Luttrell, C. *The Creation of the First Arthurian Romance*. Evanston: Northwestern University Press, 1974.

Pollock, F., and F. W. Maitland. *The History of English Law before the Time of Edward I*. 2 vols. Cambridge: Cambridge University Press, 1898.

Rémy, P. "La lèpre, theme littéraire au moyen âge." *Le Moyen Âge* 42 (1946): 195–242.

Ritual Brotherhood in Medieval Europe. Spec. no. of *Traditio* 52 (1997).

Reference Works

Aarne, Antti. *Verzeichnis der Märchentypen*: *The Types of the Folk-tale: A Classification and Bibliography*, trans. and enl. Stith Thompson. 2d rev. ed. Helsinki: Suomalainen Tiedeakatemia, 1964.

Birch, W. Gray de. *Cartularium Saxonicum*. 3 vols. London: Whiting and Co., 1887.

Davies, J. G. *A Dictionary of Liturgy and Worship*. London: S. C. M. Press, 1972.

des Gautries, Adigard J. *Les Noms de Personnes Scandinaves en Normandie, 911–1066*. Lund: C. Bloms boktr., 1954.

Ferguson, George. *Signs and Symbols in Christian Art*. New York: Oxford University Press, 1966.

Flutre, L.-F. *Table des noms propres dans les romans du Moyen Âge*. Poitiers: C.E.S.C.M. Publications, 1962.

James, M. R. *The Ancient Libraries of Canterbury and Dover*. Cambridge: Cambridge University Press, 1903.

Jensen, G. Fellows. *Scandinavian Personal Names in Lincolnshire and Yorkshire*. Copenhagen: Akademisk Forlag (D.B.K.), 1968.

Langlois, Ernest. *Table des noms propres de toute nature compris dans les chansons de geste imprimées*. Paris: Bouillon, 1904.

Moisan, André. *Repertoire des noms propres de personnes et de lieux cités dans les chansons de geste françaises et les oeuvres étrangères dérivées.* 2 vols. Publications Romanes et Françaises. Geneva: Droz, 1986.

Morawski, Joseph. *Proverbes français antérieurs au XVe siècle.* Paris: CFMA, 1925.

Reaney, P. *A Dictionary of British Surnames.* 2nd ed. London: Routledge & Kegan Paul, 1977.

Thompson, Stith. *Motif-Index of Folk-Literature: A Classification of Narrative Elements in Folk-Tales, Ballads, Myths, Fables, Medieval Romances, Exempla, Fabliaux, Jest-Books, and Local Legends.* Orig. Copenhagen: Rosenkilde and Bagger, 1955–58. Rev. and enlarged ed. Bloomington: Indiana University Press, 1989-.

Ward, H. L. D. *A Catalogue of Romances in the Department of Manuscripts in the British Museum.* 2 vols. London: British Museum, 1883–1893.

THE ROMANCE OF HORN

1. You will have heard, my lords, from the verses in the parchment, how the noble Aalof came to his end.[1] Master Thomas does not want to end his own life without telling the story of Horn, fatherless and brave, and his fate at the hands of the wicked Saracens. One of them, a scoundrel descended from Cain, was called "Malbroin" in the African language.[2] He was the first to find Horn hidden in a garden, with fifteen other boys of his race; all good counts' sons, they acknowledged the young Horn as their lord. Each wore a crimson or blue tunic, while Horn was clad in Alexandrian silk.[3] His eyes were clear and bright, his face rosy, his bearing noble. He looked like an angel. Like the day-star, rising in the morning, Horn shone brighter than his nearest companions: the boy surpassed all his friends in splendour. (1–18)[4]

---

[1] I **Verses in the parchment** *Vers del parchemin:* Thomas refers several times to a written source: *escrit*, v. 192, *letre*, v. 1656, and *parchemin* again, vv. 2933, 3981. His use of the perfect tense here suggests either that his audience has recently heard about the death of Aalof, which is backed up by a written narrative—and thus what they heard could have been Thomas's account of it—or that they heard it a while ago, from another source. Because Thomas's version of the life of Aalof, emerging piecemeal throughout the poem, is suspect, the second statement is more likely. See Judith Weiss, "Thomas and the Earl: Literary and Historical Contexts for the *Romance of Horn*," in *Tradition and Transformation in Medieval Romance*, ed. Rosalind Field (Cambridge: D. S. Brewer, 1999), 1–13, at 7.

[2] 7 **Malbroin** *Malbroin:* in the Middle Ages the name "Saracen" was, in the West, attributed to all Arabs. Thomas's poem gives the Saracens' countries of origin as Africa, Canaan, and Persia (vv. 297, 1298, 2907, 1463, 3000), but the names he gives them are often Germanic. Descent from Cain, the first murderer, is used to show how wicked a particular Saracen is, as does the first part of his name, *mal* or evil: the "African language" here is thus fictitious, as with Maldran, site of a giant's fight with Hunlaf, v. 1420, and the pagan Malbruart, v. 1708. See P. Bancourt, *Les Musulmans dans les chansons de geste du cycle du roi*, 2 vols. (Aix: Université de Provence, 1982), 1:1, 47–48.

[3] 13 **Alexandrian silk** *paile alexandrin:* by the twelfth century Alexandria had become a major exporter of silk. See Burns, *Courtly Love Undressed*, 187–89.

[4] The first ninety-six lines of *Horn*, missing in the Cambridge manuscript, are supplied by Pope from the Oxford manuscript.

2. Malbroin found the children in their refuge, where all fifteen had hidden themselves from fear. He took them all and bound them, but did no harm to Horn, as fate intended. Out of His great kindness, God gave Horn this good fortune, that all seeing him would at once pity and have mercy on him. Thus this man did so, and escorted him and his companions with kindness to King Rodmund's tents in the meadow. There he presented them, and the king thanked and rewarded him. Now that Rodmund had them, he interrogated them: who were they and of which lineage? Not a word was to be concealed from him. And Horn, the cleverest, the boldest in speech and the best educated, told him everything. When the king had heard him, he carefully observed their lovely faces and their bearing. But Horn surpassed them all in every fair feature, as God in His Trinity intended him to, who moved the king's heart to spare them. For nothing He wants to preserve can perish. (19–39)[5]

3. For King Rodmund pitied the children so much that he could not bear them to perish in his presence. Then he asked for advice from those around him: "My lords, counsel me, what should be done with them? I cannot have them killed while I look on. Yet I know well that, if they live, I will regret it, because I have slain all their most notable kin, and if they survive they will avenge them. So I do not want them to escape. Tell me how they may die so that I do not witness it. From pity, I cannot see it; I have such children myself." Then Broivant spoke fiercely, a rich and powerful naval commander, and wily and cunning indeed in his counsel, though what he advised was very valuable to us, as you can hear, if you listen. For thus was the will of God, watching over them, who never lets those who call upon Him perish. "Sir," he said, "take one of your old boats and put these boys whom I see here into it. Let them have no oars to help them, no sail nor rudder to guide them. Put into another boat twenty strong men-at-arms who, like good sailors, know how to navigate, to pull them two whole leagues out to sea. Then let them cut the ropes dragging them and leave them there, tossing on the high seas. I am sure you will never hear speak of them more: the god they believe in will never save them, no more than a silly, shorn sheep[6] can." All those present said: "Broivant has spoken well." (40–70)

4. At Broivant's words, Rodmund, the African king, quickly had an old, battered boat[7] prepared. Then he placed the children in it, sure of their death. It had neither sail, oar, rudder nor steersman. Now may He protect them, who saved Moses when they threw the child into the river from the cliff, who formed Eve out

---

[5] Allusion to John 10:28–29.

[6] Allusion to Christian *Agnus Dei* imagery, here being ridiculed by the Saracen.

[7] 72 **boat** *chalan*: M. Dominica Legge's review of Pope's edition of *Horn* in *Modern Language Review* 61 (1966): 309–13, prefers "barge."

of lord Adam's rib and made Balaam's ass speak![8] He and St. John will take care of them, for many pagans are still to die at their hands—Petschenegs, Leutiz, Turcopoli, and Almicans.[9] Persia will yet be conquered by this same Horn, now in dire straits, and by his son, who will slay heathen from here to the river Jordan: neither Mahomet nor Tervagant[10] will be able to protect them. They put twenty fierce and strong men into a boat: God send them pain and misfortune! They sat down to row and pulled confidently out towards the open sea, mocking the children. Now may He who dwells on high protect them. (71–90)

5. They rowed towards the open sea; no land was to be seen anywhere. They cut the ropes pulling the boat, abandoning all the noble children to the winds. They were helpless, tossing on the waves. God was their helper, our powerful Saviour. And it will turn out as He wishes, as you will hear presently,[11] for thereupon the twenty wicked men-at-arms rowed away, convinced that the children would perish. They told Rodmund they were not to be seen, and he gave many thanks to Tervagant, believing they could no longer harm him. But what he thought, and what befell them, were quite different things. For God granted them good fortune, sending them a wind that blew from the northwest and landed them in Brittany, home of Hunlaf, a very powerful king and a wealthy, noble man. He was very devout, and set great store by loyalty. He was to nurture Horn, as ordained by God, who was a good pilot to him on the waves of the sea until He had saved him from danger and brought him to port at His behest, with the loss of not even one gold piece, apart from the boat, which was old and shattered in the surf. (91–114)

6. When the children landed on the rocks, it was no wonder they were dismayed, for they did not know what kind of people dwelt there, whether Christian, pagan,

---

[8] Genesis 2:21–23; Numbers 22:21–35.

[9] 81 **Petschenegs, Leutiz, Turcopoli, and Almicans** *Pincenard e leutiz, turcople e almican*: the Pincenard or Petschenegs were a Tartar people inhabiting the shores of the Black Sea and the Lower Danube (Turks, according to Bancourt). The Leutiz, also called Wilzes, were a Slav people, inhabiting what is now Mecklenburg. The Turcopoles, a people originally of mixed Christian and Turkish parentage, came from Syria, and "were really mercenaries in the service of Byzantium." See Pope, *Horn*, 2:126, and Bancourt, *Les Musulmans*, 1:16–17, 2:2. The Almican (who also appear in *laisse* 229, vv. 4833–47) are unidentified.

[10] 85 **Tervagant** *Tervagan*: a god frequently attributed, in *chansons de geste*, to heathen nations, but his origins remain mysterious. See Pope, *Horn*, 2:126; Bancourt, *Les Musulmans*, 2:378–83.

[11] 97 **And it will turn out as He wishes, as you will hear presently** *Si iert il, si li plest, cum l'orrez en avaunt*: with this line the Cambridge manuscript begins.

or Saracen, [12] through whom they could discover where they were, for they had no interpreter. As best they knew how, they began to praise God, for He had so well protected them from such great danger. Then they all sat down on the sand under the rocks and began to dry their wet garments, waiting the while for someone to tell them where they were and where they could obtain food. But God, who did not intend to forget them, sent them a great lord—I heard his name was Herland—who was seneschal to the valiant King Hunlaf, with the whole realm and people in his care. He well knew how to govern it rightly and lawfully. He possessed every accomplishment and was without reproach. He came riding along the seashore, with a retinue of about twenty knights. There was not one of them that did not carry a goshawk, mewed or unmoulted, with which to capture birds for their diversion. Herland saw Horn before all the others, and turned the head of his horse that way. (115–37)

7. Herland noticed Horn's noble bearing: no boy of his age—he was in his tenth year—was finer nor better equipped to give a good account of himself. He and his companions were seated side by side, drying their clothes, on the sand under the rocks. Then Herland turned to his men and spoke thus: "Bless you, my friends, look! Who are these boys? Speak, if you know them. By God my Saviour, I never saw handsomer ones! I shall discover who they are and of what allegiance. They certainly seem to be noble barons' sons. If they are shipwrecked, we shall greatly profit from it: we can offer them to the king. No finer or nobler beings have ever yet come his way. His whole realm will be held in greater honour." "Sir," they all said, "let's approach them. Depending on what we see, we shall tell you our opinion." "We shall certainly do so," said Herland. (138–56)

8. Horn could see them coming and was alarmed. His companions too felt insecure: no need to ask if they were afraid of these men they did not know, who might seek to harm them. But lord Horn advanced and greeted them first, in the name of the sovereign Lord, dwelling in majesty. He was the youngest of them and the most intelligent, the boldest of them all and the most nobly born. He asked for pledges of peace and security. When Herland heard him, he did not refuse them but saluted him in turn with an assurance of peace. Then he asked who they were: they were not to conceal it. And the child told him the whole truth, that he was Aalof's son, the good crowned king, ruler of the realm of Suddene. He told him all his history from the beginning—how pagans had killed his father and driven him out. And when Herland heard him, he pitied him greatly. Then he told him: "Neither you nor any of those with you shall be forsaken." (157–75)

---

[12] 118 **Christian, pagan, or Saracen** *crestien, u paen u escler*: the Escler were the same as the Esclavon, both Slavs. See Pope, *Horn*, 2:127.

9 "By God, my lord Herland!" said the knights, "this is very fine wreckage, much to be prized. We can certainly present them to the king with honour. This boy with the frank face, who spoke for them all, certainly looks like a noble king's son. He well deserves to command these other boys—not that one could find fault with any of them. Whatever you command, we shall carry out all your wishes for them." "Well said, my lords," the noble knight replied. "Each of you take the boy of his choice behind him on his horse. Then we shall go straight to the principal room[13] where my lord Hunlaf, our king, usually sits. There we will present him with these foundlings and he can, as king and governor, do what he likes with them. If he abides by my advice, he will do well to keep them, for they may yet perhaps render him service." As he spoke, so it happened, as you will hear our story tell later, if you wish to hear it. Everyone was of the same mind: "Agreed! What you have said is not to be denied." (176–94)

10. Each, at the lord's command, chose one of the boys, and Herland the seneschal selected my lord Horn. Very tenderly he carried him behind him on his horse. Horn should in no way suffer harm where he could protect him. Each of his companions treated his boy the same way. Then along the cart-road they went, towards the palace. They dismounted at the royal hall and their horses were taken off to the stables. The noble children attracted much attention: their silken tunics suited them well, but Horn surpassed them all as the day-star eclipses the lesser stars nearby—in such a way was he supreme lord over them.

Herland entered the hall along with them all and came into the king's presence like a noble knight. Now they would make him a gift such as he had never received before. First they greeted him as their own lord. Then Herland, Toral's son, spoke: "My lord and honoured King, steadfast above all others, today we went hawking, down by the seaport. On that rocky shore we found these children, no sailor with them, landed in the teeth of a perilous storm. (195–217)

11. "In the midst of the terrible storm they had landed there, in a battered old boat, which struck the rocks and fell to pieces. You must know they have neither rudder, oar nor sail, nor anything else to help them, except the power of God which saved them from death. As shipwreck took them there, so have I brought them to you here. Henceforth do just as you please with them. The youngest of them all is the wisest. He will certainly recount to you all his lineage. In their land he was their lord and thus he is, I think, the readiest of speech, the noblest and the handsomest. In my opinion they are well-born: no beggar would ever have arrayed them thus. When you know who they are, take counsel on what it will please you to do, whether you want to bring them up, or to sell them and profit by it. Henceforth they are yours: do what you want with them." (218–37)

---

[13] 186 **principal room** *soler*: the *soler* or *solar* is the room, usually on the upper storey, which served as a king's living-room and occasionally a dining-room too.

12. King Hunlaf received them with great pleasure. He called Horn and asked him gently: "Listen now, what is your name? Who were your kin?[14] Tell me the truth and do not be afraid. From now on you can count on my strongest support." Then Horn, reassured, gladly replied: "Dear lord, I think and believe that you are the king to whom this land belongs. Your promise encourages me, so I will tell you the truth without reserve, despite the fact that my father was indeed, because of his actions, sworn enemy to many. My father was a very noble, valiant man, of the name of Aalof, if my lineage does not lie. He was born in Suddene and ruled it a long while. He was a foundling of King Silauf's, who brought him up kindly. Later, by God's command, it became known that he was really of royal descent, the grandson of Baderof by his noble daughter Goldeburc (that was her baptismal name). I do not know if you ever heard talk of such kings: they were bold, brave, and of noble bearing, but now they have all passed away. May Almighty God have mercy on their souls! (238–61)

13. "When it was discovered that Aalof was well-born, grandson of Baderof, the good and renowned emperor of the Germans, then King Silauf, out of great affection, gave him his rosy-cheeked daughter[15] and his kingdom too when his own reign was over. I am born and bred from these. My father was thus a brave man, with enemies in many places; I do not know if he ever did you wrong, but that will not stop me telling you the whole truth. My father had governed the kingdom for nearly ten years after Silauf's death, when he was attacked by false and wicked pagans, many of whose lineage he had killed. Before he knew of it, they had taken him unawares. Their leader was a king called Rodmund. My father was captured through his stubborn pride: he wouldn't wait for his warriors to arrive. So before Hardré, his brave steward who had gone to get his army, could come, he was killed. Once my father was dead, the country yielded to the heathen, who laid it waste. Not a single nobleman remained alive; only peasants were left. Whether they were left alone or kept to cultivate the land, I do not know. I know no more of them, nor what became of them. (262–87)

14. "But as for me, I know that when we saw those pagans we were afraid of them—I and these boys, who had been placed with me by their kinsmen to serve me and do my will, sons of the powerful and high-born. So we hid ourselves for fear in a shady garden of dense foliage. A treacherous villain dragged us out of it,

---

[14] 240 **what is . . . kin** *cum as [tu] nun . . . parent?*: Burnley compares this "formal questioning [of the hero] about his family background and allegiance" with the arrival of Beowulf at Hrothgar's court: "It is lineage which furnishes the credentials of unknown new arrivals, assuring their hosts of their good faith." See David Burnley, *Courtliness and Literature in Medieval England* (London: Longman, 1998), 12–13.

[15] 266 **rosy-cheeked daughter** *Une fille. . .coluré*: at v. 4866 Silauf's daughter is identified as Samburc.

but did us no harm, thanks to the will of Almighty God. He handed us over to the African King Rodmund, who on seeing us took pity on us: he did not allow us to die in his presence. Instead, we were put into an old boat and sent out to sea, without the aid of any sailor. We had no one but ourselves to help us. Then he had us dragged out into the perilous breakers. There they left us to the winds and waves, and returned. But through the lofty commands of the sovereign heavenly Father, creator of the world, we were brought ashore here. (288–307)

15. "Thus we came to land, and such is our parentage. There is not one of us that is not of high birth; nevertheless I, the youngest of them all, am lord over them. I do not know if my father ever did you wrong: he did much injury to many men in many places, so I fear whether I have spoken too openly. But, good and mighty king, give us our freedom so that whatever happens, we are not in bondage — in the name of that most high King who for our sake was incarnate in the noble Virgin, as the angel announced: nonetheless she lost none of her maidenhood." "My fair boy," said the king, "you are indeed wise, and your face reveals your nobility and high birth. I shall do you no harm — that would be stupidity and madness — but, if I can, I shall restore your inheritance. If you survive, you will be brave in body and mind and still be able to avenge yourself on that cruel race. (308–25)

16. "Now I am well aware of your parentage, my fair boy, tell me next what you are called in the country of your birth." "Sire," said the boy, "I am called Horn there. Have mercy and pity on me, good king!" "Truly," said the king, "now believe me, my friend, you will suffer no loss through me, you will be harmed no more than my own son but carefully nurtured — and all your companions too — according to your wishes, so that you will thank me for it. When you are grown you will be armed and so I shall help you acquire your kingdom, whence the traitors have most wrongfully banished you." The barons who had listened carefully, hearing and observing every word, said: "My lord king, your goodness is great: may the sovereign Lord reward you! We believe you will turn this upbringing to good account." Then the children all fell at the king's feet and he raised them up kindly, kissing them compassionately each in turn. (326–45)

17. "Sirs," said the king, "my liege lords, now listen and do my commands. Each of you will have one child to keep, until you see that he is full-grown. Each shall educate his own to be worthy of honour until he has the strength to bear arms. Then return them to me and I shall reward you for it. No one will have the right to have any cause for complaint. And you, Herland my seneschal, will keep Horn. So, as you love me, teach him all the accomplishments you know." The seneschal said: "Sire, I consent. But there should be another with him, pleasing to him, whom I can bring up too: he can be his playmate." "Well said," replied Hunlaf the mighty, "that is appropriate: carry it out. Horn, my fair friend, now

make your choice." "Sir," said the boy, "I ask Haderof of you, for he is my age and I love him the most. He was son of lord Hardré, the best fighter my father ever had—he made him his seneschal and his chief man-at-arms. In infancy his master[16] had been King Silauf, the noble and brave, who raised him." (346–68)

18. Now, by the royal command, the noble children were well placed and well educated. But Herland the seneschal took more pains than anyone that his two charges should not be at the same level as the others. He esteemed himself not worth a farthing if they were not more accomplished. He would have taken it badly if anyone knew more than them. There was no musical instrument known to mortal man in which the princely lord Horn did not surpass everyone, and he was similarly talented at hunting and hawking. No one could equal his swordsmanship in any way, whether they wore silk or homespun. No one, compared to him, could handle a horse properly, no one carry so well a crystal-studded shield. Heavenly God made him handsome and strong, unlike any other mortal man, yet despite this he was both so true and modest that he would not have incurred physical dishonour for all the gold ever found in one day. (369–86)

19. The children were nurtured and well cared for. They were all very accomplished and well educated, beyond reproach in any way. But Horn, clever and brave, was prized above them all—deservedly, because he was their lord and also because in all ways he was the most accomplished, for such was his God-given intelligence that there was no master-craftsman he could not surpass in skill. Throughout the land he was famous for this, his great cleverness and great beauty, yet in no way did he grow arrogant on account of it. Many praised him for this, as was reasonable, for it is seldom that such handsome men are not also vain, but he excelled all others in modesty. He had so many talents that no one was worthier than he. And his renown spread everywhere: everyone talked of how noble and excellent Horn was. He was praised so much in the king's apartments that rosy-cheeked Rigmel,[17] the daughter of good King Hunlaf, came to hear of it—indeed there was none fairer than her in all Christendom. (387–407)

---

[16] 367 **master** *mestre*: on the role of the *mestre* in *Horn* and other romances, see Judith Weiss, *"Mestre* and Son: The Role of Sabaoth and Terri in *Boeve de Haumtone,"* in *Sir Bevis of Hampton in Literary Tradition*, ed. Jennifer Fellows and Ivana Djordjevic, Studies in Medieval Romance (Cambridge: D. S. Brewer, 2008), 25–36.

[17] 405 **Rigmel** manuscript H spells the princess's name throughout as Rimel; manuscript O varies among Rimenil, Rigmenil, Rigmel, Rimignil, and Rimel. Rimenil is in manuscript O vv. 405, 408, 486, 511, 519, 555, 557, 579; Rigmenil is in manuscript O vv. 588, 604, 627, 654, 663, 677, 699, 758, 774; Rigmel is in manuscript O v. 1140; Rimignil is in manuscript O vv. 4961, 4976, 4981, 4988; Rimel is in manuscript O vv 970, 1798, 2070. (This enumeration takes no account of ambiguous contractions.)

20. Rigmel was the king's daughter and a maiden of great renown. Her body was beautiful, her face rosy: there was none like her in sixty kingdoms. Many kings, dukes, and marquises had sought her in marriage, but to no avail; it had not been arranged, nor had the King of Paradise ordained it: He intended her for Horn, I believe, as you will hear, unless you are noisy. She had already heard tell of Horn many times, how very handsome he was and how active in all games and amusements. She had asked many if she could see him and to many she had offered silver, gold, furs, palfreys, pack-horses, and swift steeds, but there was no one who would do it or would undertake it. (408–21)

21. The high-born children were so carefully nurtured that now they were fully grown. They were sixteen years old. My Lord Hunlaf the king held a grand feast, to which all his feudal vassals were invited; neither wise man nor fool stayed at home, for the summons was made to all. So all the feudal lords came, for they wanted to honour their lord in this way. And all those came who were wards, the children found on the shore, whom the seneschal had presented to the king. Each lord escorted his own charge, whom he had nurtured and willingly taught every accomplishment appropriate to those of good family. They had clothed them well, each in his own manner, and irreproachably, as if they had been their own sons or relations. (422–36)

22. They assembled at Pentecost for the great annual feast which was handsomely celebrated. Many mighty lords came from many regions, and their wives with them, magnificent ladies, thus conferring more honour on the king's great court. Herland the seneschal was in charge of the court: he lodged them well, arousing neither anger nor strife, and no one complained of the accommodation nor of anything else. Horn accompanied him, his face admired by all: no lady seeing him was not deeply affected and troubled by the pains of love. His well-cut tunic was of fine cloth, his hose close-fitting, his legs straight and slender. A short mantle hung from his shoulders, its strings untied to allow him to do whatever he was ordered. Lord! How they noticed his beauty throughout the hall! And all said he must be some enchanted being, who could never have issued from the hand of God. (437–54)

23. The court was most splendid and the feasting great, as was fitting on the day of Pentecost. Each of those lords presented his boy, nurtured by him according to the king's command, and the seneschal presented Horn and his other boy, whom I mentioned earlier, to do the king's will. And the king gladly received them. Then he said to the seneschal: "My good friend lord Herland, today Horn shall serve me as cup-bearer, and all the other boys shall follow him: I wish them to attend to this office with him." The seneschal said: "Sire, I agree," and thereupon he handed the goblet to Horn. I believe he will perform good service with it: neither

knight nor man-at-arms will be able to complain that he does not appropriately attend to each. (455–70)

24. Horn served the king well with the cup that day. He carefully scanned the rows and made many a round, for he wanted no one discontented with his service. Thus he gladly had them all well served. Lord! How they praised his bearing and complexion now! No lady seeing him did not love him and want to hold him softly to her under an ermine coverlet, unknown to her lord, for he was the paragon of the whole court. Talk of him made its way to the noble chamber where so many daughters of noblemen, of noble barons and of vavasurs[18] gathered, together with the king's daughter, flower of them all. (471–83)

25 Talk of Horn made its way to the chamber and could not for long be suppressed. Rigmel, the king's daughter, listened to it attentively and kept it to herself in her heart but she did not want the maidens to notice this, for she was wily and clever at dissembling her thoughts. She thought hard about how to see him. She found a stratagem that satisfied and pleased her: the steward could contrive this meeting, so that she could see Horn in her rush-strewn chamber and speak her fill with him. So she then called Herselot, an intelligent girl and one of her intimates, and charged her with a message for her ear alone: "Go to the seneschal for me, in the paved hall, and tell him to come to me without delay, once he has seen to the clearing of the royal table. If he comes, his journey will be rewarded." (484–501)

26. Then Herselot set off—a discreet girl, daughter of the noble Duke of Albany,[19] a good country surrounded by marshland. He would rapidly and nobly avenge himself on any neighbour, however strong, who insulted him, hence he was known as "hasty Godfrey". She found Herland before the king's table, took his sleeve and drew him close to her, saying softly and quietly: "I bear greetings from my lady Rigmel, who begs you to come secretly to her chamber. She wants to speak with you and will tell you what it is about." "My lady," said Herland, "willingly, indeed, once I have served as I ought." (502–15)

27. Herselot returned, having delivered her message. She told her lady that he would follow her at once, as soon as he could after he had served. And when Rigmel heard her, she sighed for happiness, for she thought of Horn. Her heart

---

[18] 482 **vavasurs** *vavasur*: a *vavasur* is a noble of inferior rank, a vassal holding land from a great lord. The same word is used at vv. 2257, 2341, and 3667, when Horn is disguising his origins and Rigmel's birth.

[19] 503 **Albany** *Albanei*: Pope (*Horn*, 2:131) draws attention to Albania, one-third of Britain, according to Geoffrey of Monmouth's *History of the Kings of Britain*, and named after Albanactus, one of the sons of Brutus, who is its eponymous founder.

was stirred, she would strive hard to see him. I think the steward certainly stands to gain by it! If Rigmel can manage it, there will be no shortage of fine gifts, as anyone who listens to the story can hear. She looked around her and robed herself, asked for her mirror and often looked at her face. She said to her maids: "How do I look, ladies?" They replied that everything looked fine. She kept asking: "When will my lord Herland come?" And they replied: "Soon, once he has served." Meanwhile, here was the man she had asked for! And when she saw him, she rejoiced greatly. She took him by the hand, asked him to sit beside her on her bed,[20] then spoke to him in a kind and friendly fashion. Now you may hear how she begins: by blandishment she thinks she will accomplish more. (516–37)

28. "My good lord seneschal, for a very long time I have borne much affection for you in my heart, but I did not let it appear nor did I show it you. Now, so it happens, you shall know my mind, for I shall give you my possessions until I earn thanks for them—gold, apparel, horses, and minted silver, But first I want you to make merry. In there, my father enjoys himself with his barons, in here we shall drink hippocras and clarry[21] and good, rare vintages, long barrelled. I shall have you well served according to your wish and when you depart, I shall have given you so much that you will leave me happy and cheerful." "Fair lady," said Herland, "may the King of glory, omnipotent over His creation, reward you with the kindess you have arranged for me. If I live, I will make you great recompense for it, in every way you wish to bid me." "I know that well," said Rigmel. "Henceforth you shall be closer to me than anyone yet born." (538–56)

29. Then beautiful Rigmel was delighted: with this she believed it possible to procure her desire. First she gave Herland a big ring, of pure refined gold.[22] It was crafted in Daniel's time, by Marcel the goldsmith. The sapphire he put into it was worth a whole castle. Then she called one of her free-born youths to her, her cup-bearer, named Rabel. "Listen," said the princess, "do you know why I

---

[20] 534 **asked him . . . on her bed** *sur sun lit a seeir le rova*: there was a shortage of sitting space in medieval chambers: see note to v. 806.

[21] 546 **Hippocras and clarry** *Piment e claré*: the medieval apothecary *(pigmentarius)* added spices, such as ginger and cinnamon, to wine. *Piment* was already a symbol of luxury in the ninth century. Its best-known varieties were hippocras and clarry. The latter differed from hippocras only in being made from a blend of red and white wine. See H. Warner Allen, *A History of Wine* (London: Faber and Faber, 1961), 166–68.

[22] 560 **pure refined gold** *Or quit melekin*: *melekin* is one of two Oriental words (the other is *alchaie*, commander, in *laisse* 2) found only in *Horn*. F. Michel derived it from Arabic *melech*, a king: see Pope, *Horn*, 2:132. The other words of Eastern origin *(auçopart, auferant, aukube, aumazor,* etc.) occur regularly in *chansons de geste*. See M. K. Pope, "Notes on the Vocabulary of the Romance of Horn and Rimel," in *Mélanges de philologie romane et de littérature médiévale offerts à Ernest Hoepffner* (Paris: Les Belles Lettres, 1949), 63–70, at 64.

have sent for you? Have the wine, the best you have in the cask, brought to me in my great golden cup, carved and richly chased in Solomon's style,[23] king of Israel, which the king my father gave me at Bordeaux." "Willingly, my lady," replied the young man. There you might have seen many cloaks quickly cast aside[24] to serve the king's daughter handsomely and well, so that Herland son of Toral could make merry. (557–73)

30. Rabel brought the royal cup. He was well dressed in a silk tunic and with him came noble, well-born youths, carrying handsome goblets of gold and enamel—like Rabel's cup, they were beyond compare. At Rigmel's royal command he gave it to her. She took it laughing and said to the seneschal: "I shall drink first and if it is poisoned, then you can take care afterwards that it does you no harm. On such terms, Toral's son shall drink half, in order to possess the splendid cup." "My lady," said Herland, "the heavenly Father repay you for the gift! I know nothing like it. I shall certainly do your bidding." (574–87)

31. When Rigmel heard that Herland was in good humour, Rabel was once again quickly summoned. "My friend," said the princess, "bring me spiced wine, so that truly we may drink it and grow cheerful, I and my boon companion the seneschal. Then I shall give him a gift to make him genial and happy." "My lady," said the young man, "just as you wish." Then he went to fetch it, in vessels of gilded silver, and when they had drunk, one of her head-grooms, Bertin, was summoned. When he came before her, he was informed that she wanted Blanchard quickly brought to her, with the golden bit and handsomely saddled—there was no finer horse in sixty cities. Bertin departed and did not long delay, but brought Blanchard, as arranged beforehand. When Rigmel saw him, she said: "Now, seneschal, take this horse, which is very valuable. With this we shall clinch our friendship." "My lady," said Herland, "may God reward you! Neither king nor prince gave a nobler gift. I will repay you in whatever way you wish." (587–608a)

32. "My dear lord seneschal, let us celebrate once more! We shall drink the hippocras, so delightful and delicious. Because you are pleased you shall have another gift—there can be none fairer from here to Besançon: two greyhounds reared in my household, white as swans and fast as falcons." "My lady," said Herland, "the Lord in His firmament reward you for your gift! With the help of St.

---

[23] 568 **in Solomon's style** *Del oevre Salemun*: Pope, citing G. D. West, thinks this locution (also at v. 2433) indicates "a method of carving and engraving upon a precious material" *(Horn, 2:132)*.
[24] 571 **many cloaks . . . cast aside** *desfubler meint mantel*: servers of wine discard cloaks so that their arms are freer; see also v. 4150.

Simon,[25] I will obtain anything you wish in this realm!" She asked for the dogs and a page brought them: their silver chain was of the finest workmanship, their collars of gold, fashioned at Besançon,[26] were engraved and embossed with precious stones. And when Herland had them, he would not have exchanged them for Mâcon, a fine city belonging to the Burgundians. Then he wished to go, prompted by the length of his stay, but she took him by the sleeve and held him back. (609–26)

33. "By God you are too hasty," said Rigmel. "You may still stay here, sir, and amuse yourself with us and drink the bright wine. I still have fine gifts for you; moreover, I still have to talk with you. I shall give you a goshawk—there is none such from here to Muntcler—which I have brought through the seventh mewing.[27] There is no bird under heaven a falcon can strike that it will shirk, if you cast at it." Saying this, she had it brought before her. Then she said to the seneschal: "Take it, dear friend. Truly no knight carries a better one." And when Herland held it, he was filled with joy, seeing it so well formed and in such fine feather. He would have exchanged it for nothing, neither silver nor pure gold. Then he did not know how he could requite her, but she cleverly discerned his thoughts. "You can easily reward me for my gifts," she said, "if it pleases you, honest seneschal. I only ask to see Horn, the foundling on the shore, son of Aalof the proud of Suddene, for you have nurtured and cared for him." "My lady," said Herland, "agreed! (627–50)

34. "Tomorrow I shall bring you what you have asked for, once my lord the king has eaten. And if you seek anything else, it will certainly be granted." "Sir," said Rigmel, "this suits my desires more than anything else you could give me." "It is done," said Herland. Then he took his leave and went to his lodging, for it was nearly nightfall. He spent much thought on the service of the king the next day. He summoned all the royal servants to him and described all their duties to them. And when he had arranged everything, he went to bed. But he could not sleep, not for all the gold in creation, because of thinking of Rigmel and of what she had asked him and why she so wanted to see Horn, the noble foundling. "Lord!" he said inwardly, "what if she has fallen in love with him? She is daughter to the king, my sworn lord: if this is not done through him, she will be

---

[25] 618 **St. Simon** *saint Simun*: a first-century apostle, supposedly martyred in Persia (*ODS*).

[26] 621 **Besançon** *Besençon*: nicknamed Chrysopolis, Besançon was evoked in *chansons de geste* as a symbol of wealth. See Jeanne Baroin, "Besançon dans les Chansons de Geste," in *Mélanges offerts à la mémoire de Roland Fiétier*, ed. François Lassus, Annales Littéraires de l'Université de Besançon 287 (Paris: Les Belles Lettres, 1984), 67–79.

[27] 633 **I have brought . . .seventh mewing** *La setme mueisun l'ai joe ja fet muer*: hawks were mewed, confined in a cage, while moulting.

greatly dishonoured, and if it is done through me, it will be a wicked act. I shall be accused by my lord the king of disloyalty and I shall be blamed in the court for ever afterwards. This time I shall not take Horn; I shall take Haderof instead, until I have tested what show of affection she makes to him. When they meet, I shall discover from her behaviour how she would treat Horn, the brave and wise. (651–74)

35 "I've resolved not to take Horn on any account, yet I dare not refrain from going to the meeting which I arranged and faithfully promised to Rigmel. She gave me her splendid gifts on the understanding that I would make Horn known to her—his noble person, his valour unequalled from here to the East. But I don't dare take him because I do not know her mind, I do not know if now she would fall in love so suddenly. For a woman's feelings are so changeable. When she sees a handsome young man, she is quickly inflamed with love and soon, whatever the objection, she dotes madly on him and will leave him for no one, neither friend nor relative. Useless for anyone to rebuke her, for if you admonish and beat her severely, you are lost: she will only love him all the more. So I am in great perplexity as to how to behave towards Rigmel concerning this promise, but all the same I shall do what is in my mind. I shall take Haderof, so as to observe her behaviour to him at this meeting. Haderof is very handsome, not one in a hundred is like him, except Horn alone, who surpasses everyone in beauty." Thereupon he fell asleep with this intention, not waking till dawn. (675–98)

36. Now I shall describe how Rigmel passed the time, in good spirits after Herland's departure. She lay in her bed, but she could not sleep for all the gold of Milan or the silver of Pavia. She tossed and turned, and inwardly, out of her great desire, prayed to Jesus, son of Mary, that He would let her see and possess Horn. She called her lady-in-waiting,[28] Herselot, to her: "Herselot, I love you dearly because you are my friend. I shall not keep from you what I have in mind. Suffering has seized my heart, I fear it may kill me, but I do not know whence it comes or from what region. I grow pale and wan, I think: I saw it in the mirror the other day. I do not know if it is from love that I am so unhappy. I have had no experience of love nor ever wanted it. I have heard about Horn and he has caused me much grief because I cannot see his shapely form. Nor do I know if it would be on his account that I am so disturbed. May God who governs the world allow me to see him! (699–718)

37 "Herselot, sweet creature, I'm pining away. No man of my family, however close, whether parent or cousin, will stop me talking to Horn, if I can, in the morning. Lord! When shall I see him, this noble orphan? They say that he is

---

[28] 706 **lady-in-waiting** *nurrie*: a dependent educated and brought up alongside the princess (as Haderof is with Horn) and so a confidante too.

so handsome, his face is so rosy. He seems like an angel to those who have seen him. Happy she who could have him under her blanket of marten-skins! May God and St. Martin the valiant[29] yet give him to me! I would not exchange him for any sovereign king." "My lady," said Herselot, "you will have him, I foretell it. I had a dream—from which I know it will be so—that he made you a splendid gift of a peregrine falcon. You put it in your bosom, beneath the silk,[30] and would not have given it away for all Pepin's[31] kingdom. I know it will be a son that you will bear to the young man, and that he will challenge the creed of Tervagant and Apollo.[32] Many Saracens will die by his hand, should he live." "God grant it!" said Rigmel, "and St. Quentin the valiant.[33] Now, if I can, I shall sleep better till morning." (719–38)

38. Then she slept softly, as she was comforted and because Herselot had related the dream, until morning came, when the watchman with his horn showed that dawn had indeed broken. Mass was rung at the principal churches: everyone attended, high and low. Afterward, as was customary, court was held and the mighty household splendidly entertained. King Hunlaf, pleased by the festivity, was in high spirits and ordered it to be redoubled. Herland the seneschal gave them a cheerful reception and then had them served so that they wanted for nothing but found great abundance at their disposal. Horn went through the house: he looked like an enchanted being. Lord! how greatly everyone praised his beauty in all quarters! And then many good things were spoken of him. He and his companions carried both hippocras and wine in gilded goblets throughout the paved hall. The festivity continued until noon struck. (739–57)

39. Rigmel was very vexed it had lasted so long. She called Herselot and said to her with a sigh: "Go within, my dear, and tell Herland to come and speak with me, as we agreed. He well knows what it is about. I ask no more than what he promised me yesterday evening, as he left. Tell him, if he does my will, it was a lucky day he saw Horn. He will lack neither pure gold, nor silver nor rich coin. I have plenty to give, thanks to Almighty God: he and his charges will be rewarded." "My lady," said Herselot, "at your command!" Then the girl went quickly into

---

[29] 727 **St. Martin** *saint Martin*: probably St. Martin of Tours (d. 397), a Roman soldier before conversion (*ODS*).

[30] 732 **silk** *osterin*: a costly oriental fabric, possibly silk, which came to Europe from the East, via Sicily, in the eleventh century.

[31] 733 **Pepin** *Pepin*: Pepin the Short (714–768) was the father of Charlemagne.

[32] 735 **Apollo** *Apollin*: added indiscriminately to Mahomet and Tervagant (see note to v. 85) as yet another pagan god the Saracens believed in. See Bancourt, *Musulmans*, 355–83.

[33] 737 **St. Quentin** *saint Quintin*: a martyr of unknown date, supposedly a Roman who preached the gospel in Gaul (*ODS*).

the hall and found the seneschal sitting at his meal. He and the other servants were resting after they had served King Hunlaf the powerful. She whispered softly into his ear: "My lady, the noble Rigmel, summons you to come to her as you promised yesterday evening, when you took your leave laughing. I believe she will increase her gifts to you, so that you may the better be her constant well-wisher." "Fair lady," said Herland, "I will follow you!" (758–79)

40. Herselot returned, her mission accomplished. She came back to her mistress, telling her that the seneschal was coming, as had been arranged at his departure in the evening when he took his leave, and that Horn, son of Aalof, would be brought to her, the handsome and noble, the courteous and renowned. You should know that Rigmel gave a sigh of joy. Thereupon the mirror was soon in demand. She looked at every aspect of herself, to check on her beauty, to discover how well the colour showed in her cheeks. She adorned her body with the best clothes she possessed. She was lovely and accomplished, there was none like her in all the land. Then she waited for Herland to see if he would faithfully execute his promise, as he had been entreated. And Herland rose as soon as he had eaten, called Haderof and took him with him. They came hand in hand to Rigmel's chamber. The door-keeper opened the doors and greated them courteously: "My lords, welcome! and for visiting the slender Rigmel, grateful thanks." (780–99)

41. Rigmel's salutation was cordial; she was neither backward nor discourteous in welcoming them. She spoke first to the seneschal and laughing said: "Herland, God reward you! Now I know well that you neither lie nor cheat me. When the opportunity occurs, I will repay you well. Be seated with my maidens over there, on the rush-strewn floor.[34] If you want to ask anything of them, I wish them to carry it out in whatever way; no one who deceives you will find favour with me." "Fair lady," said Herland, "I don't believe I need anything that might incur my lord your father's displeasure." She went towards Haderof, with his fresh face, and took him by the hand. She did not want to be distant with him but seated him on her bed, with its finely-wrought coverlet of Alexandrian brocade. (800–15)

42. The courteous Rigmel sat beside him, thinking he was Horn, whose love had conquered her, for he was tall and extraordinarily handsome—I think there was none fairer between Poitiers and Pisa, save only Horn. He, I find, surpassed them all. She believed it was he who had such a hold over her. Then she said to him: "My dear friend, if it please you, henceforth I wish to be at your command." "Fair lady," said the young man, "you have not enquired who I am or what I am worth. You are too easily attracted. You could have a better man, worth more

---

[34] 806 **the rush-strewn floor** *la jonchiere*: chairs were still rare at this period in private rooms, which is why Herland (v. 529) and Haderof have to sit on Rigmel's bed. See note to v. 534.

than me—and so he should be, by St. Denis,[35] for there is no better than him between Friesland and Norway." Then Rigmel thought discretion made him dissemble. (816–29)

43. Haderof well understood from her manner that she was deceived in his visit, because she believed him to be Horn, his handsome friend, whom Herland the seneschal had promised to bring her; yet he had not done so. He did not wish him to bear the blame, so he replied prudently: "Fair lady, I greatly prize your words of welcome. What all men say of your liberality and courtesy is indeed true. There will not be such a one again till the end of this mutable world, which everyone awaits. I believe you will be well-matched if you have him whom you desire. He is indeed born and bred most royally, for truly he is worth a hundred of such as I." Then Rigmel thought it was a ruse and that he replied like this so as to mislead her, dissembling out of pride. She feared greatly lest he would not deign to love her. Then this inflamed her heart to love him all the more passionately. But soon she was to be set on the right track, for Godswith[36] entered the paved chamber. (830–52)

44. Godswith entered the chamber, which was paved with intricately-worked marble and limestone.[37] She was Rigmel's nurse and governess, who well knew all the royal household and she had often seen Horn's admired face. Now she had come to talk secretly about him with her mistress, of how everyone in the hall had remarked his appearance and unanimously said he either was an enchanted being or had providentially descended from heaven. At the sight of him there was no lady who did not go mad or nearly died or quite swooned away, so great was his beauty, described by all. She had come to talk of this. When she saw the seneschal, one of her close friends, sitting on the rush-covered floor and then Haderof, on the quilted coverlet, sitting beside Rigmel, the acclaimed and beautiful, then she said loudly and clearly: "Welcome, Haderof, from spacious Suddene! If only someone else from your land had come too, Horn, the good and

---

[35] 827 **St. Denis** *saint Denise*: Bishop of Paris and patron of France, who died c. 250.

[36] 852 **Godswith** *Godspiþ* Gundesuuit (Gundeswit) in the later O manuscript. The name in manuscript C contains two runic letters, wyn (here transcribed as w), and thorn (þ).

[37] 854 **limestone** *lios*: O manuscript only: *lios* or lias is blue limestone rock in southwest England. It sounds as if Rigmel's floor is made of *opus sectile*, mosaics of marble and stones of various colours. Such mosaics were costly, luxurious objects. Rigmel's floor, like Hunlaf's marble-striped hall (v. 998), indicates great wealth, though like humbler earthen floors it is still covered with rushes. See E. Christopher Norton, "Les carreaux de pavage en France au moyen âge," *Revue de l'Art* 63 (1984): 59–72, and Margaret Wood, *The English Mediaeval House* (London: Phoenix House, 1965), 389–91.

fair, resplendent in beauty!" When Rigmel heard these words she almost lost her wits. In anger and pique her colour changed. Now her words would certainly be attended to and would cause great harm if not remedied. (853–75)

45. "Oh! how shameful! By God's saints, did Toral's son think me a whore that he has mockingly brought a menial here to test me as if I were some slut? He would rue the day, if King Hunlaf knew of it. I will have my revenge, indeed I shall. I shall have him dragged to pieces at the horse's tail. No royal woman was ever so disgraced as I have been by this insolent wretch who claims to be seneschal. By God, I have few friends if they do not avenge this insult and seek his dishonourable disgrace." Then Herland understood that the princess Rigmel bore him deadly hatred. So he wisely responded, because he was prudent and true: "Mercy, my lady, for the sake of God on high! Tomorrow I will bring Horn, I will honestly do so. I did not dare to before, because of my liege lord, the king. (876–92)

46. "Because of the king, I did not dare before to bring you Horn. There are so many traitors and they are so slanderous. The good and the bad are all alike to them when they are busy backbiting in the king's presence, and at first people will rather believe the bad than the good. That is why I did it—not to test you. But now I shall bring you Horn with the radiant face—I don't give a fig for whoever grumbles at it—and you can beguile yourself with him at leisure, say what you like, jest and play. It does not matter if scoundrels think it wrong." "By God," said Rigmel, "then I must dismiss the anger and fury in my mind just now." "Have mercy, fair lady," said Herland the noble. "I must go now, for I cannot stay: I have to prepare the king's entertainment, so that tomorrow at his dinner he is satisfied as he holds his mighty court, and finds no fault with it for the many people he has summoned." "Go," said Rigmel, "be a man of your word. Do not deceive me as is your wont." (893–913)

47. When it came to the next day, the entertainment provided for Hunlaf, who governed all the others, was sumptuous. Herland the seneschal had made every effort to have them excellently served that day. Nobody could enumerate the courses they had, as was the custom, as well as the side-dishes which Herland devised for them. Lord, how many marchioness's sons served that day! But there was not one who served in his under-tunic, but in mantles of grey and white fur or ermine, or in silk tunics, the best that heathen lands could provide. Horn served there that day, surpassing in noble bearing everyone else there, from Brittany to Pisa. He acted neither proudly nor slackly to anyone, although he was the most esteemed man there. The ladies thought so much of him in every way that love tormented, provoked, and inflamed them. (914–29)

48. On this occasion Horn served in a crimson tunic. There was no such handsome boy in the hall that day: his face was rosy-cheeked and radiant. No lady saw

him, so I think and believe, who did not want to embrace him under a coverlet of ermine. That day he carried a goblet — neither Caesar nor Constantine ever had a better — carved in relief of fine, pure gold. With it he served Hunlaf his wine. Every one of the court was inferior to him in beauty and worth; everyone recognised his superiority. Herselot, the count's daughter, saw him as she crossed the marble hall. She was overcome and lowered her gaze, so much did she marvel at Horn, the orphan. Quickly she returned to her lady, in the alcove of her room (made by the mason Bertin, a skilled master prized since King Pepin's time) to tell her she had seen the young man, so splendid and shapely, so like an angel, of beauty so perfect, that no clerk or wise divine could describe or write down how full of all excellence he was. (930–49)

49. She came to her mistress where she sat under the wall-hangings talking of amusements with another girl. She laughed gently and affectionately and whispered to her: "My lady, I have just seen something which God has ordained for you — in appearance truly like an angel. He has the cure for the pain you have had: he is dressed in a crimson tunic, close-fitting and touching the ground. I believe it is Horn, who holds sway over everyone. If it is, there is none such from here to Palestine, either amongst Christians or heathens. Henceforth I would like you to be in his power, to carry out his will under an ermine coverlet. No countess on earth would be ashamed of that. Would to God he had raped me and had me all alone, whether in chamber or forest! By St. Catherine, I would do what he wished! Neither cousin nor kinswoman would know about it from me." "Be quiet, fool," said Rigmel, "you will never have him, if it please Him who made heaven, earth, and salt sea. (950–71)

50. "Tell me truly, Herselot, did you see this boy? Is he all that they say? Is he so handsome? I wonder if I will live long enough to see him! Herland delays too long in bringing him. Indeed, good seneschal, you do not keep your word: from now on your nickname in court will be 'slow-coach'." "Yes," said Herselot, "whatever is said in praise of his appearance is true. I saw him standing there and marvelled at him — I almost lost my wits and sense — but, with difficulty, I returned, for I thought of you and turned back while I could, running to tell you what I had just seen in the hall, wondered at by everyone, high and low. There cannot be his equal in the present age." "Be quiet," said Rigrnel, "you will regret saying more! The more you praise him, the more you inflame me. Would that the boat he came in, that brought him to my father's kingdom, had been burnt and destroyed, when I now so desire to see him and cannot arrange an opportunity to do so. Ah, alas! what have I said? That is what cravens do, blame what they do not have when they want it. (972–93)

51. "Herselot, fair creature, go to Herland for me. Beg him quickly to keep faith with me and bring Horn, and then you bring them back." "My lady," said

Herselot, "it shall be done as you command." She went back to the marble-banded hall and there went straight to where Herland could be found. She softly whispered into his ear the whole message with which she was entrusted. And Herland, when he heard it, readily replied: "My girl, we shall certainly come, we shall wait only until the king is served and the meal ended." Herselot stopped to watch the choice food, the splendid entertainment, and the pleasure of the king. Everywhere men were carrying both hippocras and clarry and wines too, long-stored vintages. She saw the serving-men coming and going and how they carried the cups and golden goblets, how finely they were dressed in well-cut tunics. But Horn surpassed them all as the most distinguished, the tallest, the strongest, and the most accomplished. Do not be surprised, my lords, if she was astounded: it's woman's nature to be overcome with emotion when she sees a handsome, shapely, and splendid man. (994–1016)

52. When Herselot had looked her fill at the court, she went to her lady and told her Herland the seneschal was coming — for which she had sent her — once the king was served, bringing Horn with them. Beautiful Rigmel heard her and rejoiced. She said to her women: "Girls, how do I look ? What is my colour like? Does it come and go?" They said: "You look very good"; each one extolled her. She carefully donned her best clothes, then took the mirror and looked at herself from every angle, adjusting anything amiss. Then Herland's delay seemed too lengthy to her: "Oh God! when will he come?" Herselot told her: "The festivity is lavish, he must maintain it a long while." "Herselot, go and see when the meal ends. Go, and hasten Herland, or he will forget." "My lady, I will not, for he will notice and realise you love Horn, and delay all the more. He is in great fear of the king and will put you off: by his advice Horn will never love you. (1017–34a)

53. "I counsel you not to summon him: if he notices you love him, he will treat it in jest and hinder it as much as he can, for he is very afraid of the king, who would bear him mortal hatred and whose wish would be you should never talk to each other. I can easily see and understand that there is love between you." "My friend," said Rigmel, "bless your good sense! Your advice is good, I know it well. I trust you in this: don't go now. Let them come when they wish and they please." While Rigmel and Herselot were talking, the king and his household finished their meal in the hall. Herland the seneschal did not delay but took Horn with him, to keep the pact he had made with Rigmel the previous evening at his departure. They went straight to the chamber, hand in hand, where the king's daughter, beautiful Rigmel, awaited them. The doorkeeper opened the door to them and they entered courteously. Horn's beauty illuminated the household: everyone thought an angel had arrived. (1035–54)

54 When Rigmel saw him, she was overcome with emotion. She thought it was an angel sent by the Lord above, dwelling in majesty, so handsome did he seem

to her as she looked at him. Nevertheless she rose and greeted him courteously: "Welcome, seneschal! Receive my thanks for being so true; you shall be rewarded for bringing Aalof's son here to me. And welcome, my lord Horn! Know I have much wished to see you, for a long while. Sit here beside me so that we may be acquainted. My lord Herland, who has been here before, will go over there to the many maidens. There he can enjoy himself according to his wishes. Whatever he commands will be granted." "Fair lady," replied Horn, who was wise and prudent, "I came here with him and he led me. I must do whatever he bids me here. He taught me all the good I know, so it is right he should command my allegiance." (1055–74)

55. Then Herland, I believe, said to him: "Sit here with Rigmel, my dear friend lord Horn. She is daughter to the man who rules this land. I shall be over there with the noble maidens. I shall get, if I can, sweet laughter and kisses. Grant what Rigmel, beautiful and pure of face, wants. It would be a pity if you were reluctant, because there is no more splendid creature from Rome to Paris. And would to God, King of Paradise, you had already reconquered your kingdom and were crowned, as is right and proper! Then were King Hunlaf to take advice from me about joining you both in wedlock, I would gladly counsel it without delay." "Sir," said Rigmel, "you would not be the worse for it. You would have your desires in plenty, I guarantee you. You would not lack for gold, silver, or furs; no count, duke, or marquess would be more honoured." "Fair lady," said Herland, "I am quite sure of it." (1075–93)

56. Then Herland went to sit with the maidens. No courteous person will ask what he spoke of over there: to enquire would be to no purpose. But Rigmel drew the boy towards her and they both happily sat down on her bed, whose fine coverlet was of Persian brocade. Rigmel did not hesitate but spoke first, just as I tell you: "It is quite true what everyone says about you—that you're the handsomest man alive. I offer you my love, if you consent; by this ring I hold, I take possession of you. I never said so much to any man in the world before, and nor, I believe, shall I say so to anyone else. I would rather be burnt alive." "Fair lady," said Horn to her, "Almighty God reward you! But I am not worthy of so great an offer. I am a poor orphan, I haven't a scrap of land. I was shipwrecked here like a miserable waif. I was nurtured at your father's command: may the Creator of the world reward him! As long as I can speak I shall never do him harm. A poor man is not fitting for you: you shall have a great king, that would he more seemly. You should not love me, who came here begging my bread." (1094–1118a)

57. Then Rigmel spoke, who had already spoken before: "My lord Horn, your bearing is such that in no way could I be haughty with you. It is only right that I should ask you to love me: you are of noble birth, for a king was your father, your mother was of royal stock and your grandfather the emperor of Germany.

Those who described you did not lie. You could love me, if you pleased. You will find me neither deceitful nor false to you, for I shall willingly do anything you desire. When God brought you to land, down there on the rocks with fifteen companions, good-looking boys, you all seemed born of a proud race. Not one of you looked like a man begging his bread, for there wasn't one of you without rich clothing: no poor man could ever purchase such. If it please the Lord who saved the world, you will indeed take vengeance on the wicked race who killed your father like murderous robbers. You will repossess all the land they hold. (1119–39)

58. "My lord Horn, my dear friend," said Rigmel again, "now take this ring, out of love of me. If you wear it on your finger for love, it will please me: no smith's hammer ever forged a better. I never yet saw a young man to whom I wanted to give it, but on you it will be well bestowed. So help me Gabriel, who announced God's arrival according to the Gospel, love for you has startled and subdued me; I can't free myself from its piercing arrow." Then Horn replied: "My lady, by St. Marcel,[38] I would rather be burnt alive in a furnace than wear it on my finger, so long as I am a young man who has not yet borne arms before a castle tower, nor yet struck a blow in joust or tourney. To wear it is not the custom for one of my lineage. But when I have struck a knight off his horse, or pierced a shield in the boss or the rim, then I can wear an engraved ring. Otherwise, better to be a shepherd in the field, a worker in the vineyard, or a smith at the forge. (1140–59)

59. "Now trust me, my lady, put away your ring. Do not give it to me or anyone else, I advise you, until you are certain that it will be well bestowed. Someone might receive it whose possession you will regret, should you discover he is reputed cowardly and base. So do not give it to me, for you do not know me. I do not know myself, I was never yet put to the test and so I do not wish now to make a pact of love with you. Nor do I want your gifts, neither ring nor other favours, which might displease the king, your father: I owe my good upbringing to his kindness. But when it pleases him to arm me, and I am highly praised at his court and before his baronage for whatever I have done, if, by then, he has helped me to recover my kingdom, and you, by his advice, still love me as much as now, then I do not say I would not be best advised speedily to accept your gifts and have faith in what you offer. But, my lady, you speak to no purpose otherwise, for, if I can help it, I will never incur the king's anger." (1160–80)

60. "My dear friend," said Rigmel, "do not do otherwise. Now, I make you a present of my body and my possessions. Take them as you will, whenever you desire, so that you have them to spend, lavishly, when you wish. And let us make a

---

[38] 1149 **St. Marcel** *saint Marcel*: possibly the centurion Marcellus, martyred 298 C.E.

compact of love such that you will love no other all your life, save me, so long as I am faithful to you." "My lady," replied Horn, "I would not do so unless the king agreed, whose advice I have taken ever since I came under his protection. As long as my life lasts, I shall never injure him or give him cause to be angry with me." "Sir," said Rigmel, "what you intend is right. I do not ask for a love that would disgrace me, that people would consider shameful, but for an honourable love, whose hopes are high, until such time as you recover your domain, which rightly belongs to you. Truly, I do not wantonly ask it, but because I want no other to possess you to separate you from my love." "Now let this be deferred," said the noble Horn, "for at this time I will make no such promise. (1181–1202)

61. "I shall promise you nothing now, my lady, until it is known what I am worth. When I am armed with my colours on my shield, and I enter the lists on a prized steed, if then I fell a good warrior's son, or a nobleman, offspring of duke or count, so that many remember me honourably, and if after that you talk to me of love, which will not shame the king, our lord, I shall do your will, if it please the Creator by whose order day succeeds night. But, my lady, now listen without indignation or anger: meanwhile some emperor's son will hear tell of you, for you are the flower of all women, and then he will take you for himself, to wife. You will have a husband such as will strengthen the king and bring more praise and fame to his realm. Do not wantonly bestow your great beauty: slander will quickly follow you, from scurrilous knaves who deceitfully invent lies. (1203–22)

62. "My lady," Horn told her, "we have lingered here too long; here, I believe, we have overstayed our time. I am very afraid lest the king may already have asked for us, for without us the wine will not be brought to him, and today he charged me with performing this service." Then Horn took leave to depart and she granted it most unwillingly, but before they left, they often exchanged looks. After their departure, Rigmel sighed long and often, and then called Herselot to her and said: "What did you think, as God is your witness? Did you ever in this world see a shapelier man or one with such radiant beauty? I offered him my love and all I have, but he cared nothing for them: I don't know whether it's from pride." "My lady," said Herselot, "that is truly not so: no man in the world has more humility, and his manners are so modest. Since you haven't succeeded this time, let him be summoned another time. Then, perhaps, he may be amenable to your desires." (1223–42)

63. Lady Rigmel called her companions to divert her, for she wanted to forget the pain of loving Horn which too much occupied her mind. They all flocked around to amuse her: some sang love-songs and snatches of songs loudly and clearly. But she did not listen to them, she could not give them her attention, because she thought of Horn, whom she considered too proud, who would not even look at her once the whole time they had sat and talked just now. Then she thought

in her heart: "God! Unerring judge! Why did You wish to make this arrogant
creature? His hair is long and blond, like no one else's; his eyes are large, bright,
soft and smiling, for looking at women; his nose and mouth well-shaped, for
bestowing sweet kisses; his face is open and his expression laughing, his hands
white and his arms long, for embracing women; his body shapely and slim, quite
flawless; straight legs, fine feet, in well-chosen hose. Since You have made such
a man, do not let him grow arrogant: it will greatly diminish his praise and renown. (1243–63)

64. "Heavenly Father! Jesus Christ, good King of Paradise! Let him not lose his
renown through pride. It seems to me I still see him and how he acted before
me. How sweet his voice was, his looks and his laugh! It was a bad day for me
when he came to this land; my heart is so ensnared by his perfect beauty that I
have no comfort by night or by day. And if he is very virtuous, why should I be
any the worse for it? When he sat next to me, by St. Denis, he would not look
at me, though I committed no offence. Still, he did promise me one thing: if my
father permits, he will be my beloved once he is dubbed and acquires fame. But
God, when will that be? He has fixed too long a period; my father has not even
arranged it yet. If it were up to me, the king holding Paris would attack us, or
the count of Poitiers, the marcher lord closer at hand, and my father would be so
overwhelmed with war that he would have to knight fair-faced Horn out of need!
May all-powerful God grant me that gift!" (1264–82a)

65. These were the thoughts of the beautiful and elegant Rigmel, while her companions sang in sweet voices. Some of them realised, but no one told her to
abandon these thoughts, which so dominated her heart; so greatly did they both
love and fear her that they said nothing. Now I shall return to describing how
Horn behaved. He went through the packed hall, splendidly full of wise and
noble people, and he wanted them everywhere to be sumptuously served with
good wines, with clarry and hippocras. He asked them that the king's generosity should not be tarnished on account of him and that there should be no one in
court to speak badly of him. While they were making merry, the king at his table
heard bad news about two monarchs coming to attack him with levied forces.
They came from Africa, from that hateful race which never loved God and His
angels. And when the king heard it, he did not feel like laughing, but invoked
Jesus' aid. (1283–1301)

66. Now listen, my lords, and pay attention! You will hear how lord Horn left his
childhood behind and how the King most high was mindful of him, for nothing
can perish which believes in Him.[39] There was no knight so skilled in the art of

---

[39] Allusion to John 3:16.

defence or attack from that day to this in the kingdom of France, nor of greater valour nor with less boasting, for he had put all his hope in God, and God protects well those who trust in Him. Two powerful kings had come out of Africa, who never loved God: that was deplorable and shameful. They were brothers to Rodmund, an arrogant king responsible for Aalof's death,[40] the valiant king and father to this Horn, whose life was here at a turning-point. They still held the land and all the possessions of which he was to be king when grown up, for his father had held it and had died miserably for it. But now God was to show him by an important sign that He bore him goodwill in His heart, because He gave him his first vengeance on them, as you will hear, if you make no noise. For they arrived with a proud and presumptuous army in Hunlaf's safe land. They came to a port people call Costance.[41] (1302–25)

67. Those who had now arrived in Hunlaf's land were called Gudolf and Egolf, and with them from Africa had come mighty barons, insolent, evil, and battle-hardened, continually making threats against Hunlaf. If he did not abandon God in whom he placed all his trust, they would not leave him one castle or city, nor the breath in his body, and the kingdom would be theirs. As soon as they arrived, they quickly encamped. They spread tents and pavilions over the meadows and brought out of the ships good, fresh steeds and impressive armour with gold-edged shields. Then they sent messengers to Hunlaf informing him of their wishes: he should give up his God to whom he adhered and believe in Mahomet, their lord. If he did that, he could keep his heritage and hold his domains in peace and quiet, provided that he paid tribute to them when it pleased them; and if he did not, then they would defy him, as one whom no one could protect from losing his head and all his possessions. (1326–47)

68. Then these envoys made their way to him: they were well-equipped and also of noble birth, well-spoken in their own tongue. To show their intentions they had with them interpreters who were clever and versed in many languages. They came straight to the king's principal dwelling. The porter conducted them, as was customary, to the upper room, divided into storeys. There they found the king with his barons. First they greeted him, as was proper, and then repeated exactly, without omission, what those arriving from the sea had told them to say. When the king heard them, he was inwardly dismayed, but he did not want to reveal it, for he was not so uncontrolled. (1348–61)

---

[40] 1313–14 **an arrogant king . . . Aalof's death** *un rei de surquidance / Ki ocist Aälof*: several Saracens seem to be responsible for Aalof's death: Rodmund, here and at vv. 4664, 4702, 4706 (and *laisses* 222–24 generally); Rollac at vv. 2931 and 3151.

[41] 1325 **Costance** *Costance*: possibly modern Coutances.

69. The messengers were arrogant, insolently repeating what had been entrusted to them, without omission. When the king heard it he was sorrowful and dismayed. He had the tables quickly cleared and went to his own rooms to take counsel. With him he took the best of his men, and when they were seated he indicated what he wanted and asked for advice on what he had heard. But they sat quite quiet, without boasting because they did not want to undertake any defence. Then King Hunlaf did not know what to do. At that moment Horn arrived, heard how they behaved, and saw that it was entirely to his advantage. He came straight to the king and spoke as follows: "Sire, renowned king, God protect you! I see you very angry and preoccupied: you fear these insolent messages. If I were a knight, and armed, I would maintain by force of arms that no heathen race should lord it over you and that the creed we hold from Almighty God should never be impugned for Mahomet." "Sire," said everyone, "he has spoken nobly. Arm him, we shall all be glad of it." (1362–85)

70. Then the king listened carefully to what the barons said. He remembered Aalof the fierce and how he had saved Silauf, his foster-father, from heathen wretches, him and his realm. He had faith—and he was right—that this man would do the same and be true to his birth. Then the king replied, as we will tell you: "Good sirs," he said, "by the Lord on His throne, he and his companions shall be armed. They shall fight those who have come to my house and, if God wishes them put to confusion, then we shall advance towards those left on the shore. If it please God, we shall lead them all to damnation and overthrow their great pride. Neither Tervagant nor Mahomet will protect them, nor Apollo their god, any more than a dog." "Sire," said Horn, "that's a fine speech. May God, who saved the brave Daniel in the lions' den and delivered Jonah from the belly of the whale,[42] repay your kindness." Then the king called lord Moroan, a Breton monk who was the treasurer. (1386–1407)

71. "Come here," said the king, "my dear lord Moroan. Bring me my armour that you have guarded many a year. I believe there's no better from here to the river Jordan: no matter how hard the attack it will not give way. Give it to Horn to make him more secure. Once he is equipped with it, the Saracen will have reason to fear him. He will have a gleaming high-peaked helmet, a hauberk double-meshed at the breast with yellow flaps, and an ivory shield slung round his neck—no sort of heathen can cause it so much as an acorn's worth of damage. He will have the iron greaves I took from a giant I fought with under Maldran rock, the very first year I was knighted. He will have the sharp sword that Roman the emperor of Rome gave me at St. John's abbey, when I went to Rome, straight to the Lateran See. He will have my sorrel horse, Passevent. With this

---

[42] Daniel 6:16–24; Jonah 1:17–2:1–10.

equipment he can do the heathen harm. As Aalof used to, so he will put them to scorn. (1408–26)

72. "My lord Moroan, good friend, look for other weapons, to arm the fifteen boys with him who accompanied him here from Suddene; if they resemble those who sired them, they will defy the heathen!" "Sire," replied Horn, "may God, the Almighty Lord in Trinity, reward you!" Then Moroan departed and soon returned, performing the royal command promptly. All fifteen of the boys were then sent for, and when they came, they were well-equipped, exactly as you will hear. First King Hunlaf gave the weapons to Horn — the armour which I described to you earlier — and girded the sword on his slender side. And when the others were provided with their armour, the wisest of them, Haderof, said to the king: "Great and noble king, grant us our request: that lord Horn gird on our swords at our sides, for he is our lord and we are his men." "Indeed," said the king, "you speak wisely and I would not stop you: let it be as you wish." (1427–48)

73. With the king's permission, each took his sword and brought it to the young Horn and he girded it on, as agreed: with them they would hammer the heathen. Then they left the council for the paved hall. The matter was not concealed from the messengers: the king made it quite clear to them that he would abandon neither his God nor his creed for them, and swore that not one pennyworth of what he owned would pass to them. If they wanted battle, it would not be refused them. "I have my defence ready prepared here, if anyone wants to deprive us of our redeeming religion, given to us on this earth by Jesus. We will never hold any other, for all others are false." Then a Canaanite sprang forward, huge, terrifying, and snarling. In his own country his name was Marmorin. He was unflinching, renowned in tough fighting. He had inflicted much suffering on Christians when he was with Rodmund in Suddene the spacious, at Aalof's death, yet to be avenged. Please God, Horn will requite him for being at that death. And if Horn had known he had encompassed it, he would have killed that wretch even quicker. This was Marmorin's hasty speech, in his very words. (1449–74)

74. "By Mahomet, King Hunlaf, I am an envoy of the two kings who have landed from the sea. If anyone will enter the field against me, I am ready to prove on him all that I say to you: that the creed you hold is utterly worthless. Though you don't want to, you should forsake it and embrace Mahomet, who can protect you better, and pay tribute on our terms." Then Horn retorted: "Now I hold my hand too long. What does this fellow say? I should keep quiet no longer. Go, miscreant, what you say is out of the question, and if God allows me, I'll make you recant it. I'll fight you now, man to man, to show you Mahomet's faith isn't worth a bean. If you dare to begin, here I am quite ready, first to defend our creed and next to ensure Hunlaf doesn't pay tribute." And when he had said this, he mounted his steed and grasped his weapons: he looked the perfect knight. Everyone took his

place in the courtyard. Now Horn would need Herland's teaching, who instruct-ed him so well in carrying arms. When the pagan saw him, he flew into a passion and went straight for him, full of anger. After their challenge, battle could now take place. (1475–99)

75. They slackened their reins and charged impetuously, each attacking the other like a valiant man. They brandished their lances, unfurled their banners, and struck each other on their shields painted with lions. The pagan struck Horn so hard that the lance, with its shaft of unseasoned wood, broke, but Horn was immovable as rock and returned his blow with such force that he knocked him off the horse, prostrate on the ground. When the villainous Marmorin found himself laid low, he quickly jumped to his feet to get his own back, and angrily rushed towards Horn. Now may He who saved Solomon, save him! When Horn saw him coming, he got off his stallion and drew his shield in front of him, be-cause of its thick lining,[43] and the wretch struck him without mercy. But this blow did not do him a scrap of harm, and when the scoundrel saw this he was dis-heartened, and cursed his blade, whose powers came from Mahomet. (1500–18)

76. Horn was enraged by Marmorin's blow. He drew his good blade with its pure gold hilt: now he would give the heathen a blow, if he could. He struck him on the peak of the Saracen helmet, smashing it into pieces and knocking it off. The blow fell on the cur's shoulder, breaking the rings of the double-meshed hauberk. He wounded him so badly that he nearly perished, so that the wretch cried out: "Help me, Apollo! You are too lazy to be mindful of me." Then he dealt another blow with the steel blade, but the young Horn was not in the least harmed but rushed on him with a fierce lion's heart, striking him a blow that reduced him to misery. He could not stop himself falling prone, measuring his full length in the middle of the path. And Horn did not spare him, did not treat him like a kins-man, but cut off his head in front of his clan.[44] (1519–36)

77. When they saw such a blow they were full of dismay. And Horn's companions did not spare them: each attacked his man and defied them so well that in a short time they had completely overthrown them. They presented their heads to Hun-laf, their lord, who was delighted and thanked them. The barons said: "My lord king, the armour you gave them has been put to good use. In this first deed they have fared well; with these men you will vanquish all your enemies. Make Horn

---

[43] 1514 **thick lining** *li doblun*: Legge's review of *Horn* (see n. 5, 312) prefers "cover-ing," i.e., of leather.

[44] 1408–1536 **"Come here," said the king . . . in front of his clan** "*Ça venez,*" *dist li reis. . .veänt ces de sun lin*: Horn's fight, as court champion, with Marmorin, armed by Hunlaf with his own armour, has clear parallels with the biblical fight between David and Goliath (1 Samuel 17:38–50).

constable[45] over all your people; he will lead them very well and just as you command." Then Hunlaf replied: "God be praised! I am now avenged on this one, for a start. I will do as you describe, and since you wish it, it pleases me very much for his sake. Now let Horn be called constable amongst you: in your presence I invest him as such, and I am glad that you agree." And when lord Horn heard, he rejoiced greatly. Then he said joyfully: "My lord king, mount your horse! We shall go and attack the new arrivals. They are an accursed people: not one will get away. The first blow is ours, and so, God willing, you will defeat them. God, and His creed you uphold, will certainly help you. They will find their Mahomet useless — that was clear today." "My friend," said Hunlaf, "agreed! You are constable: go, begin." Then Horn said to everyone: "My lords, to arms! I know it was God's will that we met to hold the feast: what a fortunate gathering! Indeed, God ordained it, in His goodness. Today we shall win great honour, over renegade heathen: you will easily conquer them and all their wealth!" "My lord," they all said, "God be praised! Nothing better could happen: fate decided it." (1537–71)

78. They went back to their lodgings. The town was in uproar, each man wanting to act valiantly for the sake of Horn alone. Anyone there could indeed have seen a noble assembly of young men! Not one of them did not boast of accomplishing such feats that his mistress should hear of his prowess. The news of the fighting by Horn and his company reached the royal chambers — how they had killed the messengers in an onslaught and how Horn had assumed the post of constable. Rigmel, hearing it, gave hearty thanks to God. Then she took a banner of Russian silk and sent it to lord Horn by one of her companions, begging him to receive it in this battle for love of her. And Horn took it, not wanting to refuse: it was the first token of love between them. The hateful race would pay dearly for it. There you might have seen that day many an elegant lady and noble maiden, with their rosy cheeks, ascending the battlements of the prosperous town, to see the heathen race destroyed. Horn was seated on Passevent, a horse from Hungary. He looked the right knight to be in command of all those there, so impressively did he lead them. Now may God, son of Mary, guide them! (1572–93)

79. Horn came out of the city, leading his troops: there were a good ten thousand of valiant armed men. But he wanted to take into battle only young men of repute, able to strike hard with sword and lance. The old men all stayed behind to guard the region, so that they could provide the means of recovery if anything went wrong with the rest. For the old are often tough people who can endure suffering when the need for it increases, as they have frequently borne it before. And Horn went secretly along a valley. The heathen were never to know they were about to have a battle, because Horn had forbidden any noise, wanting thus to surprise

---

[45] 1547 **constable** *conestable*: the constable was in charge of the military training of young men; in wartime, he was responsible for arranging combat or defence.

the accursed race. They rode along a thickly-wooded valley till they came to the harbour where the fleet was anchored. The fools, however, had disembarked and lay in the meadow in tents and pavilions, confidently thinking that they were so great in numbers no people could withstand them in a pitched battle. Thus they lay around, in overweening insolence. But then lord Horn shouted the battle-cry at their army and the fighting began before they realised it. The first in the field paid dearly: many a head was there severed from the body. Fellowship and loyalty were dearly bought by these, without question: not one of them did not wish to be back in Canaan, so harried was this cantankerous race. No clerk could count the numbers of dead men, to be seen with mouths agape. (1594–1623)

80. Horn, first of all, fiercely started the onslaught. No one he struck did not lose his head to him, and all his men did the same, hitting hard. And the heathen ran fleeing fast towards their ships. Horn reached King Eglaf in the midst of his men, recognising his royalty from his rich trappings. Then he struck his spurs hard into Passevent his horse, who bounded along, far from slow, and when he reached him, he made him a present[46] of his sword, cleaving him in two from his head to his lungs. As he fell, he jeered at him like this: "Go, wretch; I defend our creed against you. Such tribute and such dues do I pay you: this is the return I make you, from Hunlaf our king. Strike, noble knights! Don't spare them! Soon they will all be completely vanquished." And they pursued them all, striking bravely; before their blows hundreds and thousands fell. But Gudlof escaped the attack and, entering his ship, proudly armed himself: now he would join in the battle (if the chronicle does not lie), for already his men had rallied round him. He would do great harm before the end. (1624–46)

81. Gudlof armed in the hold of the ship and the heathen people rallied to him. They returned to land with burning ferocity. They overran the fields and the whole woodland, and our men were few against the barbarian race. But they were good knights, superbly valiant, and Horn, a lion in strength, led them. He cut off many a head, severed many a spine, and plunged his lance through many a breast. As the text says, no one could count them. The armies met beside a fir-wood. The Saracens shouted their war-cry and we ours: "St. Malo of the Bretons!"[47] Many an ashen lance was to be shattered, many a horn was blown, and many a trumpet sounded, whose noise was heard far over the sea. Horn brandished his spear, with its trailing pennon, and struck a pagan, Turlin of Tabarine—one

---

[46] 1632 **made him a present of his sword** *li fist de sun brand un present:* black humour about the infliction of injury characterises *Horn* (see *laisses* 158, 241 etc.), *Boeve de Haumtone*, another Anglo-Norman romance influenced by the *chansons de geste*, and early English romances too.

[47] 1659 **St. Malo of the Bretons** *Mallou la bretunine*: possibly of Welsh origin, sixth-seventh century, and mainly known as apostle of Brittany (*ODS*).

of Gudlof's relatives, a son of his kinswoman—so hard that his shield was not worth a chicken's wing, nor his double-meshed hauberk a weasel's skin, for he cut through his breast, liver, and entrails, flinging him down dead in the mire beside a thorn-bush. "Away with you, wretch!" he said, "may Beelzebub in hell seize you today, with his hellish company! You'll never prove our way of life is false." (1647–72)

82. Then Horn and his fifteen young men, the newly-armed who followed him, did very well, proving their valour against the evil Saracens, for they slew them wherever they found them; not one escaped who did not come to a sticky end. Haderof came across a pagan, Gibelin, the kings' constable and their own cousin; he sat well-armed on an Arab steed and poured out threats against our people. Haderof heard him, grasped his steel blade, made for him and struck him on his heathen helmet, cleaving him to the teeth. He fell prone: neither Mahomet nor Apollo could protect him from dying immediately in the middle of the field. Horn saw it and rejoiced, calling out: "Bless you, Haderof! I'm avenged on the cur! He'll never destroy our creed, nor shall we ever pay tribute to foreigners." The battle was furious; the heathen were undone and fiercely harassed. Miserably, they all fled. (1673–92)

83. Elsewhere King Gudlof was fighting courageously. Near a clearing he came across Herland, the seneschal of old King Hunlaf. He fought with him, knocking him off his grey horse. Horn the valiant nearly came too late: if he had not come at top speed, the Saracen would have slain him. He was already holding him by the nose-guard when the brave warrior came up, and the treacherous scoundrel would have cut off his head when Horn shouted to him: "Villain, don't touch him! I owe him my help: he brought me up as a lad and indeed I owe him a recompense, no question about it." Then he struck him fiercely on his shield so that both leather and wood shattered and severed, and through his hauberk he hacked into flesh and fat. With that blow he killed him. Then he made for the standard and slew its bearer, the heathen Malbruart. (1693–1708)

84. Horn rejoiced and was glad: he had won his battle. Not a pagan he reached had not lost his head, as God in advance had ordained matters, who, through Horn, had defended and protected His law. Then they went over to the ships, stocked with riches and great wealth, which was distributed there: neither high nor low lacked their portion, so that no words nor quarrels arose. The king's portion was handed over for him to do with as he pleased. Horn then made his way to the city. So many noble ladies could be seen in the streets, clad in wheel-patterned brocade or silk, to welcome back their lovers, who had brought them such joy by so great a slaughter of heathen that day. Never was a battle better fought, after that day. Many a heathen woman lost her lover there. (1709–22)

85. Horn acquitted himself very well, defeating them valiantly. He broke up the ships and took all the wealth, and so distributed it between them that there was no complaint. Then he went to the city where lord Hunlaf awaited him, and he received him with love and joy. Horn presented his portion to him, and he thanked him for the riches won in such a victory. Then he put the land under his governance, so that all his people should do his will, because he was old and could not support the burden, and lord Horn would henceforward deputise completely for him. Horn sent a strong challenge to those who had offended against the king, and summoned all those who held land from him. First of all he wanted to attack Anjou, for its count had greatly wronged Hunlaf: you should know that he first wanted to take revenge on him.[48] Everyone in the land came proudly and without delay on the appointed day. Lord Horn led them splendidly, like a noble knight. He burnt and destroyed and laid the land waste, and besieged the count with all his might. Whether he liked it or not, he came to terms entirely at lord Horn's pleasure, on whom mercy depended. And Horn made quite sure, through careful taking of hostages, that he would behave loyally towards his lord; by Almighty God, he would never transgress again. Then Horn, through this deed, was much feared. (1723–50)

86. All those who had hitherto despised King Hunlaf, on account of his great age and his weakness, Horn slew or attacked so hard that, whether they liked it or not, they begged for mercy, paid tribute, and gave hostages as a sign of keeping the peace with Hunlaf. And he who did not wish to was quickly overthrown; no town, castle, or city failed to be ravaged, and whoever was captured was killed and despatched. For this reason peace and a truce were declared throughout the realm, and Horn was held in more fear and awe than anyone else in Christendom. And King Hunlaf loved him as if he had begotten him, because through him he held his kingdom in such great tranquility that there was no neighbour to harass him, for they all feared Horn and his stubborn pride. Where he intended harm, he avenged himself very fast, and where he intended good, he behaved very soberly: because of this he was called lord throughout the land, like a valiant man, and he was so generous that his renown grew throughout the realm. And nothing he asked for was refused him; he was everywhere both extolled and loved. But Fortune cannot remain stable. Because this man was so handsome and valiant, I tell you many envied him, as I will now describe to you, if you are listening. (1751–73)

---

[48] 1739 **he wanted to take revenge on him** *de lui. . .veut prendre vengement*: on Horn's raid into Anjou as "a sudden glimpse of standard twelfth-century local feuding," see Laura Ashe, *Fiction and History in England, 1066–1200* (Cambridge: Cambridge University Press, 2007), 155–56. Brittany was part of the Angevin empire from 1158 onwards, having been acquired by Henry II (who was also count of Anjou).

87. Rigmel, the king's daughter, heard much talk of his great prowess, of his generous gifts. She could no longer conceal the love she already had. She summoned him to her. He would not refuse her, but willingly came, for diversion and entertainment. She addressed him as I shall relate: "My lord Horn, you are now a knight, thank God. Now you may easily vaunt and boast that on earth there is no better at bearing arms. You are renowned for it—I heard so recently. If you wish, henceforth you can't deny me the love I used to beg you for, for I will do whatever you command me: you can use my possessions entirely as you please. I thank you for deigning to carry the pennon I sent you in pitched battle. Now, take this ring so brilliant and fine. When you see it, you will remember me. My love will never be false to you, so long as I know you love me. Why are you silent so long? There is no avoiding it! Take the ring, along with this kiss! No need to worry about what anyone says, knave or liar: someone complaining of it would get scant reward." (1773–97)

88. Then Horn replied: "Rigmel, by your leave, I will take this ring, I will not refuse it. The other day I carried your pennon for love of you—know that it caused many a pagan to lose his horse—and I want the love between us constantly to be kept alive. I am very happy with it, provided it pleases Hunlaf, for I seek nothing that makes me ashamed before him; by St. Marcel, I would rather die, because he raised me tenderly from when I was a little boy. But, fair lady, for St. Michael's sake, beg him to help me with all his might in something I entreat: to regain my kingdom—every town, city, and castle—from which I am an outcast, as it is held by Saracens, those renegade wretches, sons of Cain, not Abel. Then, if the king permits, I will do as you wish. No need to give me anything with you—gold, silver, or plate—only your body, in nothing but a cloak. Love me truly and I will be true to you; if you are a turtle-dove, I will be your mate, taking only one spouse, as the Bible says."[49] (1798–1817)

89. As you can hear, the love-pact was concluded, which was long kept on both sides. But it was not long before they were separated by a wicked traitor who denounced them, Horn's close cousin and kinsman. Through him and his lies he was embroiled with the king and went off to serve in foreign lands. This love was nearly defeated by the forceful constraint of Rigmel the beautiful, as you will hear, if you want to listen. One day Horn was in his own lodgings and with him the companions he loved best. He had made them a feast and they were merry, so they entertained each other by making boasts. Wikele was there, grandson of Denerez, who had accused Aalof to the noble Silauf, and this Wikele was to denounce Horn, his lord. He was an evil traitor, in this way faithful to his lineage, because he was cowardly and treacherous—this is proven truth. He came

---

[49] It is not the Bible that should be referred to here but the *Physiologus* and bestiary literature.

straight to Horn, sat down by his side, and said what he wanted of him, in this way. (1818–38)

90. "My lord," said Wikele, "listen to your liegeman! I am your kinsman and loyal to you: wherever I am no harm will come to you, for I love and esteem you above all mortal men. No man alive now is so princely, and your words and deeds are always so regal that no earthly being could challenge their truth. Now grant me a gift, pray don't refrain from giving it me: it is the white horse which Herland the steward gave you the other day." "Wikele," said Horn, "that would be a shameful gift. I gave it to Haderof on Christmas Day, and a good sword too, with a pommel of crystal. But you shall have another horse, more splendid, and much swifter over hill and dale: it will never flag at crossing hillsides. And you shall have a spear with a silk pennon: there is none such to equal it in court." "Come now!" said Wikele, "I never heard such a thing before! To deny me this shows mortal hatred. (1839–58)

91. "Now I see very well," said Wikele, "that I shan't get this gift. I don't have much confidence in your friendship. I will look for a lord to serve somewhere else, if I can, who can give me fine presents and aid, if necessary. I think whoever puts too much trust in you is foolish. I will pay you back for my unanswered request, when I'm able. He is mad who asks you for anything!" "What?" replied Horn, "do you think you can get one jot from me through insolence? Do what you like; I shall see what power you have, for you shan't get a fig's worth from me." Then Wikele left, with an angry face: he would invent a lie of which Horn had no inkling. He quickly saddled his horse and set out as fast as he could for the peaceful forest, where good King Hunlaf was hunting, with his retinue. He drew him aside and uttered his tale of lies—the old saying is true: "Envy will never die."[50] "My lord king," he said, "I have heard something strange that I won't refrain from telling you, for you are the person I love most in the world, even more than Horn, whom I owe friendship and loyalty. (1859–79)

92. "Since that is so, my lord king, then I will not hide it, if I'm aware of anything shameful to you anywhere. If I knew of it, I would tell you, even if it concerned my own brother, for you nurtured me: thus I could repay you. But if I reveal it you, I must be quite sure that I'm not betrayed or accused in this affair." "My dear friend," said the king, "I assure you, tell me truly and I will never betray you." "Indeed," said Wikele, "then I shall tell you. When I was in your chambers, some days ago, I observed that Horn lay with Rigmel, which seemed to me a shameful deed. Afterwards he said, whenever he pleased, 'I shall never wed her, but make

---

[50] 1875 **Envy will never die** *Ja ne murra envie*: this proverb is cited in Joseph Morawski, *Proverbes français antérieurs au XVe siècle* (Paris: CFMA, 1925), nos. 704 and 705. See also v. 2580.

her my paramour for as long as I like. I'll seize the kingdom from that old fool and with that I'll certainly reconquer my realm.' And when I heard that, sire, I rebuked him. Ever after, he did not wish me well, so I am leaving him, for I shall cleave to you, for good or ill. (1880–97)

93. "If he will not take an oath, sire, you may trust me that what I tell you is the whole truth. It would go against the grain to tell you one untrue word." "My friend," said the king, "go now: I heartily thank you, for I know well that you love me—and if I live long, you will profit greatly from it—when you don't tolerate Horn to impugn my honour. Give no sign of this, but dissemble carefully!" And the king remained, sad and angry. Then he called all his huntsmen to him and they gathered up their venison, they had had enough hunting. Then he went back to his time-honoured city. And Horn came to greet him, as he always did, and said: "Hand me the sword and gloves, sire." He was accustomed to do this, before his indictment. But the king said neither "Come" nor "Go" to him, but held them out to two other friends, and lord Horn and many others were amazed. Then Horn asked why he was angry: "Dear lord, tell me if I am at odds with you." "Yes," said the king, "you shall hear of it at once. We shall never be friends unless you can deny it. (1898–1919)

94. "Raising you has been a bad mistake, for you have procured me harm and shame. You are sleeping with my daughter, a wicked deed; you repay me evilly for the good I did you. But, by the Lord whom penitents invoke, if you cannot deny it to me, and on oath, you will find no favour with me, for the rest of your days." Then Horn replied thus: "Now listen to me, noble king! Take two knights, chosen from a hundred: if they want to find me guilty, I shall defend myself against them. However valiant they may be, I am so sure of being in the right that I have no fear of them: I shall vanquish them utterly here, before your household. He who tells you this, and can't prove it, is mad. You should not, if you please, so foolishly believe these evil, jealous men who bear me so much envy: I have done them no harm, by St. Vincent!"[51] "By God," said the king, "I won't believe a word you say unless I get better assurance, and that on oath; and those who arrived with you shall swear likewise." "By God, sire," said Horn, "that shall not be done, for it is not the custom among those of my race. (1920–40)

95. "He whose time is up, so that he's old, lame, or maimed, should swear. I never saw a king's son asked to take an oath, for it would be base. So long as he is whole in body, if he is accused of anything, he refutes it in combat: that is how the right is determined. If he won't do so, he admits his guilt like a man who shouldn't remain in Christendom or amongst people without dishonour. My lord king, this

---

[51] 1936 **St. Vincent** *saint Vincent*: St. Vincent of Saragossa, d. 304, deacon and martyr (*ODS*).

is right and according to the law. Therefore let him who accused me come forward, and if he can prove it, take no pity on me but let me be hanged or sent to the stake. Let him besides have two of his kin with him: I will maintain against them all that it's a lie and that he accuses me of this deed through his own great wickedness. If I win, let them be justly condemned, like vile traitors who have encompassed my harm, though I never hurt them in all my life. I must defend myself thus, renowned and noble king." (1941–59)

96 "Horn," Hunlaf told him, "by the faith I hold, you shall swear me an oath, if you want me to believe you. If you won't do it, you can depart, to Norway if you like, for all I care. He who doesn't clear himself from the charge shouldn't be believed. I am no friend of yours, nor do I think I ever shall be. How could I imagine you would treat me so wickedly? If you won't swear, I won't believe you by other means, for I believe your words no more than a puff of wind. I won't appoint a champion; I would be mad to do so. Now be off, for I shall do nothing else to you, and I want my land to be rid of you. I shall take neither goods nor other possessions from you by distraint." Then Horn replied: "Here is cruel mercy. I could easily swear, if I had to, but in my heart I think I should not. I would rather have my heart and liver cut out than make an oath.[52] Any man of standing doing so is in the wrong; I would rather fight with six of your best men. Saving your pleasure, my lineage will not permit it." (1960–79)

97. Since King Hunlaf had angrily dismissed him, Horn the valiant and true departed. On his way he met Herland, the seneschal: he took leave of him as from his own lord. The royal household, all in tears, went with him. It was not surprising they did so, for he had been generous to them, valuing them far above rich possessions. A darker day never happened to him. Then he left them and went straight to his lodgings. He had a very swift horse saddled, which would not tire on mountain or valley. Then he donned a splendid hauberk, that he would not have exchanged for all the king of Portugal's gold, placed his helmet with its gold nose-guard on his head and his sword by his side: its pommel was of crystal and neither Curtein nor Durendal[53] was sharper. He had good iron greaves: why should I tell you differently? The noble Roland never wore better. He had a sharp spear with a silken pennon and a shield hanging from his shoulders with a brass boss, well gilded and set with enamel. Then, equipped, he went straight to the main gate. (1980–2001)

---

[52] 1976 **I would rather . . . than make an oath** *Ainz me larraie . . . Ke serement face*: on Horn's refusal to swear, see J. D. Burnley, "The 'Roman de Horn': its Hero and its Ethos," *French Studies* 32 (1978): 385–97, at 388–89.

[53] 1995 neither **Curtein nor Durendal** *Curtein ne Durendal*: the swords belonging to those heroes of *chansons de geste*, Ogier the Dane (in *Ogier le Danois*), and Roland (in the *Chanson de Roland*) .

98. Thus equipped and armour-clad, Horn came to the entrance of the palace and dismounted as fast as he could; someone quickly came to receive him. He left his spear there to await his return and went into the king's presence. He saluted him and walked proudly on, his shield at his shoulder, grasping his good sword, newly sharpened — no man could recover if it struck him in anger. And when the king saw him, he appealed to his friends, but he did not desist nor stop until he reached Rigmel, for that was why he had come. And when Rigmel saw him, she was so distraught that she fainted and fell under one of the vaulted arches. But when she came to, never was there such a lament as her women made for him. Then they said: "My lord Horn, you have been much feared. We commend you to God and His might." (2002–19)

99. When fair Rigmel knew that Horn wished to go, she said to him gently: "My good friend, beloved and dear, what does it mean that you won't swear this oath? You know well the accusation is false: to swear can't harm you. And thereby you can stay with us and free both you and me from blame, that wrongly brings us pain and ill-repute. If it were true, by St. Richer,[54] it wouldn't matter to me, so greatly do I love you and the pain endured for you would be sweet." Then Horn replied: "Leave your tears. I would not do it were I to be cut to pieces. I am not so cowardly as to rebut such a charge except in battle: no one will ever reproach me with that. Cowards, villainous slanderers, know that well, who want to accuse me of that deed to the king. Now I am a king's son: it is not fitting that I should clear my name by oath. But when I return, then he can pay for it, if I know who he is and can meet him. But I beg you to guard the love we have for each other, and not take another partner for yourself meanwhile. I shall set the term at seven years, if you will grant it me — for I don't think I can return sooner — but then I shall come back, if I'm not prevented. And if I can't come, you will be sent word, that you should do as you please, lead such a life as suits you, and release me." "Sir," said Rigmel, "I must consent. Since it can't be otherwise, you may go, with God's blessing." (2020–48a)

100. Then Rigmel well understood that he wished to depart. She fetched a deep sigh from the bottom of her heart. Then she said to him: "I want to keep your ring, my lord; because it's yours it will do me good to feel it. You shall wear another, a better, in my opinion, with a carved sapphire set in it. The man who has it on him can never die: he need not fear death by fire or water, nor on the field of battle nor in the joust, provided only that he is willing to keep it chastely. I beg you to wear it in memory of me.[55] I entreat you to return as soon as you can, for

---

[54] 2027 **St. Richer** *saint Richer*: perhaps Riquier/Richarius (died c. 645), French abbot and preacher (*ODS*).

[55] 2059 **I beg you . . . in memory of** *me Çoe vus pri ke . . .. de mei [pur] sovenir*: the magical ring, used also as a means of recognition between lovers (see vv. 4224–25, 4230–34,

I am bound to lose heart if you stay away too long. Close to you, I am filled with joy; far from you, I shall waste away. If it pleased you, you would not forsake me, for you are the person who gives me the greatest joy. God grant you prosper, as I wish and desire you should." "Fair lady," Horn told her, "be careful not to waver, for during this time I want you to hold fast. Meanwhile I shall go and serve some good king, who, if I do, may repay my service!" (2049–69)

101. Horn left Rigmel once they had exchanged rings. He took leave of her and courteously came away. He paused only at the dais where Hunlaf sat with his young nobles. Horn said to him: "My lord king, one thing I beg of you, that for the love of St. Marcel you treat me fairly. If there is any man here, young or old, who can say I ever behaved disloyally to you, so that in court I had to bow my head in shame, I am ready to rebut it, down there in the meadow, or here, in your court near the elm tree, against five, or six, all alike, so greatly do I trust in the God who saved Israel, delivered Susanna with the help of the young Daniel, and Daniel himself from the lions' den.[56] He would do the same for me, sending St. Michael to help. And if I'm defeated, by a sin I've never committed, then may I be condemned to burn in a furnace." (2070–87)

102. "Fellow," said the king, "don't ask too much of me. We know well enough that you are valiant and brave, so I would not find anyone to fight you. But if you will swear, then I shall believe you. If you will not, then go, for henceforth you shall not stay with me — and anyone so bold as to beg for it in future will regret it — because I shall do nothing beyond what I have said." "By God, sire," said Horn, "you are greatly in the wrong. Now I shall go, commending you to God. What the traitor said never even entered my thoughts, but I shall certainly revenge myself for it, should I ever return. But you, who nurtured me when I was little, shall not lose by it. If I hear you are in need, I shall come here quickly, to share your trouble, for that would be right. Meanwhile you will discover that he was a liar who told you untruths like a craven traitor, and then you will hate him as much as you love him now." Then he turned away and mounted his horse. He made straight for the road leading to the sea. With him came all those who wished him well, who had come in the boat with him from Suddene, except for Wikele, the traitor — he alone stayed behind, which made it clear he had accused him. All of them begged Horn to take them with him, and he replied: "I shall not do it," nor would he take knight or man-at-arms with him. (2088–115)

---

and *laisse* 201), is an old folk-tale motif, used rather more coherently in the English *King Horn* than here. There it is given to Horn before his first battle, for remembrance and also as a protective device (manuscript C, vv. 563–76); through it he recalls Rimenhild in battles in both Westernesse and "westene londe" (vv. 613–14, 875–76) before finally dropping it into the goblet (vv. 1161–90).

[56] Daniel 13 Vulg.; Daniel 6:16–24.

103. "My lords who love me so, may God reward you for wanting to accompany me, who am so forlorn. The king has nurtured you; remain with him. He has more to give you; you will be better paid. If you hear I have stayed in any one place, and you are unexpectedly in need, then come to me and I shall render you what you deserve, if I possess anything there; and if not, you shall conquer it with me. But now it cannot be otherwise. Go back, my friends, may God be with you!" Haderof lamented and nearly fainted, like the others, but he surpassed them. Then they all remained behind and Horn departed. His heart was full of pain, but he did not reveal it to them. He chose to go to Westir,[57] a celebrated realm—this was Ireland's name in the old days. There dwelt a mighty king, Gudreche by name. He had two brave and noble sons, of great renown: they greatly prized knights and for that were acclaimed. To them he wanted to go and in that direction he turned his steps. (2116–35)

104. He came to a well-known port and found a boat there that met his requirements: it was going to Westir with all its wares aboard. It stayed only for the breeze, and now the breeze was good, just as they wanted it. He came to the master steersman and spoke with him: "Master," he said, "is your voyage prepared? Where do you intend to go? Tell me truly." "My lord," said the steersman, "I will not keep it from you: I want to go to Westir, a renowned kingdom. There dwells a mighty king, Gudreche by name. He has two sons, knights of great liberality. Knights who go there are well paid." "I want to go to them," said Horn, the renowned. "Take me there with you. You shall be well rewarded: you shall have this arm-ring of pure fine gold." "My lord," said the steersman, "I shall do just as you wish. Whatever you think of, you shall have, until we get there and have arrived. As soon as night falls, we shall embark at once." And Horn dismounted and took a rest, refreshing himself with food and drink. When the time and occasion came, they went to the ship, and lord Horn entered with the sailors. He will now be called Gudmod. He changed his name from what it was at first, so that he should not be recognized in a foreign land until he had performed valiant deeds that deserved praise. When they had raised the anchors and hoisted their sail, they put out to sea and commended themselves to God. (2136–65)

105. Together the sailors put out to sea. They had a favourable wind and a good breeze. They bore Horn with them, the noble knight, for in sixty kingdoms no one was truer than he. He had his armour with him and his swift horse: there was none fleeter from here to Portugal. All night they sailed, guided by the

---

[57] 2130 **Westir** *Westir*: it has been suggested that the -ir ending of Westir indicates a Norse name for Ireland. See H. L. D. Ward, *A Catalogue of Romances in the British Museum*, 2 vols. (London: Printed by the Trustees of the British Museum, 1883–1893), 1:452–53, and *King Horn, Floris and Blauncheflur, The Assumption of our Lady*, ed. George H. McKnight (London: Oxford University Press, for EETS, 1901, repr. 1962), xx.

north star,[58] the most important star for sailors. They held their course straight
ahead until day came, when they saw quite clearly a solid rock, marking Westir's
splendid port. [59] No ship entering it is ever damaged by the wind. They made
port around six o'clock, on a feast day. Together people came to meet them at
the shore, beautiful women of high rank, dressed in silk, to see the ship arrive.
When they landed, they disembarked and Horn came ashore like a good and
valiant knight. (2166–83)

106. My lords, the ship bringing Horn arrived in Ireland, then called Westir.
He disembarked first. His face was beautifully shaped and he was especially remarked by the ladies, for among themselves they said it was some fairy creature.
Many said it would be a lucky woman who could intimately enjoy him and the
memory of it would put all later suffering out of her mind. Horn observed them
but took no notice; he donned his equipment. When he had armed his head he
swung himself on to the padded saddle of his horse and took leave of the people
gathered there, after asking where was the court of King Gudreche and his noble
household. He speedily turned in that direction, but he had not gone a league
from the port when something occurred which God had planned, for the king's
two sons had that morning gone out hawking with their own retainers. There
were only twenty of them, well-equipped. They had falcons and goshawks and
had scoured the riverside, taking so many birds that they were well satisfied.
(2184–205)

107 Between these king's sons I have just described to you there was a friendly
and happy agreement that, if any knight arrived in the land intending to take
service and obtain reward, the first two to come would be retained by the elder,
and the third by the younger, who could keep him with him, for himself. At that
moment, the arrangement I have described to you meant that the elder had as retainers two accomplished knights he loved and trusted. So now the younger was
to retain the next knight to arrive, as was his right. One of the retainers was the
kind of man who is strong in every respect, so that no one knew his equal. The
other played chess so well he beat everyone — no one against whom he competed
could defeat him. Meanwhile Horn the brave came riding along their path. His
fine horse clattered along it, he was well arrayed, and his shield became him. He
had all the appearance of a knight a man could trust, and the younger son was
the first to notice him. (2206–26)

---

[58] 2172 **the north star** *l'esturial*: this word, found only in *Horn*, designates the north
star; see Pope, *Horn,* 2:150 and the Anglo-Norman Dictionary.
[59] 2175 **a solid rock** *une roche naäl*: on this rock perhaps describing the Staine, or
Steine, near Dublin's harbour, see Weiss, "Thomas and the Earl," 5, and Legge's review
of *Horn*, 310.

108. The one to notice him first was called Egfer, and he quickly pointed him out to Guffer, his brother: "Look, brother Guffer, here comes a knight. He is nobly armed and has a fine steed; he seems valiant and knows how to handle it well. I see he's well equipped to bear his weapons. By God, brother, if he's coming here to take service, I have the right to retain him: you shouldn't refuse it me." "Brother," said Guffer, "agreed! I won't deny our agreement. No one shall ever reproach me for that, if I can help it. Now let's go and ask him all about himself: who is he? Where does he come from? What is his name, which he shouldn't conceal." "Well spoken," replied Egfer. Then they turned in the direction they thought to meet him. Egfer rode ahead, to interrogate him. As soon as he came up, he began to greet him and address him as I will tell you. "Who are you, knight? You shouldn't hide it from me: where do you come from? What do you seek? What should I call you? If you have come to this country to stay, or to serve for pay, I have to make you my retainer. It's now my affair, for I am son of the king who rules this country, a wide and rich one, to which you have come." (2227–50)

109. Horn heard clearly what he said and was not slow to reply, but answered him most courteously and in the order of his questions. "My lord, you first asked, who am I? Where do I come from? And what do I seek? And what name belongs to me? I shall willingly tell you, without any lies. I was born in Suddene, a most noble land. I am the son of a nobleman with few possessions: in feudal dues he owed the service of two armed men, beside himself, whenever he accompanied his lord to any tournament.[60] Such is my family: my kinsmen are poor. I came directly from that land to this. I am come to take service, if God grant it me, either with you or another who will retain me. And know that if I can I will perform it faithfully: I believe no one will find cause for reproach. I was called Gudmod when I was baptized. Now I have answered all your questions. If you are son of the king to whom this realm belongs, then I shall stay with you, if you agree." And when Egfer heard him, he gave him many thanks. (2251–70)

110. "You shall stay with me, my fair friend," said Egfer, "and I shall give you good horses, fine and valuable weapons, beautiful sables, grey and white furred robes, so that when you leave me, you shall be no beggar. I think these fine possessions will be turned to good account; nothing a man can give you would not be well bestowed. By St. Denis, from your appearance you could be born of a prince or marquis." Then Horn replied, "My lord, I have entered your service. From now

---

[60] 2258–59 **he owed the service . . . tournament** *aveit en tensement . . . turneiëment*: literally, he owed two knights' fees (*dous escuz*) beside his own. A knight's fief was granted by his liege lord in return for helping him with military service (or with money). The (fictitious) nobleman here would have to help his liege lord in the tournament by providing him with his help and that of two armed men drawn from his own fief. The "fee" describes the value of land, here that equivalent to the service of three knights.

on I shall not be slow about doing your command." Thereupon they returned in good spirits over the flat country straight to the city, where the king was. They went cheerfully to their lodgings: Egfer took Gudmod to the house of Malgis, his host, born in Paris. There they dismounted and their horses were taken. I warrant they had everything they needed. (2271–87)

111. Gudmod disarmed, looking every inch a knight, with his handsome body and open face. He was dressed in a close-fitting silken tunic, and his face was bruised from wearing his helmet — for those looking at him, it made him more handsome. But he remained without a mantle, for he had none to put on. When his lord saw this, he had one of his chamberlains bring him a rich cloak, and when he had donned it they went up to the principal chamber, where the sound of the horn as a signal to wash hands before the meal had been given a while ago. They mounted the staircase together, but those who saw Horn could not stop looking at him and asked amongst themselves: "Who is this warrior? He looks very handsome but also very proud. Believe me, he'll be a tough man in battle." Someone who was acquainted with him said: "Egfer has retained him, over against the two that lord Guffer retained the other day. But this man seems a braver and bolder fighter. But if Egfer takes my advice, he won't take him if he goes courting, otherwise he would surpass everyone in looks. This man surpasses Egfer by far, no one comes near him." (2288–308)

112. Gudmod stayed next to the king's son, but he surpassed them all in beauty of face and body. Lord! how his looks were remarked upon, and by so many people, because he surpassed all the company in height. When king Gudreche saw his sons enter, he at once beckoned them both towards him and they came. When they arrived they were asked about the knight they had brought with them. "Sire," said Egfer, "let him be questioned. I retained him today. He will tell you his lineage if you wish to ask it him: he speaks well." And the king said: "Indeed he is welcome here. Now have him come here, bring him to me. But one thing I will tell you, and that is, you should be careful not to take him with you if you go courting, for his beauty is so radiant that you, who previously surpassed every man in looks, would be underrated in comparison with him." "Father," said Egfer, "now you're joking. We'll pay attention to your will and pleasure." (2309–29)

113. Then they called Gudmod before them. When he came before the king he saluted him handsomely, and the king was courteous, asking him graciously who he was, whence he came, and what was his lineage. Next he asked him his name, and Gudmod told him, but not entirely truthfully, because he wanted to conceal there what he was known by in many a realm. "King, what you ask will not be denied you, although I am of poor lineage. I was born in Suddene, a noble kingdom. I am a nobleman's son with few fiefs, who had only three knights' fees,

counting his own.[61] Throughout his life he was considered a loyal man. When the land was conquered and laid waste by heathen, he was killed along with all the other noblemen. Just a boy, I escaped, by God's will. I went to Brittany, where I provided for myself, for I had acquired weapons and a fresh horse on which to depend at the start of battle. I heard tell of you and your goodness and of your sons I see here, who are so renowned, and that's why I came seeking service here, if it please you. Your younger son thus retained me and I will serve him well, just as he wishes, with all my might: no one shall ever find fault with me. I was called Gudmod when I was baptized. Now, sire, you have heard my history." (2330–56)

114. King Gudreche replied: "My friend, it is fortunate indeed if my son takes you into his service. He will show you great honour, and all my court will be the gainer through you. But I don't believe a poor man ever begot you! I know the land well—I was in Suddene once—and knew Aalof well, the good king reigning there: he made me his comrade-in-arms and gave me gifts. He had a little son, whom he showed me there. No man on earth ever resembled another as much as you do the child I saw then. If I had him here, by God who made him, I would repay him for Aalof's kindness." "Sire," said Gudmod, "it will often happen that a poor lad resembles a rich one, but there is no connection between me and the boy you speak of: I have no such luck. It irks me, God knows! May His will be done!" "My friend, you say well: as He wishes, so shall it be. If it please Him, you will soon grow rich. Whoever owns such beauty will not be altogether poor. And if there is goodness too, it will soon appear.' (2357–77)

115. "My sons, go and be seated where you usually sit. Honour this noble man as you should do. The honour you show him will be turned to good account. I shall never believe he is not well-born." "Sire," said his children, "we shall do as you command." Then they sat down, as they had washed, and they addressed Horn courteously, following their agreement and the king's orders. Then Queen Gudborc and many of her friends entered the palace and mounted the staircase. She had her two daughters, both very beautiful, with her. The elder was called Lenburc and had so many good qualities I could never enumerate them all. The younger was called Sudborc and was very wise.[62] They sat down at the high table to eat the choice food. After the first course had been brought before them, Lenburc looked long and hard at Gudmod. She called a boy and said to him: "Come here! Carry a message for love of me, my good friend, and you will earn

---

[61] 2342 **had only three knights' fees . . . own** *n'ot ke treis escuz od le soen acunté*: see note to vv. 2258–59.

[62] 2391 **The younger . . . very wise** *La joindre . . . sage assez*: with this line manuscript O stops, and resumes at v. 4586.

my thanks and gratitude." "My lady," said the boy, "I shall do as you direct me."
(2378–98)

116. "Take this cup, of African gold, engraved in the manner of the goldsmiths
of Solomon,[63] powerful David's son. Carry it to the knight I see sitting in front
there with my brothers: he looks noble. Tell him that just now I drank half of
it. Let him drink the rest, provided he keeps the cup for himself and wishes me
well. Thus he will be my friend in future. And tell me his name and what he
seeks, what is his country and who are his kinsmen. Come and tell me what he
replies." "Fair lady," said the boy, "I shall certainly do what you command." He
took the cup and went over with all speed. First he greeted him in the name of
the Almighty: "Sir, I come to you with a message. Lenburc, the king's lovely
daughter, in the name of God most high sends you a hundred greetings. By my
hand she sends you this glittering gold goblet. She drank half the cup: drink the
rest, sir, on the condition I shall tell you. (2399–417)

117. "She asks you to drink the wine for love of her. Keep the cup of fine gold for
yourself and drink from it, if you like, morning and evening. Thus you will love
her, and be more certain to love her. Remember her when you go your way. Tell
her your name and your lineage, and why you came to this foreign land." And
when Gudmod heard him, he replied: "Do your words come straight from the
parchment, my fair boy? No clerk or wise divine ever repeated his lesson better.
Tell the lady, with her rosy cheeks, that I shall indeed drink the wine, but I am
not so poor as to covet a gold goblet. I would rather have one of maple wood for
myself, or, even better, of fir or pine. (2418–31)

118. "She is too hasty, my friend, in sending me such a gift, such a cup, engraved
and so valuable. And I'm a newcomer from another land—she doesn't know who
I am or if I'm worth a button. By St. Simon, whoever gives her gold and her money to a ne'er-do-well is bound to regret it. Now let her wait till she hears whether
I am virtuous or not—then she may do as she wishes and provide for me as be-
fits my character here. So much you can tell her, that I am called Gudmod and I
was born in Suddene, now held by the Saracens.[64] I'm a vassal's son: such are my
origins. You can also give her, my friend, a message in quite a different vein: I set
no store by a straw fire, it quickly dies down. It's quickly lit and quickly put out.
Wanton love is like that, when it has no true cause." (2432–47)

---

[63] 2399a **the goldsmiths of Solomon** *de l'oevre Salemun*: see note to v. 560.
[64] 2442 **Saracens** *Esclavon*: Slavs, synonymous with pagans or Saracens.

119. On hearing these words, Guidhere returned—that was the boy's name, the king of Orkney's son.[65] He waited on Lenburc, who was destined to be his betrothed. None the less he did not refrain from giving her these words. He came to the rosy-cheeked maiden and repeated the words, hiding nothing from her. She was ashamed and blushed. "It's a good thing," she said, "to correct oneself in private. I was too hasty just now, but now I regret it. But anyone who thinks my intentions were base is mad." Then she started thinking deeply and forgot the meal, because love had attacked her and caused her torment. She said in her heart: "Lord! (son of Mary, as was earlier planned in the Old Testament), where does this man come from? Is he of this earth or some fairy creature, that he is of such a fashion? If I can't have him, I know my joys are over. I wonder whether anyone else is as wild about him as I am, for love fetters and torments me! So I can't refrain from another attempt." Her mother noticed her pallor and knew love controlled and moved her. She gently told her not to be foolish. But Lenburc was not in awe of her authority and only loved him the more. (2448–70)

120. When the king had eaten, the tables were cleared away and counts and knights went off to their lodgings. And lord Gudmod did not want to remain there any longer, but went off to his lodging where he wished to sleep. The queen had herself conducted to her rooms, but Lenburc her daughter continued pensive. She called for one of her runners and said to him: "My friend, you shall be my messenger. Go to Egfer's lodgings and tell the warrior—the man he retained yesterday, you will find him there—to come and talk with me in my rooms. If you can bring him, you will be amply rewarded. I shall give you a horse, and I'll always cherish you. Tell him he can have anything of mine he likes, for I can further his career with fine possessions of mine—chargers and palfreys, good steel weapons, minted silver, goblets of bright gold, and plenty of fine garments to supply him with a change of clothes. He should take as much as he can use, for he who has enough to give is welcome everywhere." "My lady," said the boy, "you don't have to ask: I'll willingly do whatever you command." (2471–92)

121. The boy went off to find Gudmod and first greeted him on behalf of Lenburc. Then he repeated word for word what she had told him: "My lady says she will give you possessions of hers. Nothing you want will be withheld, palfreys, chargers, or weapons. She will line your pockets with coins and refined gold. Provided you love her, she will love you." "My fair friend," said Gudmod, listening to all this, "nothing will come of all that you have said. You can tell her that that's not what I came here for. Nor did the man who first taught me instruct me to do so. Rather, let her wait now and she will hear of me, who I am, what I'm

---

[65] 2449 **the king of Orkney's son** *fiz le rei d'Orkanie*: we hear no more of Guidhere, supposedly Lenburc's betrothed, but perhaps this is why Gudreche asks the King of Orkney's advice about marrying Lenburc to Horn?

worth, and if I'll put to good use the gifts she promises me through sending me you. She may hear so much about me that she'll regret it, for if I am disreputable it will greatly vex her should any of her family hear she made friends with me." Then the boy went off and disclosed to his lady everything Horn had said and that he would take no action. (2493–512)

122. When Lenburc heard these words she was very unhappy, because love for Gudmod had hopelessly ensnared her. She was so infatuated she could not free herself. At night she could not sleep, neither early nor late, and whenever she saw him she was so overwrought that nothing anyone could do pleased or satisfied her. Lord! How many ways she planned of getting his love: none got a hearing. Her mother often spoke to her severely and threatened her in many ways, but the more she was spoken to, the more infatuated she became. She could not be deflected from getting his love. Lord Gudmod was well aware of it but did not care tuppence for it. The whole of that year it happened that the royal household did not go to tournaments or other military expeditions through which it could have distinguished itself or gained renown. Now you must know that such a life irked the brave Gudmod with his noble bearing. For the king had brought his wars to a peaceful end and made a truce, which had lasted a long while. (2513–32)

123. Meanwhile the king's household, quite inactive, took pleasure in hunting and hawking; but in every sport Gudmod surpassed them all, for no one in the land knew as much about it as he. If he were given a wild dog he would train it so well that very soon none would run better, and he would do the same with birds, training them to hawk so that none of their best birds accomplished as much; nor did this ever make him more boastful. When all his companions related their exploits, he would sit quiet, not uttering a word, as if he knew nothing about such a thing, so that the whole court marvelled and said to each other he was very discreet, surpassing them all and yet so reticent about it. Everyone praised him to the skies and spoke well of him. Three years had already passed without his ever giving a sign of knowing about anything, any more than if he were a child. If chess or backgammon were being played, he never joined in, in order not to attract ill-will. Yet there was no one in the land who knew as much about it. Until it happened one day—as I shall tell you—that the king held high court on account of a great feast. All his vassals were gathered there to augment the court, as was proper. (2533–56a)

124. The day you hear me speak of was Pentecost. The king heard mass at the principal abbey, sung loudly by Archbishop Markier. Then they went to the palace and sat down to the meal, all, without distinction, served so well and attentively that no one could improve on it. When they had eaten enough, the tables were cleared away and the cup-bearers served hippocras and clarry: plenty was brought for those who wished to drink. When they had drunk enough, they

began to amuse themselves. In the court the light-hearted young men started playing. Whoever wanted to throw the lance, or put the stone, could try his hand there if he was strong enough. They strove hard to try out everything, to see if one could surpass the others in strength. Both the king's sons went to the games, and so did the king, to watch the sport, and along with them the queen brought her daughters, to see who would claim success in the games. Then lord Egfer, the king's younger son, sprang forward, casting off his cloak, and eager to gain fame. With his first attempt he surpassed all those putting the stone, by three feet in length, as I heard tell. (2557–79)

125. I have long heard it said that "envy never dies."[66] The knight I told you of, whom Guffer had previously taken into service, could not refrain from jumping up and unfastening his cloak. Then he took the stone and threw it so that it led all the others by five feet, at his first attempt. Lord, how the young men praised him for the mighty throw he had made with strength and power, but the queen and her daughters were vexed that her son should be defeated and derided. She was so angry that she grew quite pale, and Lenburc also blushed for chagrin. But the wise king, who had often seen such games in his life, was not in the least concerned. The strong man's name was Eglaf, and he bragged exorbitantly about it, going around with arrogant boasts. Gudmod saw that his lord's face was sad at the insolence of such large boasts; he was now willing to play, if anyone asked him, in order to cut the man's arrogance down to size. (2580–99)

126. Egfer saw Eglaf going around boasting in this fashion. At heart he was very angry and sad, so he came straight to Gudmod, his brave knight, and said to him: "My good friend, why don't you avenge the shame this insolent fellow has done me? Whatever you start, you bring to a proper conclusion, so now avenge me for this! You'll be well rewarded with whatever you like, according to your will. I'm certain you will defeat him, once you start." "Sire," said Gudmod, "where I came from I wasn't used to playing such a game,[67] but nevertheless my best efforts are at your disposal, because it's proper I should act for you so long as I have the power." Then he went over to the place where the other men who had thrown before had previously stood, and the stone was thereupon brought to him. If it

---

[66] See above, note to v. 1875.

[67] 2609–10 **I wasn't used to playing such a game** *ne fui pas costumant / D'itiel geu enveiser*: this might be one of the very few indications in the poem that the Irish were regarded as less sophisticated in their habits. On twelfth-century views of them as barbaric and violent, see Ashe, *Fiction and History*, chap. 4. On the other hand, Wace's *Brut* includes stone-throwing among the games at Arthur's court: Wace, *Le Roman de Brut*, ed. Ivor Arnold, 2 vols. (Paris: SATF, 1938, 1940), v. 10528. For the comments of Giraldus Cambrensis on the Irish expertise in throwing the stone and harping, see Weiss, "Thomas and the Earl," 5.

was heavy, he never showed it and never even took off his cloak. He gave it a little shove and it flew straight to join the cast thrown by Eglaf. (2600–21)

127. When Eglaf saw the cast Gudmod had thrown and heard him much praised among the ranks of spectators, you must know that at heart he was very angry. So he seized the stone again and exerted himself so much that he threw it ahead by a full foot's length. He could not restrain himself but was once again very boastful. And Gudmod kept quiet, not saying a word. Lord, how he was begged on all sides to try and defeat this wretch once again! And his master bent his head in his direction. When he heard what they wanted, he did their will and in his turn made a cast that matched the other one. But then Eglaf was wretched at heart because he had put all his strength into his second throw. So he threw the stone a good half foot ahead, but his body followed his cast so much that he fell to his knees. Then everyone was afraid lest Gudmod had abandoned the game and did not want to throw, but his intentions were otherwise. And his master looked at him and earnestly entreated him to do him honour, just as he had at the start. (2622–41)

128. "My lord Gudmod," he said, "now listen to me! I adjure you by the love and loyalty you owe her, who must be beautiful and who gave you the ring you wear on your finger—you often look at it so I see you love it well. As surely as you hope to invoke her name in the stress of battle, you will avenge the arrogance and insult this fellow has shown me by his great insolence. For I know well that if you want to, you will staunchly support me. I shall be indebted to you, as will the king my father, and my mother (who is greatly dismayed), will repay you a hundredfold." When lord Gudmod heard him, he kept very quiet and only said: "My lord, I intend to do what you command: that's right and proper. Whatever I can do, I will not fail to do." More than three men ran to lift the stone. And Gudmod threw it with such force that it overshot Eglaf's cast by some seven feet of level ground. (2642–59)

129. Lord! what a shout went up when Eglaf was defeated! The king's two daughters gave thanks to God on high, who performs miracles for us. Eglaf went to his lodgings silent and speechless, nearly out of his mind with misery. He was not seen around court for more than a week. From that time on, Gudmod was known and prized. The king said to his sons: "I see that the new arrival shows great prowess." Now Lenburc sent him a hundred salutations, saying that with her he could have a fief with a thousand knights' fees. Gudmod gave a kindly laugh; he was not angry but said to the messenger: "You've wasted your journey. When I came here, it was not for this. Now let her wait until it first appears how well my shield hangs from my shoulders and how well my sharp spear cuts down knights." (2660–76)

130. When the king had celebrated the feast at his court, people took their leave and departed. Gudmod was very irked that they lived so quietly, not going to jousts or tournaments where a valiant man could display his courage. They took their pleasure in hunting and hawking, to relieve boredom, and went out frequently. In these sports Gudmod showed his excellent training which Herland had well and skilfully given him, so that he far surpassed all those of the court. But he never boasted about it. One day as they returned from their sport in the forest, the king's sons had the idea that they would like to go and divert themselves in Lenburc's rooms: they would drink good wine, spiced and unspiced, with her, play chess, and listen to the harp, because those were the things they enjoyed most. They dressed and equipped themselves handsomely, and each took with him those retainers he wanted to accompany him, as was fitting. (2677–96)

131. The two brothers went to their sister's chambers. The elder brother took his chess-player with him who played very well—that was his entire occupation—and his strong knight, the best he had, and the younger took Gudmod, who was no boaster. Lady Lenburc was extremely happy at their arrival—never more so—and especially with Gudmod, because she loved him. She was dressed in a tunic of costly brocade, and no queen had a finer cloak than the one hanging from her shoulders. Her shy blushes enhanced her colour; as her mirror had told her, it suited her looks. The chamber's ceiling was carved, by the art of a sculptor, into a beautifully-made vault,[68] and it was well designed. The floor beneath was completely strewn with flowers—yellow, blue, red, releasing a cloud of perfume. I cannot describe to you all the spices, but no man dwelling there would ever feel pain. When she saw them she said: "Welcome, my lords; I've never been so happy to see you as now. By God, my lord brothers, you have done me honour and I shall do whatever you want: only command it." (2697–717)

132. "My beautiful sister," said Guffer, "we're here to talk to you, drink your good wine and enjoy ourselves. Send for the chessmen and we'll see whether you or this knight makes the better moves: with his skill in such games he claims success over everyone else. When we've seen that, we'll hear you harp." "Sir," said Lenburc, "I won't refuse to do whatever pleasure you command." She called to a boy to fetch the chessmen and sat down with the expert player at the chessboard. She played four games, each one reluctantly, because there was not one game in which the others did not all advise him together, except for Gudmod, who would not look at it even once. When the beautiful girl saw that she began to wonder and said to him: "Don't you know how to play this game? For you're standing

---

[68] 2709a **vault** *umbrelenc*: this word otherwise only occurs in two Italian texts. As with Rigmel's *arcs voluz* (v. 2015, vaulted arches), "Thomas seems to be taking a term from some Continental region in which architectural development was more advanced than in England." See Pope, "Notes on the Vocabulary," 65.

aside here, when you could instruct someone." "My fair lady," said Gudmod, "I believe it might be useful, but where I grew up it wasn't the custom when two people sat down to play, for anyone else to instruct them. It would be reprehensible. And I don't know so much about it that I want to interfere, saying or advising anything to make someone angry." (2718–39a)

133. The knight, who was outplayed, was very vexed; he would have given all his property not to have come along. Lord Egfer, well aware of it, was grieved. Then he said to Gudmod: "My fair friend, play my sister and so take our revenge for us. I know, if you begin, you'll succeed. I never see you do anything which you don't bring to a successful end." Then on all sides they begged him to play, and Lenburc greatly desired it above all the rest, so much did she long for them to be close enough together that he could be touched on hand or foot. He could not refuse to do their will, but he did say this much: "My lords, pray keep quiet! Don't bother to teach me the game! I want you to know that wouldn't be a civil deed. It's not our custom, where I was born."[69] "Upon our honour," they all said, "we agree. We'll all keep quiet and see what you do." Then they sat down and set out their chessmen, and she, who had checkmated the other man, moved first. (2740–59)

134. Now they played the game in such a way that not a word was spoken suggesting discourtesy, but whatever was said expressed good manners. They played four games skilfully, one after the other, without her winning a fig's worth in any of them. Nevertheless it seemed as if it did not grieve her, because she loved him so much she did not envy him. But if anyone else had done it, she would have been very cross, even had it been the king, who had tenderly brought her up. Then Gudmod rose, and Lenburc begged him to play one more game, for the love of his sweetheart. And Gudmod, laughing, gently admonished her not to entreat or say another word about it to him, for if he played any more it would be presumptuous, since he had avenged those he had come to help. (2760–73)

---

[69] 2754–55 **It's not our custom** *nostre costume n'est*: according to Murray, citing many *chansons de geste* and romances, it was usually the case for bystanders to give advice and comment throughout a game, since chess was a social activity. See H. J. R. Murray, *A History of Chess* (Oxford: Clarendon Press, 1913), 475–76; see also Merritt R. Blakeslee, "Lo dous jocx sotils: la partie d'échecs amoureuse dans la poésie des troubadours," *Cahiers de Civilisation Médiévale* 28 (1985): 213–22: the mastery of chess shows superior intelligence, suitable for the old and wise, but also to precocious and brilliant youth (214). On Irish tales which use *fidchell*, a game like chess, to represent the public winning of a bride from her parents, see Maria A. Rebbert, "The Celtic Origins of the Chess Symbolism in *Milun* and *Eliduc*," in *In Quest of Marie de France*, ed. C. A. Maréchal (Lampeter: Edwin Mellen Press, 1992), 148–60.

135. When Gudmod had played, he rose and went back to his former seat. And the brothers asked for Lenburc's harp; she took it and played them a very famous lay, which her hearers received with kind praise. Next she played them another, which was even better, and everyone once more praised it as it deserved. Then Lenburc said to her brothers: "These lays you admire so much are very highly regarded, but I've heard one, half of which I know, that, if I knew it all, as I am a Christian, there's no fine city in our land, however dear to me and at my disposal, that I wouldn't rather lose than forget it." "God Almighty!" said lord Guffer, "if we could only hear it, how we should listen to it! And who composed it, my beautiful sister? Do you know?" "Yes," said Lenburc, "it's all been told me. Baltof, son of Hunlaf, the noble king living in Brittany (for that is his realm), composed it about his sister, the beautiful Rigmel. You've heard much talk of her in this kingdom, and of Horn's love, whom she held so dear—and she was right, for there's no man who is as good as Horn: indeed that's what I've heard tell." (2774–98)

136. "That's right, my fair sister," said Guffer, "Rigmel is admired for her beauty in many a land and I've often heard of Horn's renown, that he's valiant and brave and quietly courteous. Would to God he were here now in our service! My love and my possessions would be at his disposal. But play as much of the lay as you've learnt. Take the harp: we'll give you all our attention." "Willingly," said Lenburc, "I shan't refuse you." Now Horn heard what he desired, what most pleased him, but as far as he could he hid it deep in his heart. The girl then tuned her harp: she raised it a whole tone in pitch and after the tuning she began the song, and performed as much as she knew and as she had been taught. She was greatly praised for what she knew of it. One of those listening, who instantly recognised any wrong notes, paid close attention to all of it—that was Horn, who had kept it deep in his heart. Next they passed the harp to Guffer and they listened to the melody of the lay he performed. They praised him when he reached the end. Then the harp was passed to everyone in turn; each one was told to harp and each one did so. (2799–823)

137. In those days everyone knew how to play the harp well: the higher the rank, the greater the knowledge of the art. It was now Gudmod's turn to entertain them with it. As it was quite clear that he wanted to make excuses, they all told him he should not have to be entreated. He did not want to refuse them: they should not think he shirked the task. Then he took the harp, for he wanted to tune it. Lord, whoever then watched his knowledgeable handling of it, how he touched the strings and made them vibrate, sometimes causing them to sing and at other times join in harmonies, would have been reminded of the harmony of heaven! Of all the men there, this one caused most wonder. When he had played his notes, he began to raise the pitch and to make the strings give out completely different notes. Everyone was astonished at his skilful handling of it. And when he had done this, he began to sing the lay of Baltof, which I mentioned just now,

loudly and clearly, just like the Bretons, who are versed in such performances. Next he made the harp strings play exactly the same melody as he had just sung. He performed the whole lay for them and did not want to omit any of it.[70] And Lord, how his audience then had occasion to love him! Lady Lenburc could no longer refrain from saying what she wished, whoever might be listening: "O God, heavenly King and Redeemer, could such a man be found anywhere else in this world? Already he possesses all known accomplishments and wishes to boast of none of them. It must be Horn, I believe, the talk of everyone. If he hides from us, it's because he doesn't want to make himself known, so as not to be recognised and honoured, or else it's no mortal man. No one resembles him; he has come down from heaven to look at mankind. My brothers, beg him deign to teach me this lay we heard: I want it so. I will give him much, both silver and pure gold. Let him take many of my possessions, I have plenty to give." (2824–60)

138. "My beautiful sister," they said, "we will beg him too and, if he wishes, we'll give him plenty of our own." "My lords," said Gudmod, "it's no good to talk thus. By Him who suffered on the cross for us, I'll never take a pennyworth from you, nor her gold and silver either. I didn't come to this land for that. By Lazarus, truly I came here for something quite different: to bear arms, if I get the opportunity. May he who keeps the truce so long receive no blessing at the Last Judgement, amongst the good and the bad, but be condemned, on the grounds that he hasn't broken it. Now if I can help it, Lenburc won't incur through any fault of mine the reproach that I come and go stealthily to her in her chambers. Slanderers and knaves would soon speak evil of it. By my Redeemer, I'll prevent them; they won't have the chance to mock me for it. They'll hear nothing but good. Now let us take our leave and return: may Lenburc remain with God's blessing." Then the lords did as Gudmod bade them. And Lenburc was left in great torment because love consumed her heart and soul, so that inescapable death awaited her if she had no remedy. (2861–83)

139. Beautiful Lenburc remained, tormented by love, which blanched her cheeks and removed their bloom. She perceived it when she went to her mirror. She knew very well that this great passion was doing her no good, but none the less

---

[70] 2830–44 **Then he took the harp. . .omit any of it** *Lors prent la harpe. . .rien retailler*: the technical details of this passage reveal Thomas as either a musician or very well acquainted with music. Note that vocal and instrumental music appear to be kept separate. See G. Reese, *Music in the Middle Ages* (London: J. M. Dent, 1940–41), 203; Richard H. Hoppin, *Medieval Music* (New York: W. W. Norton, 1978), 275, 280–81; J. Stevens, *Words and Music in the Middle Ages* (Cambridge: Cambridge University Press, 1986), 141, 205; and especially Christopher Page, *Voices and Instruments of the Middle Ages* (London: J. M. Dent, 1987), 92–93. I am grateful to him for permission to quote part of his translation of this passage.

she devoted herself to loving Gudmod. But to no avail: she would never succeed, never getting the opportunity she wanted, for he cared nothing for love but instead was very dejected about the truce and the length of time his weapons, which should have increased his renown and esteem at his lord's court, lay idle. For five years already there had been no expedition where he could carry arms, and he suffered much for it. In his heart he appealed to God: "Ah God, dear Lord and true Creator who divided night from day,[71] let me see the day when I can foretell I can again mount my precious steed and break lances before castle and tower, for love of you, against the heathen killers of my people: let me avenge them." His prayer was heard; moreover he would meet with success, as you will hear, if you listen. (2884–904b)

140 One day two wicked princes came sailing with their fleet to the kingdom of Westir. They had come from the realm of Africa and were brothers of Rodmund who had usurped Suddene — slaying the brave Aalof, Horn's father — and brothers of those he had taken revenge on in Brittany, when with Hunlaf the powerful. These people were coming to avenge them, as I shall tell you. They completely overran the land through which they went. The elder of the two was called Hildebrant and the younger Herebrant. They had a nephew with them, Rollac, son of Gudbrand their eldest brother, the king of Persia: he was their lord and leader, as I have often said. This Rollac, by chance, killed Aalof, whom I have often mentioned, the best knight in the world then alive. Now Horn was to have his revenge, as you shall soon hear. Then, as I told you, they arrived at the port. They disembarked with great arrogance, leaving the ships and boats behind in harbour moored with ropes and held fast by anchors. They took their weapons and their good horses. I cannot tell you their numbers, so great they were, but I know for sure that as they went, uttering threats against King Gudreche, they entirely covered the fields. (2905–26)

141. The Saracen scoundrels arrived at the port. They sent to the king the young lord Rollac, son of Gudbrand, the mighty sultan of Persia. Of the heathen religion,[72] no knight was as good as he. He was nephew to that Rodlac whom Aalof slew and for love of him bore the same name. He killed Aalof, according to the record, and now, if it pleased God above, Horn would avenge him. Rollac went riding along the cobbled road[73] straight to the city called Dublin, where the

---

[71] Allusion to Genesis 1:4–5.

[72] 2930a **Of the heathen religion** *En la lei Apollin:* literally, of the creed of Apollo. See note to v. 735.

[73] 2936 **the cobbled road** *le feré chemin*: literally, metalled road. "Metalled" refers to the topmost layer of the roads which, according to region, could be waste iron from flint or nearby workings. Legge in her review of *Horn* remarks: "metalled roads and causeways were well known in Ireland, owing to the marshy nature of the ground" (310). According

king usually dwelt and was that morning. He knew well the message those dogs had sent, and he would deliver it well because he knew many languages. He had a good Arab steed under him, with a well-padded saddle of fine gold; the bit in its mouth was entirely of silver. On his back was a good, double-meshed hauberk, and on his head was no mean helmet; the hoops around it were of pure gold.[74] He had a shield at his shoulders and a Saracen spear, keen and sharp, with a crimson pennon. (2927–48)

142. He came to the gate very arrogantly, with the equipment I have just described to you. He called to the porter and said: "Go within to the king; give him my message. Tell him I'm a messenger from pagans and want to speak with him. I will deliver their words. I'll reward you handsomely if you do it well." "Truly," said the porter, "I'll go at once. I'll tell you his reply when I know his wishes." Then he rushed off and ran speedily up to the great hall, straight to the dais where the king was seated with no suspicion of the arrival of such people, or of war with them. When he saw the porter enter the hall in great agitation, he was very surprised. He beckoned to him, then questioned him thus: "What news have you that you run so frantically? Do you know anything likely to harm us?" "Now you shall know," he said, "what's on my mind. (2949–68)

143. "A messenger came just now to the gate outside, proud and arrogant, judging by appearances. He was very ready to deliver a message. He wants to enter the city and speak with you, on behalf of two kings over there at the seashore. I saw them arrive at the port yesterday evening already. With them I saw many men, but I couldn't tell you of it because you had retired to bed a long while before. Tell me if you wish me to let him enter." "Indeed," said the king, "I won't refuse him. Let him come forward and we'll hear him set forth his news and demands. But first, have all my men summoned here so they can hear with me what he says and give advice, if they see I need it." Those who were there said: "Agreed." Then all his knights were summoned, and they all came, his sons first. The porter went off to bring the messenger. He entered the hall without delay. (2969–88)

144. Rollac came before them, arrogant and boastful: there was no better warrior in the African realm. He remained on horseback, not dismounting, and in

---

to Corráin, however, "a cobbled or stone-paved road would have been most unusual . . . but monastic towns had streets, occasionally paved." See D. O. Corráin, *Ireland before the Normans* (Dublin: Gill and Macmillan, 1972), 67–68, 72.

[74] 2946 **the hoops around it** *Li cercles environ:* the "hoops" could refer to the vertical strips which formed a framework connecting three to six steel plates, in a type of helmet known as "spangenhelm." See Ian Peirce, "The Knight, his Arms and Armour c. 1150–1250," *Anglo-Norman Studies* 15 (1992): 25–74. Legge (review of *Horn*, 312) prefers "headband."

this position delivered his message with great insolence. Everyone in the court watched him attentively and the king, above all, wondered at him. Some people were frightened by his pride. But when he chose to speak, he began thus: "Listen, king of Westir, it's you I've come to see. This is what the kings say to you, over there in the rowdy port, brothers of lord Gudbrand, sultan of Persia, who have come from Africa the great. They come upon you as conquerors and tell you this: you shall hold this rich and prosperous realm of Westir from them. You shall pay tribute for it to the supreme sultan—I am his son, who comes to demand it—and henceforth you shall believe in Mahomet and Tervagant. If you refuse to do this, then find someone to maintain against me that you shouldn't do it: I'll make him turn tail. I'll fight the two best men you have." Both the king's sons threw down their gloves to defend their religion. They proffered themselves to the insolent prince to maintain by force of arms that they should not abandon the creed they held, nor should they render tribute. When Gudmod heard the Saracen's speech he was most indignant, and anger made him spring forward and begin speaking in this manner before them all. (2989–3018)

145. "Now listen to me, lords! Hear my words. I see before us a fellow urging us to abandon our creed and adopt Mahomet's—who was devoured, buttocks, flesh, and skin by sows[75]—and pay tribute to Gudbrand, a scoundrel who believes neither in our God nor in our way of life. If we don't do this, he wants to do battle with the two best men in the land, maintaining the creed we hold is false and if he can prove its falsehood, we should adopt his. Our king's two sons have offered to rebut everything the wretch says, but God (who suffered on the cross to get us out of Hell, as the Church tells us) forbid that two men should ever fight a man on his own, or that other lands should ever hear an evil rumour that Gudreche couldn't nurture anyone in his household to fight the Saracen[76] single-handed. I will silence him, by St. Simon. (3019–38)

146. "Now listen to me, good king, if it please you. It's been a long time since I came to the kingdom of Westir. I came to serve you and your sons faithfully. You have amply repaid me and just as I could wish. Now the time has come for me to remember that: I should repay your kindness by utterly silencing this heathen. I'll force him to confess he's told a pack of lies; I'll make him sorry he ever attacked us to destroy our laws; I'll see that he's considered a fool. When I've totally put an end to him and made him perish, we can go and attack those who came with him. Provided you don't waver, not a single one will get back to the country

---

[75] 3022 **who was devoured . . . by sows** *Ke truies ont mangé*: the story that Mahomet was originally one of Christ's prophets but got drunk and was devoured by pigs in his stupor appears in other *chansons de geste,* such as *Le Couronnement Louis* and *Le Siège de Barbastre.* See Pope, *Horn,* 2:7 and 158, and Bancourt, *Musulmans,* 367–70.

[76] 3037 **the Saracen** *l'Esclavon*: the Slav. See note to v. 2442.

they came from. I promise you this, my lords, as God is my support, the sovereign Lord and defender of all. Now I shall go to my lodgings and arm myself. Meanwhile you take care this man doesn't flee, for as soon as I can you'll see me return." (3039–55)

147. Gudmod went to the lodgings to arm himself, and everyone said: "Gudmod has spoken well." "Good God!" said the king, "this man was born under a lucky star. He certainly hid his valour from us a long while. I said as much when I first observed him: no one who looked like that could be bad." The report spread round the royal chambers that Gudmod, the renowned, was going to do battle with this heathen, whom they so feared for his proud, rash, and insolent words. Then you must know that Lenburc was full of entreaties to God, not to let Gudmod be harmed or slain. Then he returned to the hall well armed and with all the appearance of a brave knight ready for action. He had taken satisfactory revenge on the relatives of Rollac when he was in Brittany, as was earlier related; but he did not realise to what extent this man was his sworn enemy, who had wrongfully and painfully killed his father. But once he got to know it, he would reward him with harm and take more pains to destroy him. (3056–74a)

148. Gudmod, his armour on, entered the hall on his horse — there was no better, faster, or dearer in the land. He looked just the knight to obtain his rights. He looked at Rollac, who made himself out to be so fierce. "My friend," he said, "listen! You come from the coast and two kings who made you their messenger. You say we should abandon our entire creed, which ought to protect us, because it is reprehensible. You want us to renounce it in favour of the heathen creed. You want us to convert to foul Mahomet and leave God, the Creator of all, for your worthless gods which ought to be burnt. And you say we should henceforth pay tribute to Gudbrand, the sultan, whatever scoundrel *that* is. But I defend my rightful lord from all this, maintaining he should not, for any man alive, have to change his religion given to us by Jesus who suffered to get us out of Hell, so the preachers say. That is the first point; I maintain that first of all, and secondly that he whom I hear is called Gudbrand, the Persian sultan, has no right to demand tribute. To rebut this I shall now challenge you. In the courtyard outside you shall take up your position. No man will hinder you from defending what is right, if you have any knowledge of it. But you will have to pay for the wrong that you spoke." (3075–100)

149. Rollac heard all that he said to him and said very proudly that he would go outside and thoroughly justify everything he had said: not a word would be omitted in any way from fear. And Gudmod went out: he would not yield but defend God's creed like a warrior. And I know for sure that He will help him, for He never fails anyone who really loves Him in their hour of need. When they had taken up their positions, each looked at the other and each donned his weapons.

Then each angrily challenged the other and each let go his horse's bridle. Each met the other at a gallop, and Rollac struck Gudmod, breaking his lance. But Gudmod returned the blow and completely laid him low. He fell from the horse's saddle to the ground, embedding his helmet's point in the sand. His neck was almost broken by the blow, but by chance he escaped death. And the king and his court praised God heartily, hoping that in this way Gudmod would be victorious. (3101–19)

150. Rollac, finding himself overthrown, was much dismayed; never since his birth had he been so dismayed. In great fury he very quickly jumped up, sword in hand, shield over his head, and he ran at Gudmod as soon as he could. But before he got there Gudmod had dismounted, not wanting him to strike his horse. He was not taken aback by Rollac's fierce advance but met it firmly and received it angrily. And when Rollac reached Gudmod, he did not pause but struck him a great blow on the top of his conical helmet, so that sparks leapt out, kindling the turf. And Gudmod, seeing this, was infuriated: in his fierce might he would take his revenge. He gave Rollac such a blow with his keen blade that he brought him to his knees. Yet he was not totally down, so strong were the weapons protecting him—otherwise he would by now have been dead and done for. But he sprang to his feet as if undefeated. Now a great battle raged between the two, causing the king and his people much fear. (3120–40)

151. The fight was hard, its cause great, and the warriors fierce, vying with each other. They made helmets ring and devices shatter; they drove each other round the sandy ground. And many, the king and all his people especially fervently, prayed to God for the valiant Gudmod, that He would not let this evil wretch conquer him; and God, for whom he fought, heard their prayer, as you will hear if you listen to the tale. The fight lasted till the stroke of noon, so that Rollac was weary and spoke to him as follows: "Fellow, you are very brave. Never before have I found anyone so good, except one whom I saw, as I think, in Suddene when I was with my uncle Rodmund. I killed the fellow—Aalof was his name. Draw off, and let us rest, and then come with me to my country. I am the sultan's son, who holds sway, by Mahomet's authority, in the kingdom of Persia. I have a sister there: I give her to you and, with her, as many fiefs as you like will be at your disposal and with us you shall hold to the creed that we hold." "My word," said Gudmod, "this speech is not wise. I shall talk to you in quite a different fashion before we part." (3141–64)

152. Gudmod saw the infidel, too hasty in his avowal, and looked at his hand and the ring, set with precious stones, given him by Rigmel at their leave-taking. Then his heart swelled with fury and angry pride, and he was the more strengthened by it for understanding very well the other's boast: that he had killed Aalof, the crowned king. Henceforth the affair would not be brought to a peaceful end

until one of them was slain. "Fellow," said Gudmod, "now listen to me: the Aalof you speak of was my rightful lord. Now I must avenge him, that brooks no delay. I was born in Suddene, my family was there. Whoever killed the king is my sworn enemy, and on his account I challenge you. From now on, take heed!" Thereupon he rushed towards him. In his hand he held his sword, shining and inscribed, the great name of God Omnipotent written upon it. Like one infuriated, he struck him a great blow with it on top of the bright helmet, which completely shattered, and severed the golden hoop[77] and thongs. The blow came down to the left, on the shoulder, so that the shoulder and arm along with the shield were sent headlong—he would not have relinquished the shield for the value of two cities, for there was no weapon on earth that could harm it. That renegade wretch had such confidence in it because it was so skilfully tempered and cast in a metal not easily ascertained. He who made it was a master craftsman, for it was very light and yet strong too, as you will hear. Over the shield Gudmod bravely took his stand, to gain it for himself where it would be better employed. (3165–96)

153. The lethal blow made the infidel lose heart. He did not want to beg for mercy but angrily came at him. With his sword he dealt him such a blow in the face that, had it not been for the nose-guard, his nose and all the rest of his flesh would have been cut off. It would have been a shameful stigma for ever after. But the heavenly Father did not wish it so. When Gudmod the brave and true saw this, he remembered his royal birth and gave him in return a noble blow. I think Rollac never saw another day dawn, for Gudmod cut off his head like a noble knight and commended his soul to the infernal devils: Beelzebub, Tervagant, Apollo, and Belial, lord of these and of Hell. There he was welcomed to suffering and pain. (3197–210a)

154. Gudmod took the head and gave it to Gudreche, presenting it to him before all his lords. And the king thanked him heartily for it, as was fitting, for it conferred great renown. The news quickly spread everywhere that Gudmod had nobly defeated the infidel. When the beautiful Lenburc heard, she gave great praise to God. And Gudmod gave the king this advice, as I shall tell you, provided you listen quietly. "Lord king, let us go without delay and bravely attack these pagans, so that their stay here is short. We'll never find them putting up a defence, for they are utter cowards—I've often put it to the test. You would incur shame if they stayed long with you. A mere ten of your men are certainly worth a hundred of theirs." With such words he emboldened their hearts, and the king gave them great encouragement. Then the young men went together to their lodgings and very proudly each armed himself. They came out into the courtyard where Gudmod, who was to lead them at the king's command, awaited them. (3211–33)

---

[77] 3185 **hoop** *cercle*: or headband. See note to v. 2946.

155. Gudmod led them, bravely and well, straight towards the infidels on the shore, the arrogant and cruel race. But Gudmod never loved them nor their kin and thus showed them now such great violence, for there was none of them who would not pay a heavy price—their proud heads, that is: no other pledge would be taken. They met the army beside a wood. Gudmod divided his squadrons like a wise man: he formed seven brave groups, all intent on harming the infidels and bringing them to grief. If those heathen intended to defend themselves, in harbour and in dire straits, not one of them would ever return to his own lands. The outcome of the tussle would show them how ill-starred was their voyage. Gudmod made them the initial challenge, for arriving without safe conduct. First of all he came to Escofard de Durage, who had been the first to pitch his tent with rashness, and by the seashore cut him down. (3234–52)

156. There was a great battle, arduous at first. Lord Gudmod fought well like a good knight, and those with him brought him much aid. They left cold and dead upon the sand many whose heirs will never recover them. The infidels were roused, rushed to arms, and sent a message to their kings that they were under attack in a pitched battle. Anyone who could have heard the kings shouting the battle-cry, the drums beaten and the trumpets sounded, the horses whinnying and making a great racket, would have been astounded. Then the infidels gathered from land and sea, and their kings appeared, to encounter our men. Then an arduous fight was soon set to begin, for the kings were courageous, very arrogant and fierce, and, what's more, they wanted revenge for their dead. And our men were brave, hardened warriors, wanting to expel the infidels from their lands. The armies met—there was no more delay—from all directions, valley, mountain, forest, and sea. (3253–73)

157. Gudreche's sons, lords Guffer and Egfer, were in the vanguard; both were of great valour. The two African kings, the pitiless Hildebrant and the other, Herebrant, joined battle with them. Like hardened warriors, they struck them mighty blows; when their spears were shattered, their swords were drawn. They made themselves well known wherever they passed. And our king's sons did not shirk encountering the enemy, but met them in full, giving them no quarter. They left them lying dead, cold and mouths agape, so that the streams that ran along the paths were full of blood. No one could count them; never could one number so many. Horses crossed the fields, trailing their reins. Their masters had died in the heavy fighting, but none of ours looked at a single steed, for Gudmod the brave had ordered no one to take one but instead to destroy the infidels, that none might boast that Mahomet, Tervagant, or Apollo, the false gods they believed in, could protect them. Nevertheless, for their part they did great harm to our men, for Guffer died there, killed by Herebrant. But Gudmod avenged him, as I shall tell you. (3274–97)

158. Gudmod was elsewhere: he heard the news as he was in combat with the heathen, giving them mighty blows. Know that when he heard it, his blood boiled. He turned in that direction, beside a meadow, and when he saw the infidel, he called to him angrily: "God send you pain and grievous misfortune, infidel, who has killed our Guffer, bringing misery to his mother and Lenburc, his sister, the courteous and beautiful. He was her own brother;[78] I know no lady like her except for the noble Rigmel, whose turtle-dove heart never, in all her life, took wing to any man save one. Now I defy you, you villain! You shall pay for it on the field!" Thereupon he went at him, raising his shield on his left arm and shaking his spear: it was made at La Rochelle of Poitevin steel[79] and its head was sharp—now he would find its stroke harder than a fiddle-bow's. He cut through his shield, made in Tudela, and punctured his hauberk—no more use than a tunic—piercing his heart right through his breast and knocking him dead off his Castilian horse. His entrails covered the grass with blood. (3298–317)

159. When Gudmod had killed this evil Saracen, you must know the Africans lamented bitterly. Now they were weakened and in dire straits. Never again, I think, would they see Persia, nor could Mahomet or Tervagant save them. Gudmod led them towards a ravine and mocked when five thousand fell into it: they would never again help the sultan in battle. Then Cloakan, an infidel, came up, to get lord Gudmod into difficulties if he could. He was a wealthy man and owner of Corinan, a rich island, home of sailors who used to trade with its silk and buckram. He was very well armed on a piebald horse. He sounded his *olifant*[80] to rally his men and came threatening Gudmod, for he was evil and overbearing. And Gudmod, hearing him, invoked St. John for vengeance on this formidable scoundrel. Then he turned his Castilian horse towards Cloakan and struck his high-peaked helmet with his sword so that it split like an acorn. His mailed hauberk was no use to him, cut into two halves right down to the Cordoba leather[81] covering his heathen's saddle. "Away with you, wretch!" said he, "now you're done for." (3318–42)

---

[78] 3306 **He was her own brother** *Sun frere esteit germain*: Guffer was a brother by blood.

[79] 3312 **of Poitevin steel** *Del acier peitevin*: from the tenth to the twelfth century Poitiers was a rich town notable for its metal-workers, and Poitevin steel used for fine armour is mentioned in thirteenth-century records. See *Histoire de Poitiers*, ed. Robert Favreau (Toulouse: Editions Privat, 1985), 130.

[80] 3332: **olifant** *olifan*: a horn made of ivory. The most famous is Roland's, blown at the battle of Roncesvaux, in the *Chanson de Roland*.

[81] 3340 **right down to the Cordoba leather** *de si qu'al cordowan*: the soft leather from Cordoba was celebrated during the Moors' occupation of Andalusia.

160. When the infidels saw this prodigious blow, they closed ranks, dismayed, around King Herebrant, now their leader, to continue the fighting: they had confidence in him. And our men were valiant, giving them no quarter but confidently joining with them in battle. So many great blows were there given and received that neither laymen nor clerk could count them. So many hands, chests, and feet were there cut off, they would have made twenty wagon-loads. For three days they fought without separating, neither by day nor by night; they were very weary. Not a horse there was unbridled, you must know, nor did anyone eat or drink. Towards mid-afternoon on the third day, Herebrant and Egfer encountered each other with violent ferocity. They exchanged such blows on their decorated shields—breast clashing against breast so harshly—that these could not withstand them and shattered completely. They were both knocked and beaten to the ground by the blows, but as soon as they could they got up again. Then the battle began between the two of them that would end in Egfer's death, nor did the other have time to boast of it. (3343–64)

161. Egfer and Herebrant fought fiercely, the valley, surrounding woods and hillsides resounding with the blows they exchanged. Egfer struck Herebrant on his fine helmet, knocking off straps and studs together, so that he fell to his knees and gave ground, calling on his lord, Belial, infernal prince and judge over Hell, to give him vengeance on this prince. Then he ran towards him and took him by the nose-guard and struck him with his sword (its pommel was of crystal), cutting off face and flesh. He laid him low with the mortal wound, and would have taken his head with its princely helmet, when the loyal lord Gudmod noticed from afar that his liege lord was hard pressed. He quickly turned towards him his horse's head, which was bloody down to the chest, and cried loudly to him: "By God in heaven, you touch him at your peril, mercenary son of a whore!'" (3365–84)

162. The infidel heard him and did not fear him; he left the senseless Egfer and rushed at Gudmod. And that brave man came valiantly to meet him, dismounting as he reached him. Now a brutal battle began between the two, for the infidel was strong and truly evil, and fought as one defending his life. And the other fiercely and angrily attacked him, intent on avenging his lord, who had done so much for him and for whom he now grieved. They exchanged great blows without stinting. Gudmod was skilled in defence, having learnt it in youth, and, holding the naked blade—his arm was bloody from it—struck the infidel on his gleaming helm, breaking off its peak and shattering it completely. He did the same to the hauberk coif,[82] and the stroke descended without a check till it came to the girdle and there ceased. Nothing saved him from being completely cleft

---

[82] 3400 **the hauberk coif** *La coife del hauberc*: the mail coif, a cap under the helmet, was usually attached to the mail shirt or hauberk.

asunder. Then Egfer came round from his swoon. When he saw the infidel dead, he gave great thanks, yet he felt great pain and anguish; he suffered greatly from the blows he had received. Then he said: "I am about to die, but with less suffering, now I see you have killed the heathen wretch. I did very well ever to take you into my service. You have well repaid all the honour I did you, and *will* do you, if I live for long. (3385–412)

163. "My dear friend, lord Gudmod, don't stop here, although you have waged the battle so. Now all the hated race will be discomfited, since you have killed him who leads and guides them. Forward! may the Son of Mary help you." And Gudmod mounted the Serbian horse from which Hildebrant had been struck dead—God curse him! There was no better or finer in any heathen land. Gudmod shouted his war-cry and blew his horn, which far over the field was heard and known. Then a fine company of young men could be seen! And Gudmod led them, playing his part to the full. They attacked where the enemy was thickest. Many a body was transfixed by many a spear, many an inlaid sword made its mark. The hapless men could not withstand it, because all their support had completely come to an end, and when people are leaderless they are quickly destroyed. They could no longer endure it but forsook the battle and set out for their ships. (3413–31)

164. The infidels were defeated; they fled towards their ships, but our men forcibly interposed: the bridges were drawn away, preventing entrance, and whoever could not swim went to the bottom. Nearly all of them were drowned, for they got no help. And Gudmod pursued them, urging his men to strike them, and they did so splendidly. They spared no one, on hill or dale; they were all delivered to death, they would never escape. In vain they begged for mercy, for they would get none: they would all be dispatched to the pit of Hell. Gudmod fought fiercely and gladly destroyed them. The villains were wretched, knowing well enough they were to die. Then they resolved that first they would be avenged. They closed their ranks and made a shield-wall;[83] their descendants would never suffer reproach in days to come. (3432–47)

165. The vicious wretches closed their ranks and turned themselves into a mighty fortress. They suffered grievously from their lack of a leader; nevertheless, they would not be captured that day without a fierce fight. Gudmod, seeing this, went

---

[83] 3446 **made a shield-wall** *de aus chastel funt*: on the shield-wall, a method of defence used by both Romans and Germanic peoples, see Pope, *Horn*, 2:161. It was used at the battle of the Standard in 1138 by King Stephen's army against the Scots; it may be known more generally as the Saxon defence strategy against the Normans at the Battle of Hastings in 1066. See C. Warren Hollister, *Anglo-Saxon Military Institutions* (Oxford: Clarendon Press, 1962), 131–32.

off angrily and assembled his men at the end of some fallow land. Now he would smite the wretches: he would lie in wait for them and turn their good humour into suffering and wrath. He called on God who steers the course of all events. Then he joined battle with them; everyone he struck screamed aloud. They broke so many hauberks, shattered so many shields, that there was none so bold who now was not dismayed. (3448–59)

166. They fared badly, for now they were vanquished. They could not reach their boats, for Gudmod had taken them and had set the best of his men to guard them, They would never see their lands again. Gudmod was angry and eager to strike; anyone receiving his blows came off the worse — no man had struck like that since Louis' time.[84] He called to his men: "Strike, friends! Spare no one, for the love of St. Denis! They shall have the deserts I promised them: they shall live no more, now their days are at an end." (3460–70)

167. The infidels were defeated, dispatched and slain, and Gudmod was happy and his men rejoiced. He seized all the armour and he exposed the bodies. Then he ransacked the boats and took gold and silver, brocades, clothes, and other ornaments: there was no end to the goods he seized. And he behaved nobly because he distributed generously: he did it equally, so there was no grumbling. The king got his share, the queen likewise, and both daughters. Each took their share and everyone was alike enriched. He kept some for himself, as it pleased him, and no one complained of it: he had done everything so well they could not blame him. When he had done all this, he gathered his men together. The sick and wounded were led gently away, and kinsmen found and carried off their dead. Gudmod came straight to the field where his lord awaited him, mortally wounded in the face by the infidel. He found him still alive and dismounted before him. Then he asked him very gently: "Sire, can you recover? How do you fare?" Egfer replied: "My friend, very ill; but I find relief in being avenged. Because you have slain the infidels I shall die more peacefully: I seem to feel no pain." (3471–96)

168. Gudmod dismounted before his lord. He gently and lovingly comforted him: "Sire, can you recover from this great agony? If I lose you so soon, I shall be sick at heart. Your father will be plunged into great fear; never again will he feel joy, he will lose all his strength. What will your mother do? She will certainly pine away, she will tear at her beautiful face, she will grow pale, when her sons, the noble and generous, are dead, no longer caring for a valuable steed any more than for a wretched nag, fit only for the plough.[85] Who, after you, will support

---

[84] 3466 **since Louis' time** *des pus le tens Lowis*: Louis III defeated the Danes at Saucourt in 881.

[85] 3506–7 **no longer caring for a valuable steed . . . wretched nag** *Ki plus ne tindrent plai d'un destrier milsoudur / Ke d'un malvais runcin*: this has less to do with the Irish

noble knights? With whom can they find help?" "My friend," said Egfer, "what use are your tears now? I shall never aid you again in joust or battle, for today is my last day. But may the Creator on high thank you for avenging me thus on the wicked traitor who slew me. There is no recovery for me. (3497–515)

169. "My good friend lord Gudmod, blessed be the day that I first saw you and retained you. If I ever was good to you, you have repaid me indeed, by thus killing my mortal enemy, who gave me my death-blow. Now I shall die more peacefully: God have mercy on me! One thing I ask of you. Do not leave me here, and carry my brother Guffer back too. My father, I know well, will cherish you the more. Now I can speak no more, but do this, Gudmod, my good, dear friend: that is all I ask." And Gudmod told him: "I swear faithfully that everything you have said will happen forthwith." Then without delay he made a bier, on which he placed Guffer's body, as he had promised him, and had it carried straight to Bealni[86] Castle. He wept, cried, and lamented so much for him, you would not believe it. I say no more. (3516–33)

170. Gudmod took his lord, who was still alive, and very gently laid him on an ambling horse. He sat behind him and gently and compassionately supported him in his arms, that he might be tenderly carried straight to Bealni. On his arrival his friends would lament bitterly, and not they alone but the whole land. Lord Gudmod faithfully carried out whatever he had promised him. When they arrived there was neither sport nor laughter, but great sorrow, I assure you, and much weeping. The king was distraught, the queen much more so; the sisters made unimaginable lamentation. Yet they rejoiced that the infidels were vanquished, so they would never fear those vile enemies again. And they had the dead carried to the abbey of St. Maurice. There they kept vigil over them till daybreak. (3534–49)

171. Lord Egfer's wounds caused him great pain. Nevertheless a leading doctor took charge of him, but could see no recovery in his urine[87] nor knew of any cure in his books of medicine, for the brave lord was dead before cock-crow. When he was prepared for burial—what else should I tell you?—they had him carried

---

princes' interest in horses than with Horn's appreciation of their discrimination between men: they knew Horn was a *destrier milsoudur*, and cared for him accordingly.

[86] 3531 **to Bealni Castle** *al chastel de Bealni*: according to Legge's review of *Horn*, 310, Bealni/Beaunis is "either a corrupt form of Baile Atha Cliath [the old name for Dublin] or . . . a humorous name for a castle of peeled osiers constructed in native fashion" where Henry II kept Christmas in 1171.

[87] 3552 **could see no recovery in his urine** *n'i veit pas santé par [le] sun orinal*: medieval doctors, like their Greek and Roman predecessors, used the state of a patient's urine to ascertain how sick or healthy he was.

to the royal and metropolitan church, where the brothers who had received their fatal injuries lay together. The next day a magnificent service was held there and they buried them like high-born men; and when they had done so, each sought his lodging. They went to comfort the king in his heartfelt suffering. Not once, during the day, was there ever song, fiddling or dance, so great and violent was the grief everywhere. No greater was ever seen at any time. (3550–66)

172. In spite of all one can do, if it is God's will, a man must die: it cannot happen otherwise. But a man cannot keep grieving, for all that, and must return to his more urgent needs. This is what the king did, Gudreche of Westir, who now wanted to defend his kingdom in another fashion, for he was very frail: he would admit it to everyone. He summoned his wife's brother, the king who held Orkney, to come to him. He thought and it was his secret wish that he would repay Gudmod's service by giving him Lenburc, and relieve her suffering—it was great and she could not relinquish it. She was the only heir to his land, and he feared she would die of grief; by taking a husband she would thus find happiness. This was the king's will; this is what he did. But everything would be otherwise; it could not happen thus, for the High King who sustains all did not wish it so. (3567–85)

173. My lords, do not believe that anything happens in this world according to anyone's intention, if God has not previously ordained it. In spite of all that the king had wisely planned, it nevertheless did not come to pass. Everything happened otherwise, as you can hear, if you listen quietly. Now you shall hear the truth: who says differently is lying. When that king had arrived, whom I mentioned—he was the queen's brother, a man of great good sense—King Gudreche took counsel with him, as I shall now tell you, in the following terms. He said to him: "King, I look to you for help, since I have lost your nephews and my family, my two sons—for whom I grieve—past recovery. I am old and cannot, you know well, govern like one to whom the kingdom belongs. I cannot defend it against strangers if they attack me again, as happened just now. My kingdom, with all my fiefs, would have been lost, if Almighty God had not watched over me and sent me here, by His command, a noble knight: he is one in a hundred. God intended my son Egfer should take him into service. He well repaid his kindness, at his death, by killing the wretch who slew him and by destroying all the infidels for us, borne here in boats by the wind. (3586–612)

174. "I don't know who he is, but he certainly seems of high birth, so handsome, noble, and brave that he has no fellow in this world worth a button compared to him. And he has, God be thanked, restored my kingdom which without him would have been utterly lost. Now I want to give him everything freely, unreservedly and undivided, with my daughter Lenburc, if you consent. He will take care

of her so that neither infidel nor Saracen[88] will ever do her any wrong, for there is no such knight under the canopy of Heaven. He has now been five years with me in my household and never has he committed the slightest offence." "Upon my word," said the king of Orkney, "may God who brought us all to salvation pour blessings on him. Now I would speak with him and address him; I'll reveal to him our intentions. (3613–29)

175 "He is in every way inspired by God, this man, if he is as you describe. Such a man cannot now be found in our times. It is quite right that he should have the kingdom after you, and that you should give him your daughter with it; no one will then ever be able to expel you from it. If he is truly like this, it will be a good marriage." "It is all true," said King Gudreche, "and he is worth more than that. Even half his valour, for which he deserves praise, cannot be described." At that moment lord Gudmod came up into the palace. The man sent to bring him accompanied him. When he came before them, Lord! how all eyes were on him, for his body was most slender and shapely. He was very well dressed and even better shod. He was clad in a crimson cloak and easily appeared to be lord of castles and cities. When the king of Orkney saw him, he said: "Come here! My friend, please be seated here between us! It is quite true, what I have been told about you: your face reveals you are well-born and I believe for certain that you are, upon my word. Otherwise you would not have displayed such prowess or such accomplishments as you have done here. Because of this King Gudreche now wants you to assume the crown and take his daughter Lenburc to wife. The kingdom you now defend will be yours henceforth. The king leaves it all to you, he will no longer be called its king: he wants to rest and you, who are young, will defend it, whereas his time is sped." (3630–55)

176. Then Gudmod replied, courteously: "Noble and valiant king, my lineage is not such that a marriage could be made beween Lenburc and me, but I will defend my king and lord as a knight should. As long as I am with him he need have no fear of wicked heathen harassing him. But as a lad I spent my first youth in Brittany and stayed a while with a worthy man. A daughter of his made a compact with me, that she would love me and I her. She is a nobleman's daughter, and such is my parentage too: we are well-matched and of the same rank. I shall never intentionally take a wife so long as I know she is loyal to me: that will be the course of our love, if she keeps her word to me." "By God," said the king, "you speak too proudly: what I've heard of you is true indeed. But it's not very wise, in my opinion, to leave a king's daughter for one of lower birth. If a man can have a kingdom and such power, and forgoes it, it seems to me he acts like a fool." While they were talking thus, through the door of the hall came in great

---

[88] 3621 **neither infidel nor Saracen** *paen n'esclavon*: Slav; see note to v. 2442.

haste a pilgrim palmer,[89] in all appearances a penitent. He made his way straight towards Horn. (3657–81)

177. The pilgrim palmer entered the hall, with his scrip, staff, and felt cap; although he was poor, he seemed gently born. He made his way straight to where he could see Horn sitting. He knew his bearing and fresh complexion well, and as soon as he reached him he fell at his feet. He said: "My lord Horn, have mercy on me! I know and can tell you don't recognise me, because I'm dressed like a miserable beggar. I'm the son of lord Herland who brought you up as a boy—he was seneschal to Hunlaf, the good and noble king. Because he loved you, Wikele ill-treated him: he drove him from the land, without steed or nag. He lost everything for you, grey and white furs and ermine. He'd be happy just to have a sheepskin cloak. He fled the land like a miserable wretch. Wikele is seneschal and all the men in the land are subject to him and at his command. I've spent so long looking for you everywhere, my appearance has quite changed: no kinsman or friend would recognise my unkempt head. (3682–701)

178. "For three years already, I've not stopped travelling to seek you everywhere, on sea or land, but I couldn't find you anywhere till now, here. Herland sends this message: if you ever held him dear, do not stay your hand but come and help him to destroy that wicked slanderer, who through his gross lies and accusations estranged you and him from the king. There is yet more, which I won't conceal from you and which a man from Brittany told me the other day when I arrived—looking for you, like me. Exhorted by Wikele and his promises, King Hunlaf is marrying Rigmel to the King of Fenenie[90]—I've heard his name—a young man famous as a leader of men; Wikele should be richly rewarded for this act. This king is descended from Haderof, the noble king and brother of the valiant emperor Baderof, your father's grandfather, as I've heard tell. He's your kinsman—I can describe it properly when we have the need and opportunity, but there's only a month left before this matter is concluded, and the day is fixed. Make haste: delay no longer, if you want to have your revenge." (3702–25)

179. "Penitent, my good friend, what's this you say? I'm not the man you're looking for: they call me Gudmod. Go and look for Horn further afield! I don't know who he is, I've never met him. You talk just like a palmer, inventing lies. No one lies so much as pilgrims, who are used to it. They can never speak truly enough

---

[89] 3680 **a pilgrim palmer** *Un paumer pelerin*: a palmer was a pilgrim who had reached the Holy Land and returned with a leaf or branch from a palm.
[90] 3715 **to the king of Fenenie** *Al rei de Fenenie*: Legge (review of *Horn*, 312) thinks Fenenie is "probably Finland."

for me to believe them. [91] Tell me something else! In no way is it true, for Rigmel would not do it as long as Horn is alive. While I was in the land I knew her mind well: she is so loyal she would never be false." "No," said the pilgrim, "not by her own will. But her father presses her hard and Wikele vigorously encourages him. I know well you are the same Horn she loved so much. Noble sir, now help her! You are brave enough. I wonder you don't recognise me: I'm the son of Herland, who raised you so well when you were a child. That's why you don't know me, it's because I beg for my bread. All this is because of you, because I wished you well, and because of you too my father is banished; no matter where he sleeps at night, not a jot of the land belongs to him." All those in the household listening to him and hearing his words were amazed. (3726–51)

180. Horn heard it all and was sick at heart. He knew Jocerand, the messenger, well; he could not hide it because he was seized with pity. Now he replied to him as follows: "My friend, of course I know you, you can be truly sure of that. And of course I know Herland: it would be a crime not to. All the good that I know and all my attainments, he taught me. I know them through his teaching. If he is deprived because of me, it brings me much sorrow. When I can, I shall amply pay him back. I am indeed that Horn that the people talk of, son of King Aalof, the victorious. I shall not stop till I have revenge on that wicked and cowardly traitor Wikele. By God, sweet Rigmel, don't say I am slow; you will get my help, and quickly too. Now my silver and gold can be spent; now if I find troops, they can have it at will. Thank God, I have richly earned it." And King Gudreche paid close attention to it all — you never saw a man so glad. He came running up and fell at his feet. Now he would speak, beginning as follows. (3752–74)

181. "My lord Horn, my dear friend, I am very disappointed I have done so little for you; I deserve much blame. But now I know the whole truth about you. Nevertheless, when I first saw you, I did remark that your appearance and complexion indicated you came of noble birth, from good King Aalof, my ally. Good God! When I asked you, why did you hide it from me? You could have had me and my realm at your disposal: my men would serve you if you were in charge. Those set over you would then have rendered you obedience. But what was not done then can now be begun! Now take the whole domain — and receive the crown, better bestowed on you than on any man on earth — and my daughter Lenburc with her shapely body. I shall rest, since I am aged and old. With this you can then conquer Suddene at will, the realm of your famous grandfather;

---

[91] 3730–32 **You talk just like a palmer . . . for me to believe them** *Bien diz cum[e] paumer. . .ke je.s seie creant*: as pilgrims carried information, they were also suspected of lying, or inventing their tales. See Judith Weiss, "The Exploitation of Ideas of Pilgrimage and Sainthood in *Gui de Warewic*," in *Exploitation in Anglo-Norman Romance*, ed. Laura Ashe, Ivana Djordjevíc, and eadem (Woodbridge: Boydell and Brewer, forthcoming).

after him your father held it with great pride. And you can take proper vengeance on that devil Rodmund, who wrongfully killed your father Aalof. You can have all my wealth—I've plenty of it—and take with you the country's nobles. They'll follow you willingly if they're well paid." "My lord King." said Horn, "I've listened to you with care. God reward you for all you've said to me! But, so help me the Creator of us all, it can't turn out as you have planned. (3775–802)

182. "By your leave, King, you pile great honours on me, your kingdom and the fair Lenburc—she's certainly fit for an emperor's son—but this time, if you please, it cannot be. But, so help me the Creator of us all, I do not reject her out of pride or any arrogance or out of scorn for you (for that would be folly), but because I have a sweetheart elsewhere, whom I shall never betray as long as I live: may I never be accused of lying! Now, if it please our Saviour, I shall go back to that land and inquire what she has done: I'll soon get someone to tell me. If that wicked traitor has made her forsake me in order to take another husband, I shall quickly come back to you, I won't stay long. I shall trust your advice, for that would be best for me. And if it's not true, I shall marry her, and yet still be your protector: no emir or prince[92] will ever do you wrong without my always inflicting on him pain and defeat. (3803–21)

183. "You must know one thing, King: however the matter goes, I shall protect you and your kingdom with complete safety. If anyone does you wrong I shall certainly avenge you. I shall take pains to bestow your daughters. God willing, I shall give them to those as good as I am. Trust me, King, in this; if you doubt me, I'll swear it. But first I shall go to see Rigmel in Brittany. She is King Hunlaf's daughter whom I loved very much, and if she has done no wrong I shall still love her. Wikele shall pay for it, if I get the chance. If she has another lover, I know it's his fault. I shall soon take my revenge: I shall marry Lenburc. You may know this for certain, I shall keep my promise to you." "God grant it!" said the king, "I consent." "My lord," said Horn, "I shall go to my lodgings and take this pilgrim of mine with me and have him bled, rested, and bathed. Meanwhile I shall summon knights and men-at-arms and give them freely of my silver and gold: I have plenty to give, I shall make them all rich. I won it all from treacherous pagans. The time is very short: I shall delay no longer." "My lord," said Jocerand, "it would be base to do otherwise." (3823–45)

184. In her chambers Lenburc heard the news that the man calling himself Gudmod was Horn. For a very long while she had heard him talked about, how he

---

[92] 3821 **No emir or prince** *amirail n' aumazor*: see note to v. 560. According to Bancourt, *Musulmans* (844–45), the use of *aumazor* to mean "heathen prince" goes back to the career of Ibn Abi Amir, the powerful chamberlain of Caliph Hisham II, who in 981 took the honorific surname "Al-Mansur bi'llah," "the Victorious, through Allah."

loved Rigmel and she him, the daughter of Hunlaf, the good and noble king, she who surpassed all others in beauty with her shapely body and radiant face. No one in the world was her equal. Then she said to her companions: "I'm not surprised this man didn't love me when he'd chosen a wife like the beautiful Rigmel, because no one can find her peer. Jesus Christ! By God's grace, how could he conceal himself so long? There's no man on earth like him. He can easily surpass everyone in the world. In these chambers, I think, he could beat everyone in play, yet no one ever would hear him boast of it. My father's great wish was that he should reign here, and he also wished him to marry me, but he refused it all, no matter how much he begged him: it was all for Rigmel, who is so highly praised. There is none so fair under heaven within the bounds of earth and sea. The less I can compete with her. I should certainly forgive him; but had it been for another, he would have been to blame. He is very loyal and does not wish to deceive her. But if I can't have him, by St. Richer, I shall have no one else in the world for husband. I shall serve Jesus Christ: I shall take the veil as a nun. For his love I shall always dwell in the convent and there read my psalter for my benefactors." (3846–74)

185. What Lenburc had in mind came clearly to the king's ears. He uttered a sigh of grief for her, then said to his people: "I shall turn monk, and leave my realm of Westir to Horn." And lord Horn told him: "Don't give it up, but keep it carefully until my return. From that time on I want to defend it, and then I shall bestow your daughters according to their desire; and I shall in all things obey you as you will. If, meanwhile, any of your people fails in his duty towards you, you must know that I shall punish him. He won't escape death, but will be torn asunder or perish on the gallows. But first, sire, I must accomplish this journey, carry out my wishes about my inheritance, and drive into hiding the evil Wikele, who has made this man's father flee from the king. That's what I most desire in the world, to be avenged on that scoundrel; that's my aim. He will have nothing left worth taking. I shall make him confess all the perjury against me, make the king discard his advice, and quite sever the love between them." (3875–97)

186. "My lord Horn," said the king, "I know well it will happen in no other way than you have said and so I agree entirely with your will. But, when you return, keep to your undertaking, for I wholly trust your promise. I know, see, and understand indeed that there is no deceit in you. Take my gold and silver just as you like, and the élite from all my men to go with you to take revenge, and ships in harbour as you judge best. Let steersmen and brave sailors be ready, just as you wish and decide, to see to the navigation of yourself and your men." When lord Horn heard this, he thanked him heartily. Then he went to his lodging, made his preparations, and fixed the day he would make his start, giving gold and silver to those going with him. So young men flocked to him from all sides and he took them all into service, courteously, and gave them all enough that they were well-disposed to him. (3898–917)

187. So on the appointed day, those going with him all assembled and they were well equipped: they had excellent armour and good, fresh steeds. And when they had taken leave of the king they swiftly came to the ships and swiftly embarked. They hoisted the sails, for the breeze was good. They would not stop till they arrived. It was on the third day, at dusk, that they put into a very convenient harbour for them, for it was a little distant from town and people. There were woods round about in which they hid themselves in ambush. It concealed them entirely so that they were unobserved: lord Horn could hide there a long time without anyone hearing or finding him. In the morning, when it was day, Horn equipped himself well and a swift steed was brought him. He told his men: "My lords, wait for me here: don't stir a foot till I return. I'm going off into the country to visit the cities and ask for news—and they'll tell me plenty—of how the king is behaving, he and his nobles, of the lovely Rigmel with her fresh charms, whether her lover has come, if they are married. When I've asked about everything and have returned, then we shall do what God has ordained for us." "My lord," they all said, "be it as you wish! We shall do your will: you have led us here." (3918–44)

188. Horn took leave of them all and then went off. He mounted his steed, which was a swift one, and carried no weapon save only a sword with him, and when he had gone some distance further on in the land, he met on his path a penitent palmer. First he greeted him and then he inquired about the king and his court, where he was now dwelling. He asked how things were with his daughter Rigmel, if she was taking a husband, as people were saying. And he replied: "I've just come straight from there; only just now I left it, on the stroke of six. The king is at Lions, a noble city, and will hold his court there, so many nobles are there. Today Modin will arrive, a king of great renown, lord of Fenenie, a handsome young man, and today he is to marry Rigmel, with her smiling face. Everyone in the land is happy and joyful; they have gone to meet him at his place of arrival. I can stay no more, because I'm hastening back to the land where I used to live." (3945–64)

189. Horn heard it all and replied: "Pilgrim, my good friend, you've just spoken well. But, by St. Martin, when I look at you, your face seems to me to show you're well-born; although you're so poor and shabby, you seem neither wretch nor beggar. In exchange for your gown you shall have a crimson tunic; I shall have your pilgrim's robe and you this ermine cloak. For these leggings, here is this silken hose, for this staff of yours, my Arab steed, for this palm-branch on your shoulder, this good steel sword. Then keep on your way to God, palmer, and I will go to court to see what they're up to." "My lord," said the palmer, "He who made wine out of water[93] reward you for the good you've done me!" Then he went

---

[93] Allusion to John 2:1–11.

straight off towards the sea. And Horn, with his felt cap, turned his steps, according to the record, at a run towards the court, so quickly that no horse could have kept pace. He stopped near the town, under the branches of a pine. There he would see the proceedings for himself. (3965–85)

190. King Modin's people disembarked and made for the city along the grassy roads, their spears and shields gleaming in the sun. From Horn's vantage point he could easily recognise them; he would not move from it until they had passed, and he would greet those he chose. He let the first people go by, keeping quite silent and quiet, for those were squires, merry and rowdy people. And next came the young, new-bearded, newly-dubbed knights, well dressed, and he let them go by without a word. At last came some imposing men, greybeards; with these came Modin — he attended them — for they were his advisers, he trusted them. With them came Wikele who had got them all there, who had instigated the affair which angered Horn. As soon as he saw Modin he realised he was the redoubtable King of Fenenie. (3986–4003)

191. King Modin and Wikele came riding behind their companions, making merry, arms round each other's necks, laughing and sporting. They talked of Rigmel, how attractive she was — no one existed in the present age to equal her. Horn heard it clearly and was very angry: now he would say something, however cross it made them. "My lords," he said, "young men,[94] you seem like roisterers, going to a wedding to show off. You're sure to be swearing like a trooper,[95] and when you've drunk so much, you're inflamed with wine and swearing exactly that, I'll pour you a measure, if you thank me for it, and if not, you won't get anything at all." And when Wikele heard him, he was beside himself and replied in anger — but if he had recognised him, he would never have started. And lord Horn knew him, because he had looked after him from birth. Now hear what Wikele said to him, if you are listening: "Son of a whore, scum, insolent scoundrel, if it weren't for the love of God and the fact you're a penitent, you'd already have been thrashed, and with your own staff, no other stick, so that you'd be filthy. You'd never make fun of such people again." "Indeed," said Horn, "then it's a pity I ever carried it! A curse on you if you don't step forward. You'd soon know who I am and how I can strike." (4004–29)

---

[94] 4011 **young men** *bachelers*: a deliberately offensive remark, since these were either young men not yet knighted, or without fiefs. See Pope, *Horn*, 2:164.

[95] 4013 **swearing like a trooper** *Bien jur(e)rez "Witegod"*: an early Middle English oath, meaning "as God is my witness." See Pope, *Horn*, 2:165. Horn suggests that Modin and Wikele are like Anglo-French barons, revealing when drunk the English origins they would rather hide.

192. "Wikele," said Modin, "leave this lordly fellow alone. We'll never gain respect wrangling with him; he'd have the best of it and we the worst. It seems he's a rascal, alas, who's on his way to the wedding to play the drum, and is dressed so shabbily in order to gain more, if he can find someone to reward him because of his playing. He hasn't worn these clothes for long: look at his white skin and healthy colour. He's so handsome he could be an emir's son; no emperor's daughter would refuse him. Now please tell me, my friend, without anger, who you are, where you come from and where you live." "I shall tell you," said Horn, "if you listen. Once I served a worthy man here. I shall tell you my job: I was his fisherman. One day I put a net I had—good for such a task—into the water to catch fish. Almost seven years passed before I returned here. Now I've come back to inspect it: if it's caught fish, it will never have my love, and if it's still without them, then I shall carry it away.[96] I lead such a life as I tell you. If you want to hear more, ask another story-teller." "Wikele," said Modin, "this is great nonsense you hear. I could see earlier he was a joker: anyone who gets in the least angry with him is a fool. (4030–57)

193. "Wikele, my dear friend, let's go our way and commend this pilgrim palmer to God. If he comes to court, we'll give him some good wine. He doesn't seem to be base-born; he's come to grief, to go around so poverty-stricken. If he's not well-born, never trust me more: his body is so fair, and his face so ruddy, he hasn't been long in this way of life." "I don't care," said Wikele, "he's vicious and uncouth. Let's follow this path straight to St. Maurin's[97] abbey; there the archbishop is, lord Taurin, a worthy man to whom we are all subject. There the king awaits us, and with him his neighbours. There you will be wed, following the prescriptions of the divines, who had God's laws written down on parchment." "Then truly," said Modin, "let's do so." Then Horn remained alone under the pine branches. He disguised himself under his felt cap and set out along the stream, with its clear rivulets, that came from the city. He carried his good ash staff in his hand and held his head down to conceal himself better. If anyone, squire or boy, did him wrong, he would quickly repay them by laying them flat. (4058–81)

194 Horn travelled long enough that he came to the door, but they refused him entry because he was unknown. This was something that angered him and gained the porter a quite different greeting, for lord Horn approached like a man in fury, hoisted him high by the short hairs and, like a powerful man, dragged

---

[96] 4046–52 **I was his fisherman . . . carry it away** *joe fui sun pescheör. . . en ierc porteör*: the fish and the net, erotic images of the relations between the lovers, also appear in *King Horn*, where they are put to more frequent and effective use (see *King Horn*, ed. Joseph Hall [Oxford: Clarendon Press, 1901]). The image is old and widespread.

[97] 4067 **St. Maurin's abbey** *mustier saint Maurin*; manuscript O: *Martin*. Maurin could be Maurus, a sixth-century Benedictine monk.

him towards him. He shoved him forwards and backwards, striking him three times; a fourth blow would have done for him. He threw him over the bridge into the stagnant waters of the moat, then entered freely, so hidden amongst the great crowd that he was not noticed. No one took any more notice of the porter that day, except that his friends ran up to drag him out of the mud engulfing him. They asked many questions about Horn, who he was, what had happened to him. But as they did not recognise him, they had to desist. (4082–98)

195. When they had heard mass in the main abbey and the service had been performed, magnificent and festal, as befitted the wedding of that royal maiden, the noble lords came to the court. They sat down to eat: stewards served them from bowls of silver and no other metal. Cupbearers had goblets of gold and brass, well worked with enamel and precious stones; they carried hippocras and wines clear as crystal. The entertainment was lavish and truly princely: no man ever saw so fine before. The king's almoner[98] had taken the poor all together to the meal; it would have been remiss otherwise. Horn was taken with them, though they were not his equals. He kept his face down under his cap so as not to be recognised by any man there. He took his position right at the end of a bench; in spite of all their shoving, he did not want to do otherwise. (4099–16)

196. From where he sat he could easily see how everyone behaved at the meal, how the stewards served attentively, how the cupbearers bore wine and clarry, which made people on all sides merry and playful, except for the lovely Rigmel, whose mind was sadly preoccupied, so that no one could comfort her with any sort of diversion. They kept playing harps and fiddles in front of her but her heart took no pleasure in them at all, she thought so much about Horn, with whom she had to break faith. But she could not help it and was the less to blame: the king had forced her, through wicked advice. When they had eaten enough, the tables were cleared and those who wanted to, washed. And now the squires and men-at-arms were to eat, but meanwhile the king, following the custom, had to find someone to serve the wine. He did not want to prevent what his ancestors had done, so he commanded Rigmel to go, and the lovely girl could not refuse his command. (4117–36)

197. It was then the custom in that land that when a lady was to be married, if she were a virgin, she was put to the test of serving the drink for as long as the seneschal and the rest of the household were eating. [99] And when she had done

---

[98] 4110 **The king's almoner** *Li aumoniers lo rei*: the almoner's job was to distribute alms and to see to the serving of the poor, as here.

[99] 4137–41 **It was then the custom. . .were eating** *Costume iert. . .cum (li) seneschal mangast*: on the Germanic custom of the lady or daughter of the house bearing horns of drink round to the guests at a feast, and on the use of drinking-horns in England,

this, the man who married her had, after his rest, to bear arms outside the city, in meadow or field. And since it was the custom, Rigmel did not refuse, but at once entered her rooms and there splendidly arrayed herself and then quickly returned to the paved hall. There was a row of thirty girls with her, each of them divested of their mantles: they were barons' daughters, each accomplished. Rigmel then entered the buttery and took a cup of ox-horn with a jewelled rim, half a foot wide round the mouth, wonderfully worked with African gold. She filled it with hippocras—a drink everyone likes—and carried it to her husband, as was the custom. The others also served all around the tapestry-hung hall with golden cups. They had already gone round four times without stopping, and when it came to the fifth Horn pulled her towards him, as she passed, by her gold-embroidered sleeve, and smilingly spoke to her as follows. (4137–63)

198. "Lovely lady, it's a pity God created you in all your splendid beauty when you don't honour Him or any of His people. You keep passing before us to the rich men and to us alone you offer nothing. By Him who made you, you are much in the wrong. You turn to bad use the benefits He gave you when you reward His people here thus for His sake. Your renown will grow if you serve us, three times as much as for the well-dressed, for He who created you loves the poor. For the poor He came to earth and was poor enough there. So now leave off serving those high barons, for the clerks say God doesn't love the rich. Sooner will a camel go through the eye of a needle than a rich man enter the kingdom of heaven,[100] for many have quite forgotten God because of their goods. So serve those of us who are poorly clothed. He who gave you everything will reward you." "My friend," said Rigmel, "you preach nobly: no bishop or abbot could do better. So now I shall do what you bid me." Then she returned and selected a gilded goblet, of Solomon's style and high antiquity—it had been a cup for her lords a long while. When she had filled it with wine, she brought it to him and he set it before him, untasted. You will not wonder at her surprise. (4164–90)

199. She took the goblet and gave it back to him, but he never tasted it or deigned to take it. She was very surprised and did not know what to think. Very carefully she began to scrutinize him; she saw the white skin and bright face. It certainly seemed he had not been a palmer long, nor was he like a man leading such a life. But she did not quite dare to indicate what she surmised. Nevertheless, she said to him: "Now tell me, my fair friend, if you don't want to drink, why ask for it? I've brought you it twice and you wouldn't taste it: as far as I can see, you have

see Hall's notes on vv. 1109–10 in his edition of *King Horn,* and M. E. M. Dickson, "Twelfth-Century Insular Narrative: The Romance of Horn and Related Texts" (Ph.D. diss., Cambridge University, 1996), chap. 3. Rigmel's horn is a *corn de bugle* and Horn later uses it to make a pun on his own name; see v. 4206.

[100] Matthew 19:24, Mark 10:25, Luke 18:25.

a proud heart." Then Horn replied thus—he could hide no longer—"Lovely lady, know for certain, once men used to bring me richer cups. But 'horn' is the English word for what you took round just now.[101] If you, for love of him I've just named, will offer me the horn full of wine that I saw you give to your lover just now, I shall share this drink with you. But I know quite well that now you have little love for him for whom I ask this; so leave it be." And when Rigmel heard him she nearly fainted, so much did the reproach pierce her to the heart. (4191–214)

200. She felt such grief at heart she almost fainted. When she recovered, she stopped and reflected. She thought he might be a messenger from Horn. She did not dare to recognise that it was he himself, nor at heart did she expect he would be so poor. Nevertheless she scanned his appearance for a long time and, having observed him, sighed for love of him. But she did not dare reveal what she thought, but went for the horn and brought it to him full of wine. When she came to him, she put it in his hand and he took his ring, the same Rigmel gave him on his departure, and quietly threw it in. Then he drank half and turned to her, asking her again to drink it as she had promised him, for love of him he had just named. Now he would see if it was true she had once loved him. She took it, drank, and tilted the horn, and the ring brushed her mouth with the wine; and when she felt it, she was afraid. She took it up and recognized it as soon as she saw it—she knew well it was the one Horn carried away[102] when he took leave of her and left. (4215–235)

201. She said to him: "My good friend, I've found a ring in this horn, but I don't know who put it there. If it's yours, take it, you're welcome to have it, for I have no wish to keep it. It may render you service, it seems to me. Now blest be he to whom I gave it. If you know anything of him, don't hide it from me; if he's alive or dead, tell me in which land: I will seek him or die, nothing shall prevent it. I shall never leave him for the man who married me today. And if you are Horn, show me; and if you hide yourself any longer, you do great wrong." "Lovely lady," said Horn, "I don't know where he was born, the man you mention and ask of me. I heard no more of him or his family; but this ring was mine—it can't be denied. I loved him so long and dearly, he entrusted me with it. Now our friendship has quite passed away. Now you have it, it well repays you for serving me with the good mature wine. I shall have other rings, plenty of them, God willing. (4236–56)

---

[101] 4206 **"horn" is the English word ... now** *Mes "corn" apelent "horn" li engleis latimier:* literally, "the English interpreters render 'corn' as 'horn'."

[102] 4234 **she knew well ... carried away** *Bien conut ... Horn enporta*: with this line manuscript H ends.

202. "As a boy, I was raised in this land, and won, through my great loyalty, a goshawk. Before I tamed it, I put it in mew, nearly seven years ago now: that may well be too long. Now I've come back to see what it's like, and how valuable, whether it's going to be docile or flighty. And if it's unblemished, as it was in the days when I left, then I promise it will be mine; I'll carry it away with me, from here to my friends. And if it's damaged, or its tail feathers injured, so its wing is broken, and it's the worse in any way, then, by St. Denis, it will never be mine." When Rigmel heard him, she gave a laugh. Then she said joyfully: "Now I'm cured of my ills. Horn, my friend, it's you! Of course I know your face. By the High King living in Paradise, who created and rules the world, have no doubts about the goshawk you speak of; I promise you it is well guarded in every way. (4257–75)

203. "Horn, my friend, it's truly you, upon my word. By the High King who made the firmament, you must know that either I'll go with you or tonight I'll kill myself. I'll die in anguish: no one else shall enjoy me. Now let it be as you please: I surrender entirely to you." Now Horn could no longer delay recognizing the truth, which he knew to be so, hut first he would still set her a hard test. So he spoke to her like this: "It's true; I am Horn—I won't deny it—who in my first youth once loved you. But I've lived amongst evil people who've given me very little: I've gained nothing. Now I've come here destitute, like a beggar; I don't know where to take you. I've no silver or gold, no lands in all the world. Why follow me then, a miserable outcast?—and you have a king with many great possessions. Stay with him and be true to him; he can provide for you, and richly too. And I'm needy: I have only the clothes I stand up in, I have nothing to clothe you, not even one garment. Someone gently nurtured could suffer badly from the abject poverty that a wretch like me expects." "By God, my dear sweet friend, you little know my mind. I shall cheerfully suffer what you suffer, or never see another dawn. There's no king so rich from here to the East for whom I would leave you with such resources." Then Horn knew truly and certainly that Rigmel was faithful, told him no lies, and bore a loyal heart quite without deceit. (4276–308)

204. "My beautiful lady," Horn said, "now let's stop talking: you see Wikele over there, he's always on the look-out. For some time he's certainly seen us whispering here. He's observed us closely, because he's a scoundrel, and is sure I'm a messenger from Horn. Soon now he'll go to the king and accuse us. He'll easily have me caught, if he can find me here; but I can stay no longer, I commend you to God. By staying you lose, by going you gain: I have three hundred ships down there on the sea, full of many bold knights who came with me. I said I was destitute to test you. Now I find you're faithful, praise God! I assure you I don't want to leave you. But tell Modin to go out there and joust, as was always the ancestral custom. I shall come, if I can, to help the sport, and if I find you there I think I can easily defend my claim to you, and anyone grumbling at it would soon pay

for it. Now do that; already I delay too long." "My lord, as you please! God grant you success!" (4309–29)

205. Thereupon Horn the brave left the throng. Because he looked poor no one remarked it: the rich man does not notice when he sees the poor man pass, so no notice is taken of him anywhere he goes. But when he left the court he went off immediately: no fast nag or pack-horse could have kept pace. He came to his ships merry and joyful and told his men how he had fared and of his long talk with Rigmel the noble, because he had changed clothes with the penitent. You must know that his men were happy and playful and said amongst themselves: "Never was there such a brave man. Where might you find someone who would have begun this business?" "My lords," said Horn, "help me now, because we're about to have a piece of good luck: everyone in the city is going out to joust, bearing arms in the fields or meadows. And my beautiful mistress Rigmel will be there. So I'm craven and cowardly if I don't challenge them. Therefore I want us to be equipped and ready to fight so that we may enter the city with them." "By God," said everyone, "that is well devised. He's a base coward who spares his sword or doesn't strike both the hairy and the bald!" Then they armed themselves as fast as they could. (4330–54)

206. While lord Horn went back to his ships and exhorted his men to fight, Rigmel addressed Modin thus: "My lord, now I have served, it's right that you should go—as our ancestors did many a day—out there beyond the city. You'll bear arms there, and I shall see the sport and you gain fame." "Indeed," said Modin, "I shall not refuse you. Go, my lords," he said, "prepare yourselves and bring me all my equipment here. I shall go out there; lovely lady, follow me, for I want your praise for my deeds." "My lord," said Rigmel, "as you command. I shall go with pleasure to see my beloved." She meant another, whom she loved much more. She went into her chamber and summoned Haderof. When he came to her, he was told: "My dear friend Haderof, I shall take you with me. I shall show you something out there to please you. Not since Horn left will you be so pleased. You shall see someone to love as much as you loved Horn, when you parted." "Lovely lady," said Haderof, "what does this mockery mean? It could be no man in the world yet born unless it were Horn himself and he'd been found. (4355–80)

207. "By God, lovely Rigmel, where's the loyalty I thought you had? Horn the brave is very soon forgotten for others not half his worth. But you love the one near at hand—it's all over with the one far away—and not him who loved you so. To have waited so long seems too long to you. I'll never believe another woman in all my life: he's mad who believes any, that's so often proved true. Who would have believed this of you? Now I'm nearly out of my mind. Whom could I find to love as much? It wouldn't be Modin, not for his kingdom. I'll never love

him in the least; I won't consider him till I hear from Horn and where he is, that man of renown. I'll never ride a horse out there; nor do I have any fine horse to ride; no one has given me one since my lord Horn left the land." "Now," said Rigmel, "you shall say all you want, whatever you please: but none of it is true. So help me the King sitting in majesty who rules heaven, earth, and sea, I only ever loved one man, the noble Horn. Now I won't hide it any longer. Know that truly, this very day, I've had much talk with Horn; if you come to the games, you'll soon be shown him." (4381–404)

208. "Father and Lord! Jesus Christ! have I heard true? By God, fair Rigmel, I was quite wrong to blame you. If you're telling me the truth, I'll make peace with you and ride the fair and good Blanchart, which lord Horn gave me. I've still kept him, and shall continue to, for love of him. You were the one who raised him, fair lady, I know quite well, and gave him to Herland: we know very well why. Now I can't fail you, it would be shameful. I shall mount him and escort you: God willing, I shall see what you've promised me. If I see he needs me, I'll be with him and strike knights for love of him: if they're his enemies I'll soon harm them. And I'll summon all our group to be with him and see them ready furnished and equipped with arms, except the evil Wikele. I'll hide it from him alone, for he planned all this affair. If I can, I'll take revenge on him and cut off the scoundrel's head with my sword." "Come quickly," said Rigmel, "soon I shall show you Horn." (4405–24)

209. While Rigmel was making ready and they were helping her onto her palfrey, Haderof came riding on his steed, its coat as white as snow on the sand. He was well equipped with both iron and steel. Except for his master, lord Horn, there was no knight like him. He seemed a good warrior to help his lord and trustworthy in case of need. Wikele had arrived first and wanted to escort her; when Haderof saw him, he was nearly beside himself. Then he said to him: "Vile wretch, now leave her be. You don't deserve to lead her. By St. Richer, if you don't leave her at once, I'll set your head flying with this blade at my side. I never liked traitors or slanderers at any price. I can't like you because I know you're one." And when Wikele heard him, he did not dare to stop but fled like the roebuck glimpsing the archer. Then Haderof took her reins of pure gold and led her to the games to see the sport. But she came to see something else, that she held more dear. (4425–45)

210. You know all about their behaviour; now you shall hear about Horn and how he fared. He had already valiantly disembarked and came riding along with twenty thousand men — not a knight among them who wasn't well-known — who rode steeds, some thick-maned, some maneless. They had girded on the tough swords and sharpened spears; they had strong white hauberks and good pointed helmets. They were riding quietly under the leafy trees. They kept quiet so as not

to be seen. They came through the woodland very close to the city. They stopped at the margin of a copse so that none of them were spotted nor recognised. Horn commanded none of them to move until they clearly heard his own horn. If people saw them all, they would quickly rush into the city and take themselves off, and thus his business would be ruined. When he had ordered this, he went out with just ten men, galloping over the turf towards the tournament. They rode very fiercely like people in anger. Each selected his own man, then struck him, so that at the first blow they struck down ten. One of them was Modin, whom Horn smote so that his gleaming helm was soiled with mud. (4446–70)

211. Horn's blow was clearly seen by Rigmel, and she said to Haderof: "That's Horn, my lover. Now go and help him if you want his safety, for you can see how many people are attacking him. They'll soon rescue Modin whom he struck down. Go and help him, show your strength. Alas! he has too few, help will come too late." Thereupon Horn, the brave and formidable, blew his horn, so that his men very soon both heard and knew it: then the knights rushed out, leaving the thicket. When those in the city observed this, be sure of it, they did not wait, for they were very frightened of the ambush from the woods. Haderof with his men came to their aid, recognising Horn easily from the griffin on his shield; he came straight to him and greeted him. And the city folk rushed inside and left lord Modin, the king, in captivity: I don't think they would ever have rescued him. But before they entered, many a man lost his shield, shamefully relieved of it as he fled. (4471–91)

212. He who could flee fled, but Rigmel did not flee: Haderof came and quickly seized her, and handed her over to Horn, for she was his beloved, and lord Horn received her and warmly welcomed her.[103] Then they took Modin, king of Fenenie, and he was entrusted to someone who would look after him carefully. Then Horn rode to the ancient city, intending to besiege it with well-armed troops. He had given his word he would not leave till he had taken and possessed it. He had quite a hundred thousand men in his company, proud and bold people who had come with him. Anyone seeing such an assembly and who had done them any wrong would have had cause for fear. But when King Hunlaf heard the news that it was lord Horn, whose life he had saved, then he knew well that he had been very foolish ever to separate Rigmel and him. Now he would show contrition, if he could, but he did not believe anybody would want it. But Horn had his shapely daughter in his keeping, and lord Modin the king in his power—it would be great folly to contend with him. He had the upper hand and the land

---

[103] 4493–95 **Haderof . . . welcomed her** *Haderof . . . la reçut*: the rescue from the wedding feast is very close to a similar rescue in the *Gesta Herwardi*. On their possible mutual borrowings, see Weiss, "Thomas and the Earl," 9–13.

in his possession, and moreover the rightful heir, in whom he reposed his trust. (4492–516)

213. So he sent for a bishop and an abbot, who were now dispatched to Horn before he might harry or lay waste his land, to propose that he should come to terms with him and enter the city. He would henceforth entirely comply with his wishes, provided that Horn quite renounced his anger at being estranged from him by false accusation. Now he should take Rigmel and be her husband; all their lives they should not be separated. There was too close a kinship between her and Modin; he would have them separated, that he would promise on oath. Then Horn should do whatever he pleased with Modin, as with his relation: he should not be ill-treated but become his sworn vassal. He would never name any other ransom. The messengers went off, as I have related, and told it to Horn, and he gave it all his consent. (4516–33)

214. Lord Horn agreed to it all, as I have said, and he and Modin came to satisfactory terms. Lord Horn and all his men entered the city: the noble Hunlaf received them very well. Lord Herland was summoned to this meeting and his office was given him back, entirely at his disposal. Not a jot did he lose of his possessions which he could prove he had lost: Hunlaf restored him everything, on his plighted word. And next lord Wikele was rewarded as he well deserved as a wicked traitor. Then they went to the abbey to receive a blessing on the marriage to Rigmel with the lovely face, for a divorce was made between Modin and her. When the service was all duly finished, the treacherous Wikele came in, his hooded head bowed low. He did not listen to a word that lord Horn said, but fell at his feet and before the barons made him this entreaty: to have mercy on him for behaving evilly towards him and, if he ever again misbehaved, to take vengeance on him as he would on a wicked traitor. Because everyone begged it, lord Horn pardoned him on such terms as he had set forth. Then they all went to the royal household where they found stewards to receive them. Even the poorest put on mantles of grey and white fur or tunics of samite or good silk, tightly laced with thongs whose buttons were of gold. (4534–61)

215. These noble knights sat down to eat: the service was sumptuous, and mighty noblemen waited on them. Everywhere alike the dishes were abundant, everywhere the excellent cupbearers set good wines, strong and clear, which made them merry. Horn had much joy in his beautiful wife; Rigmel likewise, her face radiant, and lord Hunlaf the king could rejoice that he had made such a fine match for his daughter. When they had eaten enough, the tables were cleared. Then Horn rose to his feet, the noble and brave, and signed for attention, for he wanted to speak. They kept quite quiet and dared not say a word, for they all feared him, knowing him so proud. When he was angry, no one dared approach him, and when he was happy, everyone could relax. Now hear what he said, if

you choose to listen; now you shall hear what deserves praise, how lord Horn was to go and revenge his father. He began, then, like this, wanting to reveal his desire. (4562–81)

216. "My lord, King Hunlaf, first of all may the sovereign Lord thank you for my upbringing and the good you've done me. . .

> [At this point, after verse 4584, the text of the Cambridge manuscript of *The Romance of Horn* breaks off. Pope calculates that three *laisses* of the narrative are missing in all the extant manuscripts and fragments: these must have contained an account of Horn gathering his forces, sailing back to Suddene, and meeting Hardré, his father's seneschal. The end of the poem (4586–5240) is taken from the Oxford manuscript. It is possible that the "it" of the next preserved verse (4586) refers to Hardré's offer of help, or it might refer to Rodmund.]

"You shall have it, [or him]" said Hardré, "if God now pleases."

219. Then they went happily back to their ships. As soon as it was known that it was lord Hardré, never did men show greater joy, everyone more cheerful for love of him. The following day, when the sun rose, all those from the ships assembled at Horn's tent. Then lord Hardré addressed them thus: "Now listen, my lords, how you shall proceed: by my advice, God willing, you shall avenge the suffering of your slain friends. Divide your forces, that I see here, into two, and hide half of them where I show you; lord Horn shall stay with the other half here. When I have led Rodmund and his men here, you will surround them in this field and break cover, and from behind strike valiantly at their backs. The renegade wretches will be defeated. Before they know it they'll be struck down dead. Once you're avenged, you can seize the land: you can bring in your knights just as you please." Then they all cried: "Bless the day you were born! It shall be as you wish and command." Thereupon he took his leave and departed, but first showed them the spot he spoke of: it was very convenient to do as he said. (4587–613)

220. And meanwhile Hardré went to talk to King Rodmund, wanting, if he could, to achieve his overthrow, for whatever he pretended, he had no love for him. He wanted to avenge his lord any way he could—Aalof the brave, who raised and held him dear. Horn's men went off to hide in the moors: Rodmund would not know of it until he was in trouble. There were many noble knights of proud bearing, not one of whom did not strive to butcher Rodmund—and they would do it, too, because God was on their side. Hardré now came into the main chamber where King Rodmund and his people usually dwelt. And when he reached him he first of all said: "Sire, Mahomet, our rightful king, keep you! I shall tell you something to marvel at: in the fifteen years I have guarded all your

ports, I've never seen anyone come to harm them. Now some scoundrels or other have arrived, with only twenty ships—as far as I can estimate. If they are Christians, I can't tell. I don't know if it could be Horn, come to plunder, but your men said they saw him drown. And let's not allow them to stay, whoever they are, for it would be a great shame and reproach if they carried off anything of ours without paying for it." (4614–38)

221. "Hardré," said Rodrnund, "I shall tell you something: I greatly fear Horn and shall always do so. For not long ago I sent out a spy, who told me he lived and I'll see him yet. I shall pay back those who told me he drowned. The other day, not long ago, I had a bad dream, and the more I consider it the more I'm dismayed. It seemed to me, I went out with my dogs one morning to a wood by the sea, and there I hunted. I came upon a herd of boar and so I shouted. I found a great tusked hog with them, who wounded my horse, threw me in the mire, and pierced me through the body, so I rose no more. 'Boar' means 'men' in a dream—I know quite well.[104] If I encounter these people, I'll take good care." "Nonsense!" said Hardré, "it would indeed be shameful if they escaped us scot-free on such a pretext. I shan't believe in dreams, by Apollo! Whatever I've dreamt has turned out a fiction. So let's disregard it; I'll never pay it heed. If you won't go, I'll go alone. I'll take those of your men I can, and if it should be Horn, I'll strike him first. If you don't believe me, truly I'll swear to you, by Apollo, that I won't spare one." (4639–63)

222. Thus Rodmund was encouraged to go; yet because of his dream, he went unwillingly. With him went a thousand equipped and armour-clad pagans. They were few against our men, who were hand-picked and brave, but Hardré wanted them few. He went ahead, leading and encouraging them all, making merry, with great horn-blasts and great promises that they would make a fortune. When they conquered this rash rabble, they would have more wealth than King David. So the villains were encouraged to go. The mountains echoed with the noise they made: Horn's people in the moors could clearly hear them from afar. They concealed and hid themselves to let them pass, for that day Hardré's desire would be fulfilled: that day Arab villains would die by the sword as soon as the battle began. Our men would be valiant; they went there with no reluctance. And the others would be few compared with them, and discouraged: never again would they see their wives and sons. (4664–83)

---

[104] 4652 **"Boar" means "men" in a dream** *"Pors" senefient "gent" en sunge*: according to an eleventh-century Latin dream-book with Old English glosses, to dream of pigs portends trouble: *Porcos uiderit, infirmitatem significat*. The text is also interesting on the "anxiety" of dreams to do with swimming (see *laisse* 234). See M. Förster, "Das lateinisch-altenglische Pseudo-Danielsche Traumbuch in Tiberius A III," *Archiv für das Studium der neueren Sprachen* 125 (1910): 39–70, at 58, 63.

223. Hardré led them through a valley, avoiding our men; he well knew where they were hid. And Horn was armed, and prepared his men. The pagans came on with confidence, like arrogant people, and went straight to where the fleet was anchored. When they perceived it, they lost heart, like those who knew they were doomed to lose. Then they knew their death was planned by Horn, and saw there were so many they would not withstand them, for there were only a handful of them against them. They would gladly have returned to their land if they could have seen a convenient way, but they were quite surrounded with angry men, and already lord Horn had begun the fight and lord Hardré was with him, risking his life: striking pagans was to his taste. Now blows fell on all sides and the pagans suffered losses, for they lay all around, mouths agape. Then Rodmund knew well his life was over; he recognised the dream, revealed to him, and knew that Horn would revenge the death of his father Aalof, the much-lamented. (4684–705)

224. Rodmund knew for sure he would not escape and that Horn would revenge the death of Aalof. When he saw he would certainly die that day, he thought he would sell his life dearly. First he cursed Hardré who had so badly tricked him, who had misled him and so deceived him. He had said the men were few and so led him to this unhappy field, where he knew he must stay. When he should have helped him, he joined the other side: if possible, this man should be the first to pay for it. He brandished his spear, lowered his shield, and then, when he encountered Hardré, struck him. He gave him a great blow on his quartered shield, piercing the thongs and the wood, but damaging not a single link of his hauberk. Nevertheless, he brought him down from his horse. But his son Badelac, very distressed, brought him such good aid that he could no longer wound him. And Rodmund pressed forward, now filling them with alarm: they would pay dearly for his certain death. (4706–25)

225. Horn was elsewhere, fighting fiercely. The pagans went in great fear and trembling of him, for now he was taking revenge for the death of Aalof. There was not a single one whose head he did not take: great was the battle, heavy the strife. Haderof heard the men's loud cries and with his troops sallied forth from ambush; he came up to the pagans and violently attacked them. Whoever was there could have seen such a great overthrow that no one ever arose or saw his family again. Rodmund saw quite well he was on the brink of destruction, for on all sides he was beset so there was no escape: of the thousand with him there were now only a hundred left. He denounced Hardré, he cursed him often: "I was very wrong not to hang this evil traitor long ago, and abandon him. Indeed I always feared and suspected him, but he was saved and protected by his God. He treats His believers better than Mahomet does. Hardré never forsook Him, but pretended to do so. Now He has shown us, in this extremity, that He's on their side and against us. If I can take revenge in any encounter, I'll die more easily and in peace." (4726–49)

226. When Rodmund had spoken, he spurred his horse. In his fist he held his sword with its crystal pommel, and very angrily he scrutinized the ranks. In great wrath he went to strike a knight: he split his whole helmet open down to the nose-guard. He could not withstand it but collapsed: no great wonder, for the blow was fatal. Haderof saw Rodmund as he came down a slope, and certainly saw the mighty blow he gave the knight. Now, if he could, he would render him the same. He came up to him and dealt him such a stroke on the front rim of his fine shield that his noble sword cleft it in two. He grabbed the neck of the horse, close to the chest, and knocked the king off, prone onto the ground. This was a shameful disgrace to befall him! And he jumped up in keen anguish. He called loudly on his lord Belial to let him be a perfect match for Haderof in this fight, so he could return his blows equally, for he would never give ground to him. He would have been a most valiant man, had he only believed in the Heavenly King. (4750–71)

227. Haderof, very angry, came up to him and struck the king again, wounding him badly. And Rodmund, also furious, struck him a most powerful blow with his keen sword, throwing him and his horse to the ground: now both of them were on foot and equal in the field. Then they went on fighting unsparingly, both good, hardened warriors. They fought so long it was nearly nightfall; but now Haderof was extremely tired, so that he could not hold up his fine decorated shield and the blows from his steel blade were very feeble. It was no great wonder, for he was badly wounded, his hauberk pierced through in several places, and his wounds bled fast. It would be the end of him if no help came soon. And Rodmund was very valiant and quite undismayed, for he felt quite fresh, as if unwounded, full of vigour and as if at play. Just as he wanted to seize Haderof by the enamelled nose-guard, up spurred Horn with lord Hardré, who were slaying pagans when they were told: "Soon Haderof will die if he's not helped." Then Horn cried loudly to Rodmund: "False, cruel wretch, touch him again at your peril." (4772–96)

228. Now Horn dismounted and ran up to Rodmund, sword in hand, like a man in fury. He spoke to him and said: "Now the brave Aalof will be avenged through you. Neither Mahomet nor Tervagant will protect you from dying here like a craven dog." And when Rodmund heard him, he had not the least fear of him, but said: "I was mad to put you in the boat: if I had hanged you then like a plundering thief, you wouldn't be slaying me now. Leave me to take vengeance on Hardré, then do just as you please with me, for he has quite betrayed me, like a treacherous wretch. A Saracen who ever believes one of your religion, however much he promises, is quite mad. He used to promise me and always swore it, that if he ever saw Horn he would kill him. Now he's repaid me for all by deceiving me in all. But now, step forward: I surrender my sword, and you may do with me as you wish." And Horn approached him, expecting no harm, but the treacherous dog

went quite berserk, striking under his shield towards his heart, thinking to kill him through his mail. But the good hauberk was tough and strong, and against his blow it gave him excellent protection. (4797–822)

229. Now Horn saw that the villain intended him harm and would kill him if he were not stopped. Before, had he cried for mercy, he would have had it and been kept alive, whole and sound. Had he wished to serve God, he would have been baptized. For Aalof's soul, Horn would have quite forgiven him. Rodmund would never have been blamed for Horn's death, because he did not kill him, but sent him out to sea, and thus the Lord of heaven protected him. But this deed of his did him great harm, when like a traitor he wanted to send Horn to his death. Now Horn would repay him, if he could: he would not pardon him. He struck him on the helm with his steel sword and cleft him in two down to the girdle. With this blow the brave knight won his battle and rescued his true friend Haderof. Then he had his men brought before him and his peace proclaimed throughout the army. He wanted next to travel through the land, seizing everything for himself like a man meaning to rule. Were he to find Persian, Slav, or any other heathen,[105] he wanted them to go. He would remove them all, either by death or by making them renounce their creed. He would give the land to his good knights, who had come to serve under him from afar. (4823–47)

230. What more should I say? He seized the land and completely took possession of it; not a single one of the pagan folk remained. Either he put them all to death or they gave up their creed. Then he divided it fittingly amongst his knights, according to their rank, so no one grumbled, no one felt any envy. He gave power to lord Hardré above all, who well knew how to govern those in his keeping. Where the churches had been, he everywhere restored them; there where the bishopric and the abbey had been, he quite rebuilt them and increased their goods. The praise of Jesus Son of Mary was everywhere. Meanwhile, everyone heard the news that lord Horn had trampled on the hated nation and everywhere restored Christianity, which before had been quite abandoned from fear. Then something happened which it is right I should tell you: Queen Samburc the slender, mother of Horn, heard talk of him — how happy she was! When her husband was dead, she was terrified and fled to the great forest of Arden[106] near the sea, and with her took one of her maidens. She then hid herself in a cave by the sea. (4848–71)

231. When the queen heard of her husband's death, she hid herself for fear in a cave by the sea. The heathen people never found her — indeed the Creator

---

[105] 4843 **Persian, Slav or any other heathen** *persan, almican u escler*: see notes to vv. 7, 81.
[106] 4869 **the great forest of Arden** *Ardene la grant*: I have taken this to be the forest, but the word is not used, and Pope calls it "an unidentified place."

protected her well—and she lived henceforward on herbs, with great difficulty. She had a maid, Answit, with her, raised lovingly at court, who never failed
her, in spite of pain or suffering. She would go to the towns and often make the
rounds, asking bread for the sake of God our Saviour, and her lady fed on it: that
was her task. She did this until, one day, she came to a meadow with a hundred
shepherds. They had a ball and were playing *pelota*.[107] One said to his comrade:
"Strike hard, friend! From now on we have an excellent protector. Horn the brave
has come, who will respect our rights—son of King Aalof, the valiant conquer-
or—who has put to death all the heathen folk. The wicked traitors will never
return. My father told my mother it last night at home, with great joy: I was listening." (4872–92)

232. The girl heard him; she approached them to hear and make sure of the news.
When she was certain of it, she went to her lady, who, when she saw her, quickly
asked her why she came back so soon and brought nothing with her.

[Missing verse or verses between 4897 and 4898]

For her son had come, who would henceforth feed her. When the lady heard her,
she was deeply stirred. If one had a hundred tongues—which will never be—her
great joy could not be described. She kept saying: "My dear girl, how do things
stand? Is Horn my son then alive? My fair one, who told you? And God! Can this
truly ever come to pass?" She fainted four times for joy, and when she recovered,
she began again: "My son is surely dead; he will never return! Fool, if you've lied
to me, great harm will come of it." And when she heard her, she comforted her:
"Indeed Horn has come." She solemnly swore it to her. Then she came to herself
and said she would go and see if what she affirmed was true. (4893–913)

233. With the clothes she had on, poorly dressed, Queen Samburc[108] began her
journey and the girl with her, who brought her straight to where the king's court
was held that day. The lady stopped just at the door. And the king came riding
on the road from the forest; he had caught venison and men were blowing the
horn for return. And when Samburc saw him, she presented herself to the king.
Then in a clear voice she said to him these wise words: "King, blest be the day
and hour of your birth, that you are safe and sound and possess the land: if your
mother were alive now, she would be very happy. King, for the better salvation

107 4884 **They had a ball and were playing pelota** *Une pelote urent, si.n furent zoleur:*
today *pelota* is played with a ball and wicker baskets, so my translation may be a little free.
See Pope, *Horn,* 2:115, and Adam le Bossu, *Le Jeu de Robin et Marion,* ed. Ernest Langlois, CFMA (Paris: Champion, 1924), v. 161.
108 4915 **Samburc** *Suanburc:* I have regularised the name here, as in vv. 4927 and
4940.

of Aalof's soul and for Samburc's soul, which I mention now, feed me henceforth as long as I live." And the king replied: "To refuse would be too cruel!" Then he had her brought into the paved hall and well served next to a fireplace. He gave orders she should be well served and looked after, for she certainly seemed to be nobly-born, despite her poor attire.[109] Lord Hardré caught sight of her and watched her carefully. He remarked her bright eyes and face and mouth, and realised it was his lady, so much admired. Then he came to Horn and said under his breath: "Over there I see your mother, whom you brought in here: it's the noble Samburc, my honoured lady. I don't know where God has preserved her for us!" Then Horn jumped to his feet and rushed towards her, hugged and kissed her a hundred times, and as soon as possible led her to the chamber where she was splendidly prepared for the bath. Next she was arrayed in magnificent clothes and the feast was then celebrated in splendour, all out of love for her whom they had found. Answit was joyfully summoned to the court, and happiness was heightened when she was reunited in the chamber with her lady. There was great festivity all day long, until the light failed and night came. Then they all went to lie down and rest. The queen went to lie in her chamber, and the king and noble household did likewise. (4914–57)

234. In the middle of the night, when the king was asleep, he had a dream that greatly frightened him. He was by a river—but he did not know where—and in the middle of the river he saw lovely Rigmel, right up to her chin in great raging waves. Wikele, on the other side, wanted to drown her. He held an iron fork in his hand and, as she emerged, pushed her back in. Horn was in great anguish, but when he came to himself, he shouted loudly and vehemently that if Wikele did not leave her at once, he would pay for it. Wikele did not stop but struck her all the more. Horn was greatly distressed that he could not help her. Then he found a boat and climbed in, and when he got across, the other fled. In his great misery he followed him closely, and when he reached him he cut off his head. Then he raised a gallows and finally hanged him on it. Thus he saved beautiful Rigmel from danger, and for this she gave him great thanks. (4958–77)

235. The ominous dream made the king awake, so alarmed he thought it was true. He sat up in his bed and looked around him, but found neither lovely Rigmel nor Wikele. Then he knew he had had a dream while asleep. He called Haderof, sleeping at the foot of his bed, and told him the contents of the dream, and when he heard it, he wondered greatly and then replied: "Please God, all is well. But I fear lest Wikele do something to anger my lady Rigmel." "Indeed," said the king, "I can easily believe that's the way of it." Then he said he would get ready, wait until it was day, and then go straight to the ships with his men, for he had to

---

[109] 4934 **despite her poor attire** *Parmi tut ço k'el ert povrement conree*: fragment 2 preserves vv. 4934 to 5072.

see Rigmel without delay. He left his kingdom in Hardré's care: he could serve his mother until he returned, for on his return he would bring Rigmel with him. Haderof, hearing him, approved all he said, and had no more sleep till daybreak. When they saw the dawn, King Horn rose and assembled the barons in the great hall. (4978–999)

236. When day broke and the king rose, then all the barons were assembled in the hall, and the king told them his thoughts, in just the same way as I shall now tell you. "My lords," said the king, "God be praised! I have conquered my kingdom with your help. I have given my lands to those who served me: I arranged it according to their service and in my mind I deserve no blame. Now it seems to me that I've stayed long enough. I want to return—that is my will—to fetch Rigmel: there shall be no more delay. Meanwhile the good Hardré shall keep my realm and serve my mother Samburc as she pleases. My lords, for love of me, come with me. I don't know what to tell you: some people are my sworn enemies, nor do I know for sure how Hunlaf will act, for in a man's absence hearts often change. So it's good to take along one's noble knights, if they're such as I have, and so famous. If we find the land at peace everywhere, then we shall accept it and thank God; and if we find it otherwise, then it shall be avenged. Now let's go to the ships! Nothing shall prevent it. Now, my lords, it will be seen how much you love me!" "Sire," they all said, "there shall be no opposition. It shall be as you wish and command." (5000–26)

237. So King Horn made his preparations. He embarked, and they had good breezes and wind. Now God, the Lord Almighty, guide them! We shall now tell what Wikele had done, for his behaviour needs no concealment: he had acted wickedly towards his lord, spending his treasure, both silver and gold. As it cost him nothing, he spent it lavishly. Next he built a castle, very fine and strong; he made it of stone and cement in an impregnable spot. He stocked it full of abundant provisions, like flesh and wine, straw and corn. He took many knights, and men-at-arms too, into service, for he wanted, without Hunlaf's consent, to take Rigmel with the lovely body by force from him: he would marry her—that was his intent. But he had a brother, who acted loyally—his name was Wothere—and he observed Wikele was about to turn traitor. He came to him and rebuked him thus: "What are you up to? Have you now forgotten you made the serious accusation to Hunlaf, for which Horn in his goodness has pardoned you? If you offend him again—you well know the agreement—he'll not again forgive you, and he was right to say so. He who wrongs his lord deserves to be punished. If you do as you intend, you will surely die. And that will be right, I'm sure of it; I'll be a villain and traitor if I permit you it." When Wikele heard this, he nearly burst with anger: he would never be content unless he got revenge. He planned to go and murder him that night, and to do it secretly, so no one would know he was dead. (5027–59)

238. But Wothere, from his looks, realised enough of this. He went to his lodgings, as soon as night fell, and quietly equipped himself with his armour. He mounted the best horse he had and slipped out through the postern gate towards the meadows. He was not spotted by any man living and thus, by God's will, escaped the villain. He travelled all night and never finished his journey until he came to where the wise King Hunlaf spent his time. He did not stop till he was brought directly to the king and his privy counsellors. He drew him on one side, away from the others, and Rigmel with her great beauty was sent for. When she came, then he told and revealed to them the reason why he had hastened to see them. "My lord king, I'm telling you, so you must believe me! You must with all speed stock the city with provisions: my brother is about to attack you, you will either be besieged or have to give him my lady Rigmel to wife. If you won't agree, and he captures you, he's sworn firmly you'll be slain. He doesn't care what he does, he's accursed: he has broken his oath to Horn, his lord. Because I rebuked him, I have defied him. If he had caught me tonight, I would have been torn limb from limb. I've travelled all night to warn you." (5059–84)

239. But when Hunlaf heard him, he was much dismayed; nevertheless he furnished his city with provisions as well as he could. What a man does impromptu does not last long, and many of the people lived inside: if they were there for a while, they would live in want. And Wikele knew this well and made haste accordingly, came straight there, and besieged them. Because of his great wealth, he had very many knights, whom he kept with him: they had made him their lord. He chose two messengers, to send word to the king that he should give him rosy-cheeked Rigmel and surrender to him—or be starved out. And when Hunlaf heard it, he took counsel, and his counsellors said he would never get help from any man alive unless he sent word to Horn. He did not know how Horn had fared, so he made a truce up to an appointed day—it was in a fortnight, he was allowed no more. If Horn arrived meanwhile, the matter would be settled, and if he did not come in time, he would surrender the city. Thus the matter was agreed on both sides. Meanwhile, there was neither sniping nor shooting and no wounded men either within or without. Lord, who could describe the anguish suffered in the meantime by beautiful, rosy-cheeked Rigmel? No wise or learned clerk could ever call it to mind. Lord, how often she said that Horn had forgotten her! But she had no notion how he had made ready and would come on the day determined—she would not have wept so much, had she known. (5085–114)

240. When the day that had been fixed arrived, King Hunlaf pondered—and was right to—what he should undertake if lord Horn did not come and food was short for his men within. There were great numbers of people within, and the king was tender-hearted and did not wish them to be killed. For this reason he had to surrender his city: if he had other help, he could not in any way detect it. So he had the gates opened and received Wikele, and handed over to him

Rigmel, who lamented bitterly. Wikele took her gaily, for he had no fear of Horn, quite sure that he was dead; but in her heart she did not believe it. Then he led her to the abbey of St. Benedict.[110] The bishop of the place celebrated the wedding. You should know that Wikele made great boasts about conquering such men and wedding such a wife. But Rigmel lamented and cursed the day she was ever born and that she lived so long. But however she lamented, Wikele did not care. The wedding was performed despite all her grief, and he sat down to eat with a smiling face—but he did not know, truly, how he would rise. (5115–36)

241. His brother went out—he could not watch them—and on a swift horse went towards the sea, to see if he could hear any news of Horn.[111] And when he reached it, he saw the sails of the fleet and recognised them as those of the noble Horn. They were not far off but about to land. He could not stop himself and, to hasten their arrival, he began swimming, for he wanted to meet them, and rushed towards Horn to tell him the news. He did not fear death, so much did he trust in his horse. And when Horn saw him, he had the boat put out and said to his men: "This man is in great need. I'll go to find out his news and if he is hard-pressed, I'll help him." Then the sailors cast out boats all around and made for land as hard as they could row. They picked him up: he was near death. But once drawn in, he could not care a whit and told Horn of the pain and wrong his brother had done to Rigmel with the radiant face, and begged him for God's sake quickly to go and take revenge on him. He would find him seated at his meal, being served with hippocras and bright wine. And lord Horn replied, filled with anger: "I shall indeed be there, if I can, as his minstrel; I'll play him a Breton lay with my steel sword."[112] (5137–61a)

242. The city where Hunlaf was that day was not far: Horn wanted this time to go there entirely on foot. He took a hundred companions, full of valour. Some carried harps, most fiddles: lord Horn wanted them to seem like minstrels. They donned strong hauberks that shone brightly, and over them, cloaks of different colours. They girded their hardened blades on their sides, like doughty fighters.

[110] **of St. Benedict** *de saint Beneit*: St. Benedict (c. 480-c. 550), author of the Benedictine Rule, was abbot of Monte Cassino.

[111] 5139 **if he could hear . . . Horn** *Si [la] peust . . . noveler*: fragment 2 here preserves lines from vv. 5139 to 5239.

[112] 5161–61a **I shall indeed . . . steel sword** *Certes j'i serrai . . . od m'espee de asier*: these lines are taken from fragment 2. Manuscript O has: *Sertes ja serum la* (indeed we shall certainly be there); the rest of the line is missing, as is v. 5161a. On heroes disguised as minstrels, see Hall, *King Horn*, 174–75, and Hereward in the *Gesta Herwardi* where he harps at a wedding-feast from which he rescues the bride. See *De Gestis Herwardi Saxonis*, transcr. and trans. S. H. Miller and W. D. Sweeting, *Fenland Notes and Queries* 3 (1895–1897): 7–72, at 17–21.

Now they would turn Wikele's joy into grief, and the songs they made would finish in misery. Horn would take total vengeance on the evil traitor who wanted to sever the love of him and Rigmel. This should be the fate of all deceivers, for he who tricks his lord will never come to a good end: take this man as an example. They came up to the porters and asked them for pity's sake to let them go up into the great hall and enhance the entertainment with their playing. Some knew how to harp, some played the *rote*,[113] some were good singers of songs; no one about to hear them would hold back their tears. "My word!" said the porter, "even the emperor hasn't got such people. There's no nobleman alive not honoured by such as these. Enter then, my fair friends, I shan't stand in your way." (5162–83)

243. Then Horn and his men gladly entered, to make Wikele and his followers such a present that they would all consider themselves miserable, angry, and sad: there would never be worse entertainment at a wedding. They entered the palace, came to the paved hall, and saw Wikele sitting on the highest dais, next to lovely Rigmel with the bright face. Then Horn was angered — and furiously too. They quickly shed their cloaks, which had been their disguise. The instruments fell from their shoulders to the floor, they did not care where, nor take heed of them. They were left in their hauberks, drew their sharp swords, and went round the tables giving them bad service, quite different from dishes or dispensing the best wine, for no one they touched escaped unbloodied, whoever held Wikele as lord or was one of his people. But King Hunlaf's people were spared. And menacingly Horn approached Wikele; he gave him such a blow on the head that he cleft it in two. Then he had him dragged out like a stinking cur and hanged at the crossroads as a spectacle: he repaid his service as he had deserved. (5184–205)

244. When the hall was emptied of traitors, King Horn summoned all his men from the ships and, when they came, the feast began and lasted sumptuously for a fortnight. Horn told the king how he had fared, how he had valiantly regained his land, how concluded his war with the heathen, and of his joy at finding his mother. Of all he had done, nothing was hid. After the feast, each one departed to his own land: Horn gave every one of them good pay. Then he left Rigmel with her father and made his way to Westir with his kinsman Modin, king of Fenenie. He gave him Lenburc, with a great dowry, and married the other girl to his friend Haderof; she brought with her the whole country, granted them by King Gudreche, who had retired from the world. When matters were thus concluded, he returned to Brittany and glorious Rigmel, and remained there as long as he pleased. (5206–24)

---

[113] 5179 **some played the rote** *asquant sunt roteor*: the *rote* was a triangular zither, with strings on both sides of the soundbox. See Page, *Voices*, 123 (with a picture of a twelfth-century *rote*).

245. In the time he stayed there, he fathered on Rigmel the valiant Hadermod, who conquered, and then ruled, Africa and took revenge on the heathen for all his kin. In bravery and wisdom he surpassed them all, as he who knows the story can reveal. I leave this to my son Wilmot to tell, who after me will compose the poem well—he will be a good poet: he inherits that from me. Now back to Horn! Let us tell how he returned to Suddene the great. He brought his wife and led a good life with her for a very long time, ending his days there in prosperity. Now let him who knows any more of the story, say so! Thomas will say no more, but sing "have mercy"[114]:
"And thou, O Lord, have mercy upon us."[115]

---

[114] 5239 **he will sing "have mercy"** " *'Tu autem' chanterat"*: in fragment 2, after v. 5239 and instead of v. 5240, are the words *Issi finist de Horn* [here Horn ends]. *AmeN.*

[115] 5240 **And thou, O Lord, have mercy upon us** *Tu autem domine miserere nostri:* with this formula, which concluded the chanting of the lesson during the office of Matins, and was also used at the end of meal-time readings in religious houses, Thomas brings his romance to an end. The formula was sometimes sung, and might, if the romance was sung also, provide "a suitable cadential laisse." See Stevens, *Words and Music,* 247–48.

LA FOLIE TRISTAN

Miserable, dejected, sad, and downcast, Tristran dwelt in his land.[1] He meditated on what he could do, for he lacked all solace: a cure would solace him or, if there were none, better to die. Better to die once and for all than for ever to be so distraught, and better to die once and for all than for ever languish in pain. To live in anguish is death itself; anxiety defeats and destroys man. Just so did pain, grief, anxiety, and distress defeat Tristran. He saw there was no cure for him: without solace he would have to die. Death, then, was certain, since he had lost his love, his joy, since he had lost Ysolt the queen. He wished to die, he desired to die, but only so long as she knew he was dying for love of her, for if she knew it, he would at least die more easily. He suspected everyone and hid his mind from them, fearing betrayal. Above all he hid his mind from Kaherdin, his friend, for he feared that if he told him his plan, he would prevent him. For he wished and intended to go straight to England, not with a horse but entirely on foot, so as not to be recognized in that land. Because he was well-known there, he would be soon spotted. But no one notices a poor man on foot; no one at court takes heed of a poor, bare messenger. He intended to disguise himself and so change his appearance that no one would ever know he was Tristran, however hard they looked. Neither family, neighbours, fellows, nor friends would discover his identity. He kept his thoughts so quiet that he said nothing to anyone; he was wise, for disclosing secrets beforehand often brings great harm. No misfortune, I believe, will ever befall the man who thus hides, and will not reveal, his thoughts.

---

[1] **I In his land** *en sun païs*: from the subsequent reference to Kaherdin (v. 28), we know that Tristan's "land" is Brittany, home of Kaherdin and his sister, Ysolt Blanchesmains, whom Tristan marries: compare Thomas, *Les Fragments du Roman de Tristan*, ed. Bartina H. Wind (Geneva: Droz, 1960), v. 661 (Sneyd manuscript, 1). According to Gottfried von Strassburg's *Tristan* and Friar Robert's *Tristramssaga*, Brittany is also Tristan's homeland; in Eilhart von Oberg's *Tristrant und Isalde*, that is *Lohenois*, variously interpreted as Lothian, Scotland, or Loenois, a district of Brittany. See Gottfried von Strassburg, *Tristan*, trans. A. T. Hatto (Harmondsworth: Penguin, 1970); *The Saga of Tristram and Isönd*, trans. Paul Schach (Lincoln: University of Nebraska Press, 1973); Eilhart von Oberg, *Tristrant*, ed. Danielle Buschinger (Göppingen: Kummerle, 1976).

Telling and disclosing secrets is often the cause of many disasters. People suffer from their own thoughtlessness.[2] (1–56)

Tristran prudently held his counsel and thought hard. He did not long delay: in bed at night he took his decision, and early in the morning he set out on his road. He did not stop till he reached the sea. He came to the sea and found the ship ready and all that he needed. The ship was large, fine and strong, a good merchants' boat. Its cargo came from many lands, and it was bound for England. (57–70)

The sailors hauled up the sail and weighed anchor. They were eager to be on the high seas: there was a good wind for sailing. Then Tristran the brave appeared and said to them: "My lords, God save you all! Where are you going, God willing?" "To England, with luck!" they replied. Tristran said to the sailors: "I wish you a good voyage! My lords, take me with you: we both want to go to Britain." They said to him: "Agreed: come along then, embark." Tristran approached and went on board. The wind swelled the topsail and they went speedily through the waves, cutting through the deep sea. They had their will and plenty of good wind. They ran straight for England, spending two nights and a day on the voyage, and on the second day, if the record is true, they came to the port, at Tintagel. (71–94)

King Mark dwelt there, as did Queen Ysolt, and a great court was gathered there, following the custom of the king. Tintagel was a very fine, strong castle, impervious to attack or siege-engine . . .[3] It stood by the sea, in Cornwall, its tower large and strong: it was built by giants long ago. All its stones were of marble, superbly laid and joined. The wall was chequered with red and blue blocks. There was a gate to the castle, handsome, large, and strong; the entry and exit were well guarded by two valiant men. (95–114)

There dwelt King Mark, with Britons[4] and with Cornishmen, because of the castle, which he loved, and so did Queen Ysolt. Round about were many meadows, many woods for game, fresh water, fish-ponds, and fine fields. Ships sailing by on the sea would arrive at the castle's port. People from other lands, both friends and strangers, looking for the king would there come to him from over the sea, and that is why he loved it so. The spot was lovely and delightful, the

---

[2] 56 **from their own thoughtlessness** *de so ke n'unt suvent pensé*: the faulty manuscript reading, *De ke vunt suvent pelise,* is corrected by Lecoy (*Les deux poèmes de La Folie Tristan,* ed. Félix Lecoy [Paris: Champion, 1994]) and Short (*The Anglo-Norman Folie Tristan,* ed. Ian Short, ANTS Plain Texts Series 10 [London: ANTS, 1993]), among others. I have adopted Lecoy's interpretation (88).

[3] 101 **impervious to attack or siege-engine** *ne cremout asalt ne engin*: after v. 101 there is a gap in the text of a line and a half.

[4] 116 **Britons** *Bretuns*: following Hoepffner, I take *Bretuns* here as Britons; it can also mean Bretons. See *La Folie Tristan d'Oxford,* ed. Ernest Hoepffner (Paris: Les Belles Lettres, 1938), 177.

land good and fruitful, and thus once upon a time Tintagel was called the enchanted castle. It was rightly called so, because twice a year it would completely
disappear. The peasants say that twice a year, once in winter and once in summer,
truly no one can see it, neither a local man nor anyone else, however hard they
try—so say the people in the neighbourhood. Tristran's ship arrived and carefully dropped anchor in the port. (115–42)

Tristran jumped up and left ship, and sat down on the shore. He sought and
asked for news of King Mark and his whereabouts. They told him he was in town
and held a great court. "And where are Queen Ysolt and Brenguain, her lovely
handmaid?" "Indeed, they are here: it's not long since I saw them. But Queen
Ysolt, as usual, certainly looks very sad." When Tristran heard Ysolt's name, he
fetched a sigh from his heart. He decided on a trick to help him see his mistress.
(143–58)

He knew well there was no device to be found to enable him to talk to her.
Prowess, knowledge, intelligence, skill—all were of no avail, for King Mark, he
well knew, hated him above all things, and if he could catch him alive, he was
convinced he would kill him. Then he thought of his mistress and said: "What
does it matter if he kills me? I ought to die for love of her. Alas! I already die
every day. Ysolt, for you I suffer so much. Ysolt, for you I so much wish to die.
Ysolt, if you knew I was here, I'm not sure you would talk to me. I've gone mad
for your love, yet I'm here and you don't know it. I don't know how I can talk to
you, hence my anguish. (159–78)

"Now I want to try something else, to see if I succeed: I'll pretend I'm a fool,
behave as if mad. Isn't that clever and a stroke of cunning? That's shrewd: since
neither time nor place are on my side, nothing wiser can be done. Whoever holds
me silly, I'll be wiser than he, and whoever holds me a fool will have stupider
men at home." (179–88)

Tristran kept to this decision. He saw a fisherman coming towards him. He
wore a tunic of coarse wool, with open sides, and a hood. Tristran saw him and
beckoned to him and led him off with him in secret. "My friend," he said, "let's
change clothes. You shall have mine, which are good. I will have your tunic,
which pleases me greatly, for I often dress in such clothes." The fisherman saw
the clothes were good, took them, and gave him his, and when he had them he
was delighted and went off like a shot.[5] (189–204)

Tristran had some scissors, which he would carry about with him. He trea-
sured them: Ysolt had given him them. With the scissors he shaved his hair on the
top of his head:[6] he certainly looked idiotic and crazy. Then he cut a cross-shaped

---

[5] 201–4 **The fisherman . . . went off like a shot** *Li peschers . . . s'en parti chaut pas*:
compare *The Romance of Horn*, *laisse* 189, vv. 3965–80, where the hero exchanges clothes
with a delighted palmer.

[6] 209 **With the scissors he shaved his hair on the top of his head** *Od les forces haut
se tundi*: Hoepffner (*Folie Tristan*, 155) translates *haut* as "on top of the head," Ménard as

tonsure. He knew how to transform his voice completely. He stained his face with a herb he had brought from his own land: he smeared it with its juice and then it changed colour and went dark. No man alive, seeing and hearing him, would have recognized him or claimed him as Tristran. He took a stake from a hedge and held it on his shoulder. He went straight towards the castle; everyone who saw him was afraid. (205–24)

When the porter saw him, he summed him up as a mad fool. He said to him: "Come here! Where have you been so long?" (225–8)

The fool replied: "I was at the wedding of the Abbot of St. Michael's Mount,[7] my old friend. He married an abbess, a fat nun. There was not a priest, abbot, monk, or clerk in orders, of whatever kind, from Besançon to the Mount, who was not invited to the wedding, and they all brought staves and crosses. There, in the pastures below Bel Encumbre, they jump and play in the shade. I left them, because today I've got to serve the king at table." (229–42)

The porter replied: "Come in, Urgan the Hairy's son. You are large and hairy, to be sure, and thus very like him."[8] The fool entered by the wicket gate. The young men ran up to him, shouting at him as men do to a wolf: "Look at the fool! Hu! hu! hu! hu!" The young men and the squires were intent on attacking him with branches of boxwood. They accompanied him across the courtyard, following the mad boy. He turned on them many times, pelting them at will.[9] If one attacked him on the right, he turned and struck towards the left. He came to the door of the hall and entered, stake over his shoulder. (243–60)

At once the king, from his seat on the royal dais, noticed him. He said: "There's a good servant. Make him come forward." Many jumped up and went to meet him, greeting him in accordance with his looks. Then they brought the fool,

---

"totally" (P. Ménard, "Les Fous dans la société médiévale," *Romania* 98 [1977]: 433–59, at 437); both agree on the "grotesque and derisory tonsure" of two strips of hair, forming a cross, left on the shaven head. The Oxford *Folie* is the only Tristan text to give this detail.

  [7] 230 **The Abbot of St. Michael's Mount** *L'abe del Munt*: Hoepffner (*Folie Tristan*, 100) acknowledges there is a Cornish St. Michael's Mount, but thinks this is "certainly" the Norman Mont St. Michel, no doubt because of the reference to Besançon (though this is a formula with little geographical significance) and to *Bel Encumbre*, which he and Bédier located in Normandy, near Dieppe. But Hoepffner admits this might also be a name drawn from fantasy.

  [8] 244 **Urgan the Hairy's son** *fis Urgan le Velu*: Urgan appears in Gottfried's *Tristan* (250–54), the *Saga* (96–99), and *Sir Tristrem* (vv. 2304–94) as a giant defeated and killed by Tristrem (*Sir Tristrem*, ed. G. P. McNeill [Edinburgh and London: Blackwood and Sons, 1886]).

  [9] 256 **pelting them at will** *Estre kili gacte a tanlent* emended to *est vus ki li gatte a talent* (Short), *es vos ki li giete a talent* (Bédier): a corrupted line. Hoepffner (*Folie Tristan*, 102) gives as the general meaning of the passage "there he plays the fool at will."

stake over his shoulder, before the king. Mark said: "Welcome, friend. Where are you from? What do you seek here?" (261–70)

The fool said: "Indeed I'll tell you whence I am and what I seek. My mother was a whale and dwelt in the sea like a siren,[10] but I've no idea where I was born. But I well know who brought me up: a great tigress suckled me, in the rocks where she found me. She found me under a block of stone, thought I was her cub, and fed me from her breast.[11] But I have a most beautiful sister: I will give her to you, if you like, in exchange for Ysolt, whom you love so much." The king laughed and then replied: "What would the wonder of the world say to that?" "King, I'll give you my sister for Ysolt, whom I love dearly. Let's make a bargain, let's make an exchange: it's good to try out something new. You're quite tired of Ysolt: get to know someone else. Give her to me, I'll take her. I'll be of service to you, king, out of love." (271–94)

The king listened to him and laughed, and said to the fool: "God help you, tell me what you would do with the queen, or where you would put her, if I gave her into your power, to take away?" "King," said the fool, "up there in the air I have a hall where I live. It's large and splendid, made of glass, and the sun comes streaming in. It's in the air, hanging from the clouds; the wind neither rocks nor shakes it. Beside the hall is a panelled room made of crystal. At daybreak, the sun floods it with light." (295–310)

The king and the rest laughed at this. They spoke among themselves, saying: "This is a good fool; he talks well. He can speak on anything." "King," said the fool, "I adore Ysolt: my heart suffers and aches for her. I am Trantris,[12] who loved her so, and will as long as I live." (311–18)

Ysolt heard him, sighed deeply, and was angry and furious with the fool. She said: "Who let you in here? Fool, you aren't Trantris, you lie." The fool listened more carefully to Ysolt than to the others; he was well aware she was angry from the changed colour in her face. (319–26)

---

[10] 273–74 **My mother was a whale. . .siren** *Ma mere fu une baleine. . .sereine:* the whale mother appears in the *Folie Berne*, v. 156, but the siren comparison occurs only here. Wace's *Brut*, vv. 735–64, has a long description of sirens in the "Western sea" (see Hoepffner, *Folie Tristan*, 102).

[11] 273–81 **My mother was a whale. . .fed me from her breast** *Ma mere fu une baleine. . .me nurri de sa mamele:* as Schaefer points out, Tristan's flights of fancy about the whale and the tigress also evoke the extraordinary circumstances of his birth and upbringing by parental substitutes trying to save his life. See Jacqueline Schaefer, "Specularity in the Mediaeval *Folie Tristan* Poems or Madness as Metadiscourse," *Neophilologus* 77 (1993): 355–68, at 358.

[12] 317 **Trantris** *Trantris:* this permutation on Tristan's name for the purpose of concealment can be spelled variously: Tantris in *Folie Berne* (vv. 125, 181) and *Sir Tristrem* (vv. 1187–88); *Trantris* in *Saga* (46).

Then he said: "Queen Ysolt, I am Trantris, who loves you. You must remember when I was wounded—many know it well—in fighting the Morholt,
who wanted to claim tribute from you.[13] In fighting, I had the luck to kill him, I
don't deny it. I was badly wounded, for the sword was poisoned. It damaged my
hipbone and the virulent poison fomented, clinging to the bone and turning it
black; there was then such pain there that no doctor could cure it and I thought
I would die of it. I put out to sea, to die there, so badly did the suffering torment
me. The wind got up and a great storm drove my boat to Ireland. I had to land in
the country I most had reason to fear, for I had killed the Morholt, your uncle,
Queen Ysolt; hence I was afraid of the land. But I was wounded and wretched. I
tried taking pleasure in my harp, but it gave me no comfort, despite my love for it.
Very soon you heard tell of my skill at harping. At once I was summoned to court
just as I was, in my wounded state. Thanks to the queen, there I was cured of my
wound. I taught you fine lays to the harp, Breton lays from our land.[14] You must
remember, my lady Queen, how the medicine cured me. There I named myself
Trantris: am I not him? What do you think?" (327–66)

Ysolt replied: "No indeed! For he was a fine and noble man and you, who call
yourself Trantris, are coarse, ugly, and horrible. Now be off: stop shouting at me.
I don't care for your jokes or for you." The fool turned about at these words and
began playing the madman to perfection. He struck those he found in his way,
escorting them from the dais to the door. Then he shouted at them: "Madmen, be
off, out of here! Let me confer with Ysolt: I've come here to court her." The king
laughed, for he enjoyed this very much. Ysolt flushed and kept silence. (367–82)

And the king was well aware of it. He said to the fool: "Rascal, come here.
Isn't Queen Ysolt your mistress?" "Yes indeed! I won't deny it." (383–86)

---

[13] **332 who wanted to claim tribute from you** *Ki vostre treu aver volt*: the "you" can
only refer to Mark and his people, not to Ysolt, the Morholt's niece. The scribe may have
misread *nostre* as *vostre*; it was not uncommon for *n* and *v* to be confused. Gottfried, Eilhart, and the *Saga* all depict Mark's kingdom as having to pay tribute to Ireland, first in
money, then in beautiful children. The Morholt (perhaps from Irish *mór*, big) is a huge
warrior who comes to enforce the tribute and is slain by Tristan in single combat. A piece
of Tristan's sword is left embedded in the Morholt's skull, and is removed and kept by
Ysolt and her mother.

[14] **361–62 I taught you . . . from our land** *vus apris . . . de nostre païs*: Tristan's skill
at the harp is one of his most famous characteristics, depicted in art as well as literature.
In this he is like Horn, and several critics have pointed out how the stories of both resemble the sixth-century Latin tale of another harper, Apollonius of Tyre, which was
very popular in the Middle Ages and available in Anglo-Saxon prose from c. 1000. See
M. Delbouille, "Apollonius de Tyr et les débuts du roman français," in *Mélanges offerts à
Rita Lejeune*, 2 vols. (Gembloux: J. Duculot, 1969), 2:1171–204, and Page, *Voices*, 103–5.
"Our land" is Tristan's native Brittany. Bédier, Lecoy, and Short read the manuscript as
ure (vostre) païs (as against Hoepffner's *nre (nostre)*); they emended to *nostre*.

Ysolt answered: "You're a liar! Throw the fool out!" The fool laughed in reply, and spoke as he wished to Ysolt: "Don't you remember, Queen Ysolt, what the king did when he wanted to send me on a mission? He sent me to get you, whom he's now married. I went there as a merchant, seeking my fortune. I was much hated in the land because I had killed the Morholt: that's why I went as a merchant and that was very shrewd. I was to seek you for the king's use, your lord, whom I see here, who was hardly loved in that land, while I was bitterly hated. I was a splendid knight, enterprising and brave, afraid of no one, from Scotland to Rome." (387–408)

Ysolt replied: "That's a good story. You're a disgrace to knights, for you're a congenital idiot. A pity you're still alive! Get out, for God's sake!" The fool heard her and laughed. (409–14)

Then he continued, like this: "My lady Queen, you must remember the dragon I killed, when I arrived in your land. I struck its head from its body,[15] cut out its tongue, and removed it, thrusting it in my hose. And from the poison I got such a fever I was sure I would die; I lay fainting by the road. Your mother and you came and saved me from death. With skill and powerful medicine you cured me of the poison.[16] (415–28)

"Do you remember the bath I sat in? You nearly killed me there. You were about to perform that amazing feat once you had unsheathed my sword. When you drew it out and found the notch in it, then you thought, rightly, the Morholt had perished by it. You quickly thought of a clever idea: you opened your casket and found inside it the piece you had taken out of his head. You matched the piece to the sword: it fitted at once. You were very bold, at once to try and kill me in the bath with my own sword. How full of fury woman is! And at your cry, the queen came, for she had heard you. You know how I made my peace, for I kept begging for mercy; and besides, I had to defend you against the man intent on taking you.[17] You would not have him at any price, for you found him odious. Ysolt, I defended you from him. Isn't what I say true?" (429–56)

"It's not true, it's a lie; it's your own fantasies you relate. You went drunk to bed last night, and drunkenness made you dream." "True: I am drunk, from such a drink that I'll never be sober. (457–62)

---

[15] 419 **I struck its head from its body** *La teste la sevrai del cors*: in the *Saga* and in Gottfried, it is the cowardly seneschal who, anxious to claim Ysolt's hand, cuts off the dragon's head as proof he's defeated it.

[16] 428 **you cured me of the poison** *me garistes del venim*: this is the second time the two Ysolts save Tristan's life (for the first time, see vv. 327–66), and the repeated use of *guarir* (vv. 426, 428) reminds us of the same feature in the opening lines (vv. 5, 15), when Tristan is hoping for the cure and salvation of love (vv. 5, 15). The *Saga* (47) particularly emphasises the older Ysolt's healing arts.

[17] 452 **the man intent on taking you** *celui ki vus voleit prendre*: the seneschal; see note to vv. 273–81.

"Don't you remember when your father and mother gave you to me? They put you to sea, on the ship; I was to bring you here to the king. When we were on the open sea, I'll tell you what we did. The day was fine and hot, we were in our tunics[18] and thirsty from the heat. Don't you remember, king's daughter? We both drank from the same cup: you drank it, I drank it. I've been drunk on it ever after,[19] but that intoxication costs me dear." (463–76)

When Ysolt heard this, she wrapped her mantle around her and stood up, wishing to go. The king seized her and made her sit down; he seized her by her ermine cloak and sat her down again beside him. "Patience, Ysolt my love; let's hear this folly through to the end. Fool," said the king, "now I'd like to hear the ways you can be of service." (477–86)

The fool answered Mark: "I have served kings and counts." "Do you know about dogs? And horses?" "Yes," he said, "I've had some fine ones!" The fool told him: "King, when I want to hunt in woods or forest, with my greyhounds I take the cranes flying up there in the skies; with my leash-hounds I take swans and white and grey geese, one after another. When I go out with my hunting-dogs[20] I take many[21] coots and bitterns." Mark laughed heartily at the fool and so did everyone, great and small. Then he said to the fool: "My friend, my dear brother, what can you catch in the marshes?" (487–502)

The fool began to laugh and replied: "King, whatever I find, I take, for with my goshawks I take the forest wolves and the great bears. I catch the boars with my gerfalcons; neither hills or valleys protect them. I'll take roebuck and fallow deer with my little high-flying falcons, and with my sparrow-hawk, the fox, with his fine tail. With my merlin I'll take the hare, with my falcon[22] the

---

[18] 470 **In our tunics** *nus fumes ben en haut*: the line, thought by Lecoy to have no sense, is a syllable short, and Hoepffner (110–11), referring to similar lines later, suggests *nus fumes en bliaut*; his emendation is followed by Baumgartner and Short (381). See *Le Roman de Tristan par Thomas suivi de La Folie Tristan de Berne et La Folie Tristan d'Oxford*, trans. and intro. Emmanuèle Baumgartner and Ian Short (Paris: Champion, 2003).

[19] 475 **I've been drunk on it ever after** *Ivre ai esté tut tens puis*: in some Tristan texts, the effects of the love-potion wear off after three or four years (Beroul, Eilhart), whereas in others they endure for life (the *Saga*, Gottfried, *Sir Tristrem*, and Thomas [Douce fragment]).

[20] 497 **hunting-dogs** *berser hors*: amended by Hoepffner to *berseret*, in medieval English *bercelet* or *barslet*, a large mastiff, released only to retrieve game. See the *barselettes* in *The Awntyrs of Arthure*, ed. Ralph Hanna (Manchester: Manchester University Press, 1974), v. 38. The passage seems to call for a third kind of hound.

[21] 498 **many** *mainz*: Bédier and Hoepffner (112) emend to *malarz* (mallards); I prefer to follow Payen, Lecoy, and Short and keep *mainz*.

[22] 514 **falcon** *hobel*: hobby, a small, long-winged falcon, as is the merlin. See Gerald Lascelles, "Falconry," in *Coursing and Falconry*, ed. Harding Cox (London: Longmans, Green, 1892), 199–304. The fool's "hunting" is now in an upside-down world where birds

wildcat[23] and beaver. When I come back home, then I'm a good fencer with my stake: no one escapes a blow of mine, no matter how well he covers. I know how to share out the logs[24] between the squires and the grooms. I know how to tune both harp and rote,[25] and then sing to the melody. I know how to love a noble queen, and no lover under heaven is my equal. I know how to cut wood-chips with my knife, and throw them into streams.[26] Am I not a good servant? Today I've served you with my stake." Then he struck those around him with the stake. "Leave the king's presence!" he said. "All go back to your lodgings! Have you not eaten? Why do you stay?" (503–32)

The king laughed at every word, delighted with the fool. Then he summoned a squire to bring him his horse, saying he wished to go out and amuse himself, as was his custom. His knights went with him, and so did the squires, to relieve boredom. (533–40)

"By your leave, my lord," said Ysolt, "I'm ill, my head aches. I will go and rest in my chamber. I cannot listen to this din." Then the king let her go. She jumped up and left, entering her chamber in deep thought. She called herself miserable and wretched. She came to her bed and sat down; the lamentation she made was very great. (541–50)

"Alas!" she said, "why was I born? My heart is heavy and sad. Brenguain,[27] my fair sister," she said, "really, I'm almost dead. If I were dead, I'd be better off, since my life is so bitter and hard. I meet hostility wherever I look. Indeed, Brenguain, I don't know what to do, for a fool has arrived over there, his hair in a cross-shaped tonsure. He arrived in an evil hour, for he has caused me much pain. Really, this fool, this mad scoundrel, must be a soothsayer or magician,[28] for he knows my life and my situation from top to bottom, my dear friend. Indeed, Brenguain, I wonder who revealed my secrets to him, since no one except you, I, and Tristran was privy to them. But this beggar, I think, knows them all by magic. Never did any man speak more truly, for he never got a single word wrong." (551–74)

---

catch animals bigger than them. Tristan in his usual guise is an accomplished hunter: see Gottfried (78–79), Beroul (vv. 1279–89, 1752–66), and *Sir Tristrem* (vv. 445–510).

[23] 514 **the wildcat** *li cat*: emended from *li kac* by all editors.

[24] 519 **the logs** *les tisuns*: these are fire-brands, half-burned logs, or just big sticks. Bédier, Hoepffner, and Lecoy are baffled by this allusion; Baumgartner and Short (385) translate "I know how to distribute blows of a stick."

[25] 521 **rote** *rote*: the rote was a triangular zither. See *The Romance of Horn*, n. to *laisse* 242.

[26] 525 **wood-chips** *cospels*: see note to v. 794, below.

[27] 553 **Brenguain** *Brengain*: Brenguain is the waiting-woman and confidante of Ysolt.

[28] 563–64 **this fool . . . magician** *cist fol . . . enchanteres*: fools were tormented but also revered for their supposed special access to wisdom and things concealed from others: see Ménard, "Les Fous," 451, 458.

Brenguain replied: "It's Tristran himself, I'm sure I'm right." "No, Brenguain, for he's ugly and hideous and deformed, and Tristran is so shapely, a handsome man, well made, well educated. You could not find in any land a knight of greater renown. So I'll never believe it's my lover Tristran. But curses on this fool! Cursed be his life and cursed be the ship that brought him here! Pity he didn't drown in the waves, out there in the deep sea!" (575–90)

"Be quiet, my lady," Brenguain said. "Now you are offensive. Where did you learn such talents? You're well acquainted with cursing!" "Brenguain, he put me out of my wits. Never did I hear a man talk so." "By St. John, my lady, I believe he's Tristran's messenger." "Indeed, I'm not sure, I don't know him. But go to him, my dear friend, speak with him, if you can, and discover if you know him." (591–602)

Brenguain, who was courteous, jumped up and went straight to the hall, but there she found neither freeman nor serf, only the fool, sitting on a bench. Everyone else had gone to their lodgings in the city. Brenguain saw him and stopped, at a distance, and Tristran recognized her very well. Then he threw down his stake and said: "Welcome, Brenguain. Noble Brenguain, I beg you, for God's sake, to have pity on me." (603–14)

Brenguain replied: "And why do you want me to pity you?" "Oh come! I am Tristran, living in pain and grief. I am Tristran, in misery for the love of Queen Ysolt." Brenguain said: "No, it's my belief you're not." "Indeed, Brenguain, I really am. Tristran was my name when I came here and I truly am he. Brenguain, don't you remember, when we left Ireland together, how I had you in my care, you and Ysolt, who now won't recognize me? When the queen came towards me, holding you by the right hand, she gave the charge of you into my hands. You must remember, beautiful Brenguain. She charged me with Ysolt and you; she required me, she begged me, to receive you into my care and guard you as best I could. Then she gave you a flask, by no means large but small, telling you to guard it well if you desired her friendship. When we were on the open sea, the weather grew warm. I wore a tunic, I was hot and sweating, I was thirsty, and asked for drink: you know if I'm telling the truth. A lad sitting at my feet got up and took the flask. He poured into a silver goblet the drink that he found there, then placed the goblet in my hand and, needing it, I drank. I offered half to Ysolt, who was thirsty and wanted to drink. Beautiful Brenguain, would that I had never drunk that drink, or known you. Beautiful Brenguain, don't you remember?" Brenguain replied: "No, indeed." (615–60)

"Brenguain, since I first loved Ysolt, she would tell it to no other: you knew and heard of it and you allowed the affair. Nobody in the world knew of it, nobody except we three." Brenguain heard what he told her; she went off quickly towards the chamber. He jumped up and followed her, begging for mercy.

Brenguain came to Ysolt and smiled at her, according to their custom.[29] Ysolt's face changed colour and paled, and at once she feigned illness. The chamber was immediately emptied because the queen was unwell. (661–76)

And Brenguain went for Tristran and led him straight to the chamber. When he entered and saw Ysolt, he approached her, wishing to kiss her. But she retreated, much mortified; she stood, sweating, not knowing what to do. Tristran saw that she shunned him. He was crestfallen and ashamed. He stepped back a little to the wall, near the door. (677–88)

Then he gave vent to some of his desires: "Indeed, I would never have thought that of you, noble queen, nor of Brenguain, your maidservant. Alas! to have lived long enough to see you treating me with such scorn and repugnance! In whom can I trust, when Ysolt won't deign to love me, when Ysolt considers me so base that she now has no memory of me? Ah! Ysolt, ah! my dear, the loving heart is slow to forget.[30] We prize the leaping fountain, whose fine stream runs freely; but the moment it dries, and the water neither rushes nor springs, it is worth praise no longer. Nor is love, when it's disloyal." (689–708)

Ysolt answered: "My brother, I can't tell. I look at you and I'm dismayed, for I see nothing in you to say you're Tristran the Lover."[31] Tristran replied: "Queen Ysolt, I am Tristran, who loved you. Don't you remember the seneschal who put the king against us? We were both young then and shared a lodging. One night, when I went out, he got up and followed me. It had snowed and he traced my footsteps. He came to the palisade and crossed it, spied on us in your chamber, and the next day accused us. I believe he was the first to denounce us to the king.[32] (709–26)

"Again, you must remember the dwarf, whom you so used to fear. He had no love for our pleasure: he was about us day and night. He was put there to spy on us, and carried out this service in a crazy fashion. Once we were together: like any lovers in distress, who plan all kinds of cunning, ingenious, and artful tricks in order to achieve meetings, pleasure, and delight, we did the same. We were

---

[29] 672 **smiled at her according to their custom** *si li surrist cum faire solt*: this seems to be an agreed signal between Ysolt and Brenguain.

[30] 702 **the loving heart is slow to forget** *hom ki ben aime tart ublie*: proverbial. See Morawski, *Proverbes français*, no. 1835, and Grace Frank, "Proverbs in Medieval Literature," *Modern Language Notes* 58 (1943): 508–15, at 510–11.

[31] 712 **the Lover** *l'Amerus*: a sobriquet of Tristan in Thomas, vv. 927, 1014 (Douce fragment).

[32] 725–26 **he was the first to denounce** *Ço fu li premer. . .encusat*: in the *Saga* (80–81) and Gottfried (219–21), the seneschal is a friend of Tristan's, called Mariadokk/Marjodö; Meriadok in *Sir Tristrem* (vv. 1926–62) plays the same role but is not called a seneschal.

lying on our beds in your room. But that bastard dwarf sprinkled flour between our beds, thus thinking to discover whether there really was love between us. But I noticed it: feet together, I jumped into your bed. The wound in my arm spurted from the jump and bloodied your bed; I jumped back the same way and made my own bed bloody. (727–50)

"Then King Mark arrived and found your bloodstained bed; at once he came to mine and found my bloody sheets. Queen, for love of you, I was then banished from court.[33] Don't you remember, my darling, a little love-token I once sent you, a little dog I got for you? That was Petit Cru,[34] whom you dearly loved. And there is one thing, Ysolt my love, which you must remember. (751–64)

"When the Irishman came to court, the king showed him honour and affection. He was a harper, he knew how to harp; you knew him well. The king gave you to the harper: he arrogantly carried you off and was about to enter his ship. I was in the forest and heard about it. I took a rote and followed on horseback at a gallop. He won you through his harp, and I won you through my rote.[35] (765–75)

"Queen, you must remember when the king banished me and I longed to speak to you, my love. I thought of a ruse: I came to the orchard where we had often been happy. I sat under a pine in the shade and cut wood-chips with my knife, which served as signs between us when I wanted to come to you. A spring rose in that place, which ran by the chamber. I threw the chips into the water and the stream carried them along. When you saw the chips, you would know for sure that I would come that night, to delight in taking my pleasure.[36] (776–94)

---

[33] 727–56 **Again, you must remember the dwarf. . . banished from court** *del naim vus redait ben membrer. . .fu de la cort lores chascé*: the dwarf does not appear in the Thomas fragments except in the orchard scene (Cambridge Fragment, vv. 1–11). His flour-trick appears in Beroul (vv. 73–777), the *Saga* (88), Gottfried (241–42), Eilhart (92–93), and *Sir Tristrem* (vv. 2194–222), where he is not a dwarf but conflated with the earlier figure of Meriadok.

[34] 761 **Petit Cru** *le Petitcru*: this is a magical dog, appearing in Gottfried (249–54), the *Saga* (95), and *Sir Tristrem* (vv. 2419–20).

[35] 776 **through my rote** *par roter*: this is the episode known as "the harp and the rote," which appears in the *Saga* (76–80), Gottfried (214–18), and *Sir Tristrem* (vv. 1810–1914). The Irish harper, having asked and been granted an unspecified reward for his music, demands Ysolt, and Mark is bound, by his promise, to hand her over. The *Folie Berne* does not refer to this episode.

[36] 783–94 **I sat under a pine . . . my pleasure** *desus un pin . . . mun deduit*: pieces of wood, sometimes carved, often appear in the Tristan texts as messages from Tristan to Ysolt: *Saga* (86), Gottfried (231–35), *Sir Tristrem* (vv. 2038–44, where runes are carved on the wood), Eilhart (86–88), and most famously of all, in Marie de France's *lai*, *Chevrefoil* (vv. 48–82). See G. Frank, "Marie de France and the Tristram Legend," *Publications of the Modern Language Association* 63 (1948): 405–11. In Eilhart and his continuators, the stream goes *through* the women's chambers, indicating a primitive domestic arrangement

"At once the dwarf took notice: he ran to tell King Mark. That night the king entered the garden and climbed into the pine. I came later, knowing nothing, but when I had been there a while, I noticed the shadow of the king sitting in the pine above me. You approached from the other direction. Then I was indeed terrified, for you must know I feared lest your haste were too great. But thank God, He didn't permit it. You saw the shadow, as I had; you stepped back, and I begged you to reconcile me with the king, if you could, or else ask him to pay my wages and let me leave the kingdom. This saved us, and I was reconciled with King Mark.[37] (795–816)

"Beautiful Ysolt, do you remember the oath you went through for me? When you left the boat, I held you gently in my arms. I had disguised myself thoroughly, as you told me to; I kept my head well down. I well remember what you then told me — to fall, holding you. Ysolt, my love, isn't that true? You fell gently to the ground, opening your thighs and letting me fall between them, and everyone saw it. As I see it, that's how you were saved, Ysolt, at the trial from the oath that you made in the king's court."[38] The queen listened to him, carefully noting every word. She examined him and sighed deeply; she did not know what on earth to say, for he did not look like Tristran in face, appearance, or clothes. But from what he said, she understood very well he told the truth, without a word of a lie. This filled her heart with anguish and she had no idea what to do. It would be mad and deceitful to recognize him as Tristran, when she saw, thought, and believed he was not Tristran but another. And Tristran could see very well that she quite failed to know him. (817–50)

Then he said: "My lady Queen, how well you showed your nobility when you loved me without disdain. Now I can truly complain of your treachery. Now I see you distant and false; now I've convicted you of deceit.[39] But I've seen the day,

---

older than the one portrayed in Gottfried and the Saga. The *Folie Oxford* is unclear on the matter: the spring *de la chambre curreit* (v. 788), emended and interpreted by editors variously as "ran near, in front of, or underneath, the chamber."

[37] 797–816 **That night the king . . . I was reconciled with King Mark** *Li rais vint la nuit . . . e al rei Marke fu acordez*: the episode of Mark in the tree above the lovers appears in Beroul (vv. 1–234), Eilhart (87–90), the *Saga* (88), Gottfried (234–37), and *Sir Tristrem* (vv. 2103–56).

[38] 833–34 **the oath . . . king's court** *del serment . . . la curt le rai*: Ysolt undertakes to clear herself of the charge of adultery by undergoing trial, either by oath or by the ordeal of the red-hot iron. On the day, she has arranged that as she lands from a boat, the disguised Tristan should offer to help carry her to shore, and stumble in the process. She can then safely swear that nobody, except the king and this "feeble pilgrim," has ever been between her thighs. (Beroul, the "Mal Pas" ford, vv. 3882–4208; *Saga*, 92; Gottfried, 246–48; *Sir Tristrem*, vv. 2225–77).

[39] 856 **convicted you of deceit** *ore vus ai jo de feinte ateinte*: although I have translated it by various synonyms, the same word, *feinte*, and its cognate, *feintise*, is played with over three lines here.

my love, when you truly loved me. When Mark banished us and drove us from the court, we took each other by the hand and left the hall. Then we went to the forest and found a most beautiful place there, a grotto in a rock. In front, the entry was narrow; inside, it was vaulted and well shaped, as beautiful as a picture, the stone finely and richly carved. In that vault we lived as long as we stayed in the forest. There I trained Hudein,[40] my dearly-loved dog, not to bark. With my dog and with my hawk, I kept us fed every day. (851–76)

"My lady Queen, you're well aware how we were then found. The king himself found us, and the dwarf he took with him. But God was shielding you, when he found us lying apart and the sword between us. The king took the glove from his hand and put it over your face, gently and without a word, for he saw a sunbeam which had burnt and reddened it. Then the king went away and left us sleeping there; after that, he had no suspicion of anything wrong between us. His anger disappeared and at once he sent for us.[41] (877–94)

"Ysolt, you must remember: it was then I gave you Hudein, my dog. What have you done with him? Show him to me." Ysolt replied: "I have him, upon my word! I have the dog you speak of: indeed, you shall see him at once. Brenguain, go and get the dog; bring him, along with his lead." She rose and jumped to her feet; she came to Hudein, who frisked for joy. She untied him, letting him go. He bounded off. (895–906)

Tristran said to him: "Come here, Hudein! Once you were mine: now I'm taking you back." Hudein saw him, at once knew him, and greeted him, rightly, with joy. I have never heard tell of a dog making a greater fuss of his master than Hudein did, so much love did he show him. He rushed at him, head high, rubbing him with his muzzle, patting him with his paws. Never did an animal show such joy: it was pitiful to see. (907–18)

Ysolt was amazed. She was ashamed and blushed to see him giving him such a welcome as soon as he heard his voice, for he was vicious and badly bred, and would bite and harm all those who played with him and all those who handled him. No one could get to know him or handle him except the queen and Brenguain, so obnoxious had he been since losing his master, who had nurtured and trained him. (919–32)

---

[40] 873 **Hudein** *Hudein* (*Huden* at 896, 904 and 907): Hudent appears in the *Folie Berne* (v. 486), Béroul (vv. 1589–96, etc.), in Eilhart as Utant (97 ff.), and in Gottfried as Hiudan (267). In *Sir Tristrem*, Hodain licks up the rest of the love potion (v. 1675) and is thereafter bound to adore the lovers, a perhaps characteristically English addition.

[41] 877–94 **My lady queen . . . at once he sent for us** *Reïne dame . . . e sempres pur nus envoiat*: this central episode of the discovery of the lovers in the forest occurs in all versions of the story. The separation of the lovers by the sword is taken by Mark to indicate their chaste love. In all the versions derived from Thomas's poem, the king is brought by a huntsman. See G. N. Bromiley, "Narrative Development in the Early Tristan Poems," *Modern Language Review* 70 (1975): 743–51, at 746.

Tristran held Hudein and stroked him. He said to Ysolt: "He remembers me, who nurtured and trained him, better than you do, whom I loved so much. There's such great nobility in a dog, such great deceit in a woman." Ysolt heard him and changed colour; she shuddered and sweated with anguish. Tristran said to her: "My lady Queen, how loyal you once were! (933–42)

"Don't you remember how we were lying in the orchard when the king appeared, discovered us, and quickly withdrew? He planned a wicked deed: out of spite he would kill you. But thank God, He wouldn't have it, for I realized in time. I had to leave you, my love, for the king wished to disgrace us. Then you gave me your beautiful ring, richly made of pure gold, and I received it and left, commending you to the one true God."[42]

Ysolt said: "Tokens will convince me. Have you the ring? Show it to me." He drew out the ring and gave it her. Ysolt took it and looked at it; then she burst out weeping, she wrung her hands, she was distraught. "Alas for the day I was born!" she said, "I've finally lost my love, for I know well that no other man would have this ring if he were alive. Alas, I will never be comforted!" But when Tristran saw her weep, he was seized with pity, and rightly so. (957–70)

Then he said: "My lady queen, now you are beautiful and true. Now I will no longer hide, but make myself heard and known." He altered his tone and spoke in his true voice. (971–75)

Ysolt realized at once. She threw her arms around his neck and kissed his face and eyes. (976–78)

Then Tristran said to Brenguain, who was overcome with delight: "Give me some water, my beauty: I'll wash my dirty face." (979–82)

At once Brenguain brought the water and he soon cleansed his face: he washed off all the stain from the herb and its juice, along with the sweat. He resumed his own looks, and he held Ysolt in his arms. Such was the joy she had from her lover, whom she held by her side, that it knew no bounds. She would not let him leave that night, and promised him good lodging and a fine, well-made bed. Tristran desired only queen Ysolt, nothing but her. He was joyful and happy; he realised now he was well lodged. (983–98)

---

[42] 943–56 **Don't you remember . . . one true God** *Remenbre vus . . . al vair deu vus cumandai*: this episode appears in the first of the fragments of Thomas's poem (Cambridge manuscript).

THE LAI OF HAVELOC[1]

Men should gladly hear, repeat, and remember the noble deeds of antiquity, both the good acts and the brave, to imitate and record them for the improvement of honourable men. Bad breeding and vice — these should form the homily with which to admonish them, for the uncouth are much in need of it. Everyone may take heed of this as if it were directed to them.[2] (1–11)

I shall tell you, quite briefly, of the fortunes of a noble king, and of several other barons whose names I shall give you. The king was named Haveloc, and is still called Cuaran. I want to tell you about him and record his destiny, because the Bretons made a lay about it[3] and called it by his name — both Haveloc and Cuaran.[4] I shall begin with his father: his name was Gunter and he was Danish, holding that land as king. This was during Arthur's reign, who crossed the sea to Denmark, wanting to subjugate the land and to claim tribute from the king. He fought King Gunter and the Danes and defeated them all. The king himself was slain, and many others in the land: Odulf, whose heart had always been wicked, killed him. When Arthur had brought the war to an end, he bestowed the whole land, and the homage of its barons, on Odulf; then he and his Britons departed. Whether from compulsion or from fear, most people served Odulf, and there

---

[1] The Lai d'Haveloc: the two manuscripts provide titles: Bodmer (P) has *de Aveloc*; Arundel (H) has *dHaveloc le Danois*.

[2] 11 **Everyone may. . .to them** *Chescuns s'en gart cume pur sei*: the Prologue's conception of literature's function — to recollect the past, that it may provide examples of virtuous behaviour to follow, and unworthy actions to avoid — is characteristic of twelfth-century romance. The Lai's epilogue returns to the idea of poetry as commemoration.

[3] 21 **because the Bretons made a lay about it** *K'un lai en firent Bretun*: Marie de France's *Lais* are the first to tell us of the Bretons' role in recording memorable stories in verse, and to mention the fact that they may carry more than one name: see the Prologue and Epilogues to her *Le Freine*, *Bisclavret*, and *Laustic*.

[4] 23 **Haveloc and Cuaran** *E Aveloc e Cuarant*: apart from its appearance in romance, the name "Haveloc" is first recorded around 1210, in Cornwall: see P. Reaney, *A Dictionary of British Surnames*, 2nd ed. (London: Routledge & Kegan Paul, 1977), 168. Its etymology is uncertain, but the latest scholarship does not think it is derived from Norse Olaf via Anglo-Saxon Anlaf. Nevertheless, the Irish name "Cuaran," meaning "[with] the leggings," was the nickname of the tenth-century Dane Olaf Sihtricson, sometime king in both York and Dublin, who died in 981. It must have been transferred to the Haveloc story some time after this.

were some who wished him harm, aided by Sigar Estal, a good and powerful man who well knew how to wage war. He was in charge of the horn, which no one could sound if he were not, by descent and inheritance, the rightful ruler over the Danes. (12–50)

Before King Arthur arrived and fought the Danes, Gunter owned a fine, strong castle by the sea. It was well provisioned with food. In it he put his wife and his son, and entrusted a baron of the land with its protection. His name was Grim,[5] and Gunter had much faith in him: he had always loyally served him. Above all he entrusted him with his son, whom he loved dearly, so that if the war he was going to should turn out badly for him, Grim should protect his son as best he could, and flee the country so the boy should be neither found nor captured nor handed over to his enemies. The child was not very big, no more than two years old. Every time he slept, a flame issued from his mouth, such great heat was there in his body. The flame gave out such a perfume that no one ever smelt anything better.[6] Those in the land who were in the know considered it a great wonder.[7] (51–78)

When King Gunter, his barons, and his army were dead, Odulf hated and persecuted all those he knew he had loved. The queen and the good man guarding

---

[5] **59 Grim** *Grim*: in Gaimar's *Estoire* (see Introduction, 20–23), Grim is a fisherman and trader in salt, but also, mysteriously, an intimate of the Danish queen (v. 406). Though the *Lai* tries to ennoble him, he appears to be well-known to the pirates who board his ship (v. 120). Edmund Reiss, "*Havelok the Dane* and Norse Mythology," *Modern Language Quarterly* 27 (1966): 115–24, thinks the story was originally one in which the Norse god Woden played a prominent part. He was the most popular of the Scandinavian deities in pre-Christian England and "Grim" (*grima*=the masked one, one who disguises himself) was one of his by-names, appearing in place-names like Grimsdyke. In Scandinavian literature there are several works in which Odin (Woden) protects and rescues younger men, as Grim does Havelok. The hypothesis that "Grim" in the Havelok story once had far more prominence, and possibly supernatural strength, could be tentatively supported by other legends, all admittedly late. One perhaps appears in the town seal of Grimsby (thirteenth century), which seems to know both Anglo-Norman and English versions of the Havelok story and depicts Grim as a giant warrior with sword, shield and helmet (beneath his legs).

[6] 75–76 **The flame . . . anything better** *La flambe . . . meilur*: lines omitted in manuscript P.

[7] 77–78 **Those in the land who were in the know . . . great wonder** *A grant merveille . . . kil saveient*: according to S. R. T. O. d'Ardenne, "A Neglected Manuscript of British History," in *English and Medieval Studies presented to J. R. R. Tolkien* (London: Allen and Unwin, 1962), 84–93, a legend, Germanic in origin, held that the royal origin of a human being was revealed by the emission of flames from his (or her) mouth. She links this to a picture of Woden in a thirteenth-century manuscript, transmitting breath to all the Anglo-Saxon royal dynasties claiming descent from him: "Woden is god of life, specifically breath" (quoting *Voluspa* in the Poetic Edda).

her were very frightened lest their castle should be taken from them and the king's son killed. They had no power to defend themselves; they had to take other advice. Grim had his ship made ready and well stocked with food; he wished to flee the land, to protect the rightful heir from death. He would take the queen with him, for fear of the wicked king who had killed his lord, for he would soon dishonour her. When the ship was ready, he made his household enter, his stewards and his servants. He brought his wife and his children and put the queen into the boat, who was holding Haveloc under her cloak. Then he himself entered, and commended them to God in heaven. Out of the harbour they weighed anchor, for they had a good breeze. They crossed the sea but did not know where to go in order to protect their lord. Then bad fortune befell them, for pirates[8] met them, issued a terrifying challenge, and fiercely attacked them. Those in the ship put up a defence, but they had few fighters. The pirates killed them all; the ship was plundered and damaged, and the queen slain. No one, great or small, was left, except Grim, their acquaintance,[9] and his wife and little children. Haveloc too was spared. (79–122)

After they had escaped them, they rowed and sailed till they came to a harbour, and left the ship for the land. It was at Grimsby, in the north. At the time of which I tell you, no one lived there or frequented this harbour. Grim first raised a house there: Grimsby takes its name from him. When Grim first arrived, he split the ship into two halves, raised up the two ends, and they camped inside. He went fishing, as he knew how,[10] and bought and sold salt until he was well known there and recognised by the country folk. Many joined together with him, taking up their quarters at the harbour, and because of his name, which they had heard, they called the place Grimsby.[11] (123–44)

---

[8] 111 **pirates** *utlages*: *utlages* is Anglo-Saxon and the origin of the word 'outlaw', which entered Anglo-Norman.

[9] 120 **Grim, their acquaintance** *Grim ki ert lur conuissant*: the puzzling suggestion that the *barun* Grim is known to pirates is left unexplained. It is much more likely that the pirates would have come across him as a trader, so this probably indicates the *Lai*'s tendency to "courtlify" the tale. See above, note to v. 59.

[10] 137 **as he knew how** *si cum il sot*: manuscript H: *soloit*, "was accustomed to." See *Le Lai d'Haveloc*, ed. Alexander Bell (Manchester: Manchester University Press, Longmans, Green, 1925), 233.

[11] 144 **They called the place Grimsby** *Le liu appellent Grimesbi*: though the *Lai* does not actually state that Grim and his company arrive in England, it certainly refers to his arrival at Grimsby often and in a way which suggests "civic propaganda" (*Le Lai d'Haveloc*, ed. Bell, 28). The place-name is of Danish origin and possibly to do with Woden/Grim, but equally well it may be called after a prominent figure in the Danelaw. A Grim calling himself *dux* (the equivalent of Anglo-Saxon *eorl*) appears four times as a witness in charters between 930 and 949, in the company of other Danelaw magnates apparently visiting the king's court (W. Gray de Birch, *Cartularium Saxonicum*, 3 vols. [London: Whiting and Co., 1887], 1:350, 578; 3:37–38, 39; F. M. Stenton, "Personal

The worthy man nurtured his lord, and his wife cherished him dearly. Everyone held him to be their child, for they knew no differently. Grim had made him change his name so that he should not be recognised. The child grew and flourished, getting stronger in body and limbs. Before he was in the least mature, no bearded man who wanted to wrestle with him could be found whom the child could not defeat. He was very strong and courageous, daring and hot-headed. Grim, the brave man who nurtured him, took enormous pleasure in him. But one thing saddened him: that he was not raised amongst the kind of people where he might learn of something and acquire instruction and wisdom, for he believed at heart that he would still get his inheritance back. One day Grim summoned him. "My dear son," he said, "listen to me. Here we live quietly, with fishermen, with poor folk, who support themselves by fishing. You know nothing of their trade: here you can acquire nothing good or ever gain anything. Go to England,[12] my dear son, to learn wisdom and seek your fortune, and take your brothers with you. Enter the court of a mighty king, dear son, and take service with his servants. You are very strong and extremely tall and can easily carry great loads. See that everyone likes you, and give yourself over to service, when you reach the place; and may God grant you behave so as to earn something." When the good man had directed him, and dressed him in new clothes, with some anguish he sent him on his way. Haveloc took the two boys with him; all three thought they were brothers, as their father had told them. (145–92)

They kept on the right road until they came to Lincoln. At the time of which I tell you, a king called Edelsi[13] had the land in his control. He had also inherited Lincoln, all Lindsey (that part towards the north), Rutland, and Stamford. But he was Breton[14] by race. The kingdom bordering the men of Surrey was

Names in Place-Names," in *Preparatory to Anglo-Saxon England,* ed. D. M. Stenton [Oxford: Clarendon Press, 1970], 84–105, at 99). Grimsby may alternatively date from the ninth-century Danish invasions of East Anglia and Northumbria: Snorri Sturluson, in the thirteenth century, connected it with the attack on York in 866. It is not recorded until the Domesday Book. According to Gervase Holles's remarks, made between 1634 and 1642 (see *Lincolnshire Church Notes,* ed. R. E. G. Cole, Lincoln Record Society [Lincoln: W. K. Morton & Sons, 1911], 2–4), Grim built the town near to the place he found Havelok, and a blue boundary-stone in Briggow-gate (separating Grimsby parish from Wellow) was still known as "Havelok's stone"; according to Anderson Bates, *A Gossip about Old Grimsby* (Grimsby: A. Gait, 1893), 33, this stone was one of three church turrets thrown down by Grim.

[12] 175 **Go to England** *Va t'en . . . en Engleterre*: considering that Havelok is only making a journey from north to central Lindsey, this direction sounds as if the *Lai*'s author was here rather vague as to topography.

[13] 196 **Edelsi**: manuscript H: *Alsi* here and throughout.

[14] 202 **Breton by race** *Brez par linage*: compare Gaimar's *Estoire*: *Li altre reis esteit Bretun* (v. 59). Gaimar uses "Bretun" to mean both "Briton" and "Breton," according to context, but whereas he appears to think of Edelsi as British, the author of the *Lai,* having

then governed by another king, called Achebrit,[15] a most splendid lord. He had married the sister of Edelsi—they were companions and friends—Orwein, a noble lady; but they had no children except for one beautiful daughter. The girl was called Argentille. King Achebrit fell ill and great suffering afflicted him; he knew he could not recover. He had Edelsi brought to him, and entrusted him with his niece and all the kingdom. Straight away he made him, in the presence of his household, swear and pledge that he would loyally raise her, and keep her land for her, until she was of an age to be married. When she was grown, Edelsi should, with the advice of his vassals, give her to the strongest man that he could find in the land. Then Achebrit surrendered to him his strongholds, his castles, and his cities, and the custody of his niece and sister, and all the men of the domain. But the queen sickened after King Achebrit's death, and in her turn promptly died and was buried beside her lord. (193–236)

Now I should leave them there and return to Haveloc. King Edelsi, who now reigned and controlled the two kingdoms, held a fine court with many people, and often stayed at Lincoln. Haveloc arrived at his court. One of the king's cooks took him into service, because he saw how tall and strong he was, and how handsome. He could carry great loads, hew logs, and carry water. He took charge of the plates after the meals—that was his job—and when he could obtain a piece of meat or a whole loaf, he most willingly gave it to the boys and the squires. He was so honourable and kind that he wanted to please everyone. His generosity made them privately consider him an idiot, and they made fun of him, all calling him Cuaran, because that is what the Bretons in their language call a scullion. Because of his strength, the knights and servants would often bring him forward. Since they knew of his great power, they would make him wrestle, in front of them, with the strongest men they knew. And he would lay them all low and, if any of them abused him, by pure strength he would bind and subjugate him until he had renounced it and they were reconciled. The king himself very often made Cuaran wrestle before his retinue, and marvelled at his strength. Ten of the strongest in his household could not resist him; twelve men could not lift the load which he alone could carry. (237–82)

He was a good long time at the court, until there was a gathering of barons there, who had held their lands from Achebrit and now held them from

---

created a fictitious "Breton lay," seems to conceive of Edelsi and his court as Breton too. It is interesting that there was a colony of Bretons in Lincolnshire, brought by Earl Alan of Richmond after the Conquest, whose names still survive in late twelfth-century records: see F. M. Stenton, *The First Century of English Feudalism, 1066–1166* (Oxford: Clarendon Press, 1931), 24–26. The name Edelsi/Alsi does not seem to be Breton or British, however.

[15] 205 **Achebrit** *Achebrit*: emended by Bell from manuscript P's *Esehebrit*; at vv. 213 and 234, *Echebrit*; at v. 286, *Ethebrut*; at v. 323 *Ethebrit*; manuscript H: *Ekenbright* here and throughout.

Argentille, the girl who was his daughter. She was now tall and well-grown and could certainly bear children. They spoke to the king and asked him to marry his niece to such a man as would advise and protect them, and to faithfully discharge his duty by keeping to his oath. The king heard what they said and the request they made. He asked them for a delay and said he would take counsel in order to ask and discover to whom he should give her. He fixed a time and named a day with them, commanding them to return when he would have taken advice. Edelsi was very cunning; he talked to his intimates and revealed his mind to them, asking them for advice about those now demanding that he give a husband to his niece to govern them and the realm. But he would rather endure hostility than be dispossessed of the land. His councillors said to him: "Have her sent far away, over the sea to Brittany, and entrust her to your family: she can be a nun in an abbey and serve God all her life." "My lords," he said, "I've planned to get rid of her another way. When King Achebrit died and entrusted his daughter to me, in front of his household he made me swear an oath and pledge that I would give her to the strongest man I could find in the land. I can faithfully carry out my duty: I will give her to Cuaran, the boy in my kitchen. She shall be queen of the cooking-pots. When the barons return and make their demand of me, in the hearing of them all I'll show them that I shall give her to my scullion,[16] who's very strong and powerful: those who have seen him know it. If there is anyone who opposes it, or charges me with wickedness because of it, I shall put him in my prisons and give her to the scullion." (283–342)

Thus the king arranged it. On the day he had named to them, with his close friends he got seven score armed men ready in his rooms, for he anticipated conflict when it came to her marriage. The barons came to court and the king showed them his conclusions. "My lords," he said, "now that you're gathered here, listen to me. The other day, when you came to see me, you requested me to give my niece a husband and entrust him with her land. You well know, and I'll remind you, that when King Achebrit died, he put his daughter in my care and made me swear, on oath, to give her to the strongest man I could find in the realm. I've sought long and hard until I found such a man. I have a boy in my kitchen to whom I shall give the girl: he's called Cuaran. The ten strongest in my household cannot resist him, nor endure his wrestling or his games. The truth is that from here to Rome, there's no man so strong in body as him. If I wish to keep my oath, I can give her to no other." When the barons heard what he wanted, they said openly amongst themselves they would never allow it. Blows were about to be exchanged, when he summoned his armed men. He had his niece brought before them and married her to Cuaran. (343–82)

To disgrace and dishonour her, Edelsi made her sleep with him that night. When they were both brought to bed, she felt greatly ashamed of him, and he

---

[16] 331–36 **the boy ... give her to my scullion** *celui ki est ... K'a muu quistrun la voil doner*: these lines are missing in manuscript P and are taken from manuscript H.

much more so for her. He lay down and went to sleep; he did not want her to see the flame that issued from him. But later they trusted each other so much, from words and looks, that he loved her and lay with her, as he should have done with his wife. The night that he first spoke with her, she gave him so much joy and he felt so much love for her that he fell asleep and forgot, lying face up and taking no heed. And the girl went to sleep, throwing her arm over her lover. In a dream, it seemed to her she had gone, with her husband, overseas and into a wood. There they found a wild bear; there were foxes accompanying him, quite covering the countryside. These were about to attack Cuaran, when, from the other direction, they saw pigs and boar coming, who defended him and protected him from the foxes. When the foxes were defeated, one of the boars went at full strength towards the bear and attacked it, laying it low and killing it. The foxes which had followed it came in a body towards Cuaran and lay prone before him, as if asking for mercy, and Cuaran had them bound. Then he wanted to return to the sea, but the trees in the forest bowed down to him on all sides. The sea rose and the tide advanced towards him: he was full of fear. He saw two ferocious lions coming towards him in terror, devouring the beasts of the forest which they found in their way. Cuaran was terrified, as much for his beloved as for himself. They both climbed a tall tree for fear of the lions. But the lions advanced and knelt beneath the tree, showing him affection and considering him as their lord. There was such a hue and cry throughout the forest that Argentille awoke. She was very frightened of the dream, and then still more so of her lord, because of the flame she saw issuing from his mouth. She sat up and cried out so loudly that she woke him. "My lord," she said, "you're burning! Alas, you're all on fire!" He embraced her and drew her closer. "My dear," he said, "why are you so frightened ? Who has terrified you so?" "My lord," she said, "I had a dream: I shall tell you what I saw." She told and informed him, mentioning the fire she had seen, that issued from his mouth. She thought his whole body was ablaze and for that reason had cried out. (383–457)

Cuaran comforted her. "My lady," he said, "fear nothing. The dream you saw is certainly to the advantage of both of us; tomorrow it may be revealed. The king is to hold a feast and is sending for all his barons. There will be plenty of venison, and I shall give many big joints to the squires and the boys who've been good to me. The squires and the basest grooms are the foxes; and the bear was killed yesterday, and put in our kitchen. Today the king had two bulls baited: I account those the lions. We can put the cauldrons forward as the sea; their fire makes the water rise. I've expounded your dream; have no more doubts. As for the fire ejected from my mouth—I'll certainly tell you what that means. I believe our kitchen will catch fire, and I shall be frightened and in pain carrying out our pots and pans and cauldrons. But still, I won't tell a lie: fire always comes from my mouth when I sleep, I don't know why. That's what happens and it troubles me." (458–88)

Then they left the dream alone, and the young people went to sleep. But next morning, when Argentille rose, she told and narrated her dream to a steward of hers, whom the king her father had raised. He interpreted it favourably for her, and then told her that in Lindsey there was a man leading a holy life, a hermit living in the woods. If she spoke to him he would tell her what the dream might be about, for God loved him and he was a priest. "My friend," she said, "I put my trust in you: for the love of God, come with me. If you will go with me, I want to talk to that hermit." He readily agreed to go with her secretly. He cloaked her in a mantle, took her to the hermitage, and made her talk to the holy man and recount her experience: the dream which had frightened her, and the flame she had seen coming from her husband's mouth but did not know what it could be. She asked and entreated him, out of charity, to advise her and tell her his opinion and his will. The hermit sighed, began a prayer to God, and then expounded the dream to her. "Lovely lady," he said, "all that you dreamt about your husband you will see happen. He was born into a royal family and will soon have a great patrimony; men of rank will bow down to him; he will be king, and you queen. Ask him about his father and if he has brothers or sisters, and if he will take you to their country; there you will hear of his life, who he is and where he comes from, and may God in heaven give you the courage and let you hear such things as may change your future for good." Argentille took her leave and the holy man commended her to God. She went back to her husband and in private lovingly asked him where he was born and where his kin were. "My lady," he said, "at Grimsby; I left them there when I came here. Grim the fisherman is my father; Seburc, I believe, is my mother's name." "My dear," she said, "let us go and find them and quit the king's land of which he has wrongly deprived me; he mortally hates both you and me. I would rather be a beggar elsewhere than despised amongst.my people." Cuaran answered her: "My lady, we shall soon get there. I will willingly take you with me. Let us go and take leave of the king." (489–556)

That is indeed what they did in the morning, and then they set out, taking Grim's two sons with them, and went straight to Grimsby. But the good man had died, and the lady who had raised them. They found Kelloc, her daughter, there; she had married a trader. They greeted the husband and spoke to their sister. They asked her about their father and how their mother fared. They told them they were dead, and the children mourned for them. Kelloc called Cuaran and asked him, smiling: "My dear, on your honour, who is this woman with you? She is very beautiful. Is she maiden or wife?" "My lady," he said, "some time ago, King Edelsi, whom I have long served, gave her me to wife. She is his niece, his sister's child, a king's daughter of high birth, but he owns all her land." Kelloc heard what he told her, and great pity seized her for him, a king's son, and for his wife. She called her husband forward, and on his advice asked Cuaran if he knew his kin and whose son he was. He answered her: "Grim was my father, you are my sister, these are my brothers, who came here with me. I know well that you are our sister." Kelloc told him: "It is not so. Hide it well if I tell you. Now have your wife come forward, and I will make you and her rejoice. I will tell you whose son you are: I will relate the truth. Your father was King Gunter, lord of the Danes. Odulf treacherously killed him, when the British attacked him. King Arthur made an ally of Odulf and gave him Denmark. Grim, our father, escaped, leaving the country to save you. Your mother died at sea, because our ship was attacked by pirates, who met us and killed most of our people. We escaped death and arrived at this harbour, but we altered your real name and called you Cuaran.[17] Your name is Haveloc, my dear. If you want to go to your land, my husband will take you there and give you food and clothing. The other day, not a month ago, he heard for certain that the Danes would like you to rule them, for the king is much hated. There is a powerful man in the land, who has always been opposed to the king. He is called Sigar Estal,[18] and we advise you to go to him. He has a relative of yours, often very distressed that she can hear no news of you. If you can reach them, you will get your inheritance yet. Take your two boys with you." (557–634)

When Argentille heard this, she was overjoyed, and promised them love and loyalty; if God raised her to any honours, she would richly reward them, she said. Then there was no more delay. They prepared their ship and their journey, and crossed the sea to Denmark. When they arrived in the country and disembarked, the trader, who brought them, attired them in new clothes. Then he taught them what to do and to which town to go, and about the court of the seneschal men called Sigar Estal. "Haveloc, my dear friend," he said, "when you come to his lands, take your lodgings in his castle and go and eat at his table, asking food for charity's sake. Take your wife with you: when they see her beauty, they will very soon ask you who you are and from what land, and who has given you such a wife." They parted from the trader and went on their way. They travelled and wandered for so long that they reached the city where the seneschal dwelt. They went directly to the castle and found the lord in his court; for charity's sake they asked him if he would grant them food and lodging that night. The seneschal

---

[17] 615–16 **we altered your real name and called you Cuaran** *vostre dreit nun changames / E Cuaran vus apellames*: in manuscript H, these two lines are omitted and replaced by ten lines: *Ne vout mon piere avant aler / Ici li estoet demorer / Sus cest havene se herberga / Sile vendit e achata / Mult se pena de toi nurrir / Et de celer et de coverer / Poverement estoit vestuz / Qe ne fussez aparceu / Nout si hardi en sa maison / Qui osast dire ton droit non* (My father did not want to travel any further; here he had to stay. He lodged below this harbour and bought and sold. He took great care to bring you up, and to conceal and hide; he was poorly clothed). On these lines, see *Lai*, ed. Bell, 97.

[18] 627 **Sigar Estal** *Sigar Estal*: manuscript H: *Sigar lestal* here and at v. 650. According to Bell (*Lai*, 265), the second part of Sigar's name "is the title given in the eleventh century to a royal officer corresponding to the later marshal" and derives from Old English *steallere*.

gave it them. He sent them into the hall until it was time for dinner and every-one went to wash. The lord sat down to his food and had the three boys seated, with Argentille placed next to her lord. They were served with great respect. (635–78)

The squires and young men, who served at this meal, kept looking at the girl and praised her beauty highly. Six of them went apart and together decided they would take the boy's mistress away. If he got angry, they would beat him up. When they had risen from the meal, Haveloc and Argentille went off to their lodging. The seneschal had them taken to a house to rest. Those who desired the lady—who was very beautiful and accomplished—followed them down a street. They seized the boy's mistress. They would have led her off with them, but Have-loc found a strong sharp axe—I don't know by what sort of luck one of them held and carried it—seized it and took revenge. He killed and despatched five, and cut the right hand off the surviving one. A hue and cry arose in the city. They turned and fled, and came running to a church. To protect themselves, they en-tered, closing and locking the door behind them. Haveloc climbed up the tower; the townsfolk besieged him round about. They attacked him on all sides and he defended himself very well by taking the stone from the top of the wall and throwing it down with vigour. (679–714)

The news reached the castle and the seneschal—and did not please him—that the man he had harboured, who had eaten at his table and been in his company, had killed five of his men and maimed the sixth. Now he had escaped to the church tower where the citizens had besieged him. They had attacked him strongly and he was defending himself fiercely, hurling the stone blocks down on to them from the tower. He had injured many and killed more. The nobleman asked for a horse and commanded all his knights to accompany him to the fight-ing that had arisen in the town. First of all they went to the church, and saw him doing so well that he made them all beat a retreat; everyone was afraid of being hit. The seneschal went forward and saw Haveloc, tall and well-formed, hand-some of body and splendid in height, long-armed and wide-hipped. He looked at him closely; he reminded him of his lord, King Gunter, whom he had loved so much. He gave a bitter sigh, for this man resembled him in face, height, and build. He had the attack stopped and forbade anyone to proceed. He called up to the young man: "My friend, stop throwing. I assure you, you can speak to me and tell me the reason you've killed my men in this way. Which of you was in the wrong?" "My lord," he said, "I will answer you, and tell you no lies. When we left our meal with you just now, and went to our lodging, coming out of your house we were pursued by knaves. They wanted to seize my wife and rape her before my eyes. I seized one of their axes and defended her and myself. The truth is, I did kill them, but did so in self-defence." (715–66)

When the seneschal heard of this crime, he answered: "My friend, come down, and have no fear of any kind. Tell me where you were born; take care not to hide it from me." "My lord," he said, "in this land, according to one of my

friends, a rich man called Grim, who raised me in his house. After the kingdom was conquered and my father killed, Grim fled with me and my mother,
on account of my father's death, carrying much gold and silver. For a long time
we voyaged over the sea, and were attacked by pirates. They killed my mother, I
survived, and the good man, who raised and loved me so much, escaped. When
our ship arrived in a deserted region, the good man built a house there. Straight
away he took up lodging there and found us plenty to eat, through selling salt and
fishing. Then so many people came to live there that a town and a market grew
up. Because men called him Grim, the town's name is Grimsby. When I grew up
I left him and worked for the cooks in the kitchen of King Edelsi's household.
Edelsi gave me this girl, his relative; I don't know why he brought us together.
I took her away from that land, and now we are come to look for my friends. I
don't know where to find some, for I couldn't name a single one." The seneschal
replied: "My dear good friend, tell me your name." "Haveloc is my name, my
lord, and I was called Cuaran when I was in the king's court and served in the
kitchen." The nobleman reflected, and at the back of his mind remembered that
that was the name of the king's son, whom Grim had taken with him. He was
on the point of acknowledging him, but yet he was in doubt. By pledges, he reassured him and took him, his wife, and his two companions into the castle with
him—he called them his "prisoners." That day he had them very well served, and
that night they slept in his chamber. (767–824)

When the children were in bed, he sent one of his personal servants to discover if, when Haveloc slept, the flame issued from him. The nurse, who had
tended him, had often acknowledged that it happened to him in his sleep, but
that the fire did him no harm.[19] Haveloc was extremely weary and fell asleep
at once. The moment he slept, fire came out of his mouth. The servant was very
frightened and went to tell his lord, who thanked God they had found the rightful heir again. He asked for his scribes, in order to write and seal letters. He
charged his messengers with them, and sent them to his friends, his vassals, and
his relations. (825–45)

The next day, many people gathered, all those living in the land who hated
King Odulf. In the morning, baths were heated and Haveloc was washed and
bathed, and he, and his wife with him, were dressed in costly robes. They were
brought into the hall. Haveloc, seeing the multitude of people, was very frightened. You must know that the boy was afraid whether, on account of the men he
had killed, it was the custom of the country for men to use him thus, to bathe,
wash, and dress him, and then consider his misdeed and bring him forward for
trial. It was no wonder he was afraid. He grabbed a big axe—it hung from a hook
in the palace—and held it in both hands. He intended to defend himself fiercely

---

[19]   829–32 **The nurse . . . no harm** *La norrice . . . ne li nuseit*: manuscript H substitutes
Car ceo avenoit au fiz ke roi / Que Grim od mene od soi (because this happened to the king's
son whom Grim and taken with him). See *Lai*, ed. Bell, 239–40.

should they condemn him to be hanged. The seneschal looked at him, drew him close, and embraced him. "My lord," he said, "have no fear; return the axe to me. Don't be afraid, I tell you, I pledge you my word on it." Haveloc gave him back the axe and he hung it up again on the hook. He made him sit on one side, with his wife next to him. He called his servant and asked him for the king's horn[20] to be brought from his treasury, the horn no one could sound.[21] He said they could all try it, to discover whether they could sound it: to him who could he would give his gold ring. In the hall there was no knight, servant, page, or squire who did not put it to his mouth, but none of them ever made it sound. The seneschal took the horn and put it into Haveloc's hands. "My friend," he said, "now try if you can make it sound." He replied: "My lord, I don't know how. I've never touched a horn before. I don't want to be made a fool of, but, since you order me, I shall put the horn to my mouth and, if I can, I'll sound it." Haveloc stood up and got ready to blow the horn. He blessed it and made the sign of the cross over it, and blew it loudly and clearly.[22] He blew it so violently that it could be heard a long way off.[23] Those in the house considered it astonishing. The seneschal called them and showed him to them all together. "My lords, this is why I summoned you, because we have had a visitation from God. Behold here our rightful heir: you should rejoice." Straightaway he bared his head and knelt before him, becoming his man and swearing to serve him loyally. The others followed his example, each most readily. When they had acknowledged him, they all became his men. (846–922)

The news spread, it could not be hidden long. Those who heard it poured in from all sides, both rich and poor, made him their leader and dubbed him knight. The seneschal, a valiant man and a good vassal, gave him so much aid that he gathered a mighty host. He ordered King Odulf, in a letter, to hand his land over to him and speedily depart. When King Odulf heard this, he mocked and made great fun of it. He said he would fight him: he assembled men from all sides, and the young man also acquired many. On the day appointed between them, when the armies were gathered and prepared for battle,[24] Haveloc saw the common

---

[20] 879–80 **He called . . . king's horn** *Sun chamberlenc . . . ad demandé*: omitted in manuscript H.

[21] 881–82 **to be brought . . . no one could sound** *De sun tresor . . . ne poet soner*: omitted in manuscript P. After v. 882 manuscript H adds: *Si dreit heir nest de lignage / Sur les Danois par heritage* (if he wasn't the rightful heir by descent, by inheritance over the Danes).

[22] 903–4 **He blessed . . . loudly and clearly** *Le cor benesquit . . . ben le sona*: omitted in manuscript P.

[23] 905–6 **He blew it . . . long way off** *Le cor sona . . . de loinz oïr*: omitted in manuscript H.

[24] 941–42 **when the armies were gathered and prepared for battle** *Quant li ost furent assemble / E de bataille conreië*: manuscript H omits and substitutes: *Que li dui ost sas-*

people, who had come to his aid, and he did not want them slain. He sent word to King Odulf, through his friends, that he would fight him man to man, and if he won, all the people would obey him and support him as their lord. Haveloc did not see why they should die when they were not at fault. The king did not deign to refuse; he had all his men disarmed, as did Haveloc in the other army. He dearly longed for their encounter and to capture or destroy him. The warriors met and attacked each other like lions. Haveloc had great strength: with an axe he had brought, he struck King Odulf so as to lay him low—he rose no more. Haveloc slew him there before his men, who all cried loudly to him: "My lord, mercy, don't let us die, for we shall willingly serve you." They were all entrusted to him and he forgave them all. After that, he received his father's kingdom. The Danes made him their king, and all his neighbours submitted to him;[25] he established firm peace in the land and brought the wicked to justice. He loved and dearly cherished his wife, for she well deserved it. Once she had been quite without hope, but now God had brought her comfort. (923–80)

Once Haveloc was in power as king, he reigned for over three years and amassed great treasure. Argentille advised him to cross the sea to England, to regain her inheritance from which her uncle had banished and wickedly disinherited her. The king said he would do it, since she advised him so. He prepared his navy and summoned his people and his army. When he had arranged his voyage, there was no more delay;[26] once there was a breeze, he put to sea and took the queen with him. Haveloc had four hundred and eighty ships full of men, carrying weapons and food: wine and wheat, meat and fish.[27] They rowed and sailed until they came to Charlfleet.[28] They took up quarters on the seashore and foraged the land for food. Then, counselled by his Danes, the noble king sent a message to Edelsi to surrender to him the land Achebrit had held, which had been pledged to his niece and from which he had disinherited her. Haveloc informed him that if he would not restore it to her, *he* would capture it. The messengers came to the king and found him very hard and proud. They gave him their message and he mocked and derided it. With great arrogance he answered them: "I've heard amazing news," he said, "about Cuaran, one of my scullions, whom I

---

sembleroient / Et ensemble se combateroient (when the two armies would meet and fight together).

    [25] 973–74 **The Danes . . . submitted to him** *Li Daneis en firent lur rei / Tuz ses veisins suzmist a sei*: omitted in manuscript H.

    [26] 993–94 **When he had . . . no more delay** *Quant sun eire ot apareillé / N'id ad pus gueres atargé*: omitted in manuscript H.

    [27] 999–1000 **carrying weapons . . . and fish** *Armes portent . . . e peissun*: omitted in manuscript H.

    [28] 1002 **Charlfleet** *Carreflod* (P), *Carleflure* (H), emended to *Carleflod*: according to Bell, this is "a lost seaport on the Lincolnshire coast," near Saltfleet, southeast of Grimsby, which disappeared in the middle of the thirteenth century (*Lai*, 27).

raised in my household—that he's come to ask me for land. I will make my cooks joust with him, with trivets and cauldrons, with pots and pans." The messengers went away and told their lord of the answer the king made them, and of the date he fixed for the two armies to meet and fight together.[29] (981–1031)

Before the appointed day, Edelsi summoned his friends and all those he could get; not one was left behind. The armies met at Tetford[30] and prepared to attack. King Edelsi first of all donned his armour, mounted a grey horse, and went to inspect his enemies, to see how many men they had. When he saw the Danes, with their banners and shields, he forgot the cauldrons, the pots and the pans with which he had threatened them, but withdrew to teach his men what to do and how to fight. The fierce battle between them lasted till nightfall. Many Danes were slain there, and others were grievously wounded. They had reached the limits of endurance, when black night made them separate. Haveloc was very angry on account of the men he had lost. He would have retreated with his Danes to his ships, had the queen let him. Because of a trick she taught him, by which he could defeat his enemy, the king stayed put and trusted her. All night he had great stakes cut and well sharpened at each end. They fixed the dead men on them and set them down amongst the living, ranging them in two contingents, axes raised ready at the shoulder. In the morning, at daybreak, King Edelsi and all his knights prepared to commence battle. But when they saw those in the opposite camp, their flesh crept. Terrifying was the company of the dead they saw in the plain: they saw seven men opposite for every one of theirs.[31] His councillors told the king there was no point in fighting: the Danes' men had increased whereas he had lost many of his. He should restore her rights to the lady and make peace, before matters got any worse. (1032–84)

The king had no other course but to accept their argument. By his privy councillors' advice he was reconciled with the Danish king, made him firm pledges, and handed over reliable hostages. He restored to him all the land which Achebrit had held in his lifetime. From Holland to Colchester[32] the Danes were lords and masters. But Haveloc, when he came to the city, held a feast there; he received the barons' homage and reconfirmed their hereditary rights. After this, King Edelsi lived no longer than a fortnight. He had no heirs so rightful as Haveloc and his wife. The barons accepted them and surrendered cities and

---

[29] 1029–30 **for the two armies ... together** *Quant li dui ost ... se cumbatreient*: manuscript H omits these lines here, having already used them at 941–42.

[30] 1035 **Tetford** *Tofort* (P), *Theford* (H): I follow Bell (242) in translating this as Tetford (Lincs) rather than Thetford (Norfolk).

[31] 1060–78 **Because of a trick ... one of theirs** *Par un engine ... set en veeient*: on other instances of this trick of using dead men to deceive the enemy, notably in Saxo's tale of Amleth (Hamlet), see Heyman, *Studies*, 95–97.

[32] 1093 **Holland** *Hoilant*: southeast Lincolnshire; manuscript H: *Holande*; *Gloucestre*.

castles: Haveloc had Lincoln and all Lindsey in his control. He was king and reigned for twenty years, making many conquests with his Danes, and he was talked of far and wide. In commemoration, men long ago made a lay of his victory, that it might be remembered for ever. (1085–1112)

So ends Haveloc.[33]

---

[33] **So ends Haveloc** *Si finist Aveloc*: after v. 1112, H adds*: Ceo fut le lai de Cuaran / Qui mult fut prouz et vaillant. Explicit Haveloc.*

Amis and Amilun

Here begins the story, worthy of memory, of lords Amis and Amilun, who were such true friends and hated all treachery.[1]

Whoever wishes to hear a song of love, loyalty, and great kindness should listen quietly: I will not talk of trivia. I shall tell you, just as I found it set down in writing, about two young men, who were at a count's court and served him as knights. They were most valiant, noble, and well-born, the sons of two barons. And I shall tell you their names: the one was called Amis, the other Amilun. Nature had taken great pains over them:[2] they were as beautiful as angels. They loved each other so dearly that they swore to be brothers.[3] They showed no friendship to anyone else at all. The courtiers were jealous of their situation and the firm friendship between them, and it very often made them angry.[4] The two were so alike in face and body that, were they to dress in the same clothes, no one in the world seeing them would be able to tell them apart. They also had the

---

[1] **Here begins ... all treachery** *Ci commence lestorie / Ke devum aver en memorie / De syres Amis e Amilun / Ke furet si tro bon cumpaynun / E unke ne amerunt treysun*: these five lines, preceding the romance in the Corpus manuscript but missing in the other two, are not included in the text's numbering in Kölbing's edition except as I–V (*Amis and Amiloun*, ed. E. Kölbing [Heilbronn: Henninger, 1884]).

[2] 15 **Nature had taken great pains over them** *Bien en out en eus nature ovre*: on the common twelfth-century motif of Nature taking pains to create a special human being, see E. Curtius, *European Literature and the Latin Middle Ages*, trans. Willard R. Trask (London: Routledge and Kegan Paul, 1953), 545, and C. Luttrell, *The Creation of the First Arthurian Romance* (Evanston: Northwestern University Press, 1974), 2 ff. Manuscript L omits the motif and substitutes *Li deus estoient de vne nature* (the two were of one nature)— an astonishing borrowing from Christological discourse (and cf. below).

[3] Sworn brotherhood (the Byzantine *adelphopoiia* [see *Oxford Dictionary of Byzantium*, 1:19–20]) has been a subject of great discussion in recent scholarship. See S. Delany, "A, A and B: Coding Same-Sex Union in *Amis and Amiloun*," in *Pulp Fictions of Medieval England*, ed. N. McDonald (Manchester: Manchester University Press, 2004), 63–81; M. J. Ailes, "The Medieval Male Couple and the Language of Homosociality," in *Masculinity in Medieval Europe*, ed. D. M. Hadley (London: Longman, 1999), 214–37; and the papers in *Ritual Brotherhood in Medieval Europe*, spec. no. of *Traditio* 52 (1997).

[4] 17–24 **They loved . . . angry** *Tant s'entreamerent . . . s'en coroucent bien sovent*: the Karlsruhe manuscript substitutes twelve lines here, insisting on the men's beauty and referring to the *estorie/escrit*.

same height, shape, and nature. They were loyal to their lord, whom they treated
honourably and with good will, and he loved them most tenderly, honouring
them as they desired.[5] He knighted them in a blaze of glory, providing for them
the proper arms and equipment and holding a splendid feast for them.[6] He made
Amis his cupbearer,[7] for he could trust him completely. He did not neglect Amilun, but made him administer justice among his soldiers as governor and marshal
of them all, for he was brave and strong. In these offices they served a long while
and in every way performed them well.[8] (1–46)

Amilun stayed there a long time, so that his father departed this life. There was
no other heir but him to the land. When Amilun knew for certain his father had
died, he took leave of his lord, for he had to guard his lands, so that no one acted
treasonably or caused strife there and no other man invaded them or took away his
rights. The count was vexed at this and gave him leave, but reluctantly, and said to
him, as a good lord should, that he would not deprive him of his domain, and if he
should need him, whether in peace or war, he should send for him at once, and he
would come with many men— this he swore. And Amilun thanked him. Then he
left the count and went to talk to his friend Amis, his companion in good faith and
without deceit. They could not restrain their tears because they were so distressed
at parting. Then lord Amilun spoke: "Amis," he said, "my dear friend,[9] for your
honour's sake, I ask you a favour:[10] be on your guard in one respect. The count has a
seneschal here who is most wicked and treacherous,[11] and with powerful kin— and

---

[5] 29–34 **They also had** . . . **as they desired** *E si furent . . . a lur talant*: Karlsruhe substitutes twenty-four lines on the men's mutual love and the emperor Charles's rewarding
of them for their service.

[6] 38 **feast for them** *lur feste tint*: Karlsruhe inserts six lines on Charles trusting them.

[7] 39 **cupbearer** *boteler*: the *boteler* was one of five great officers of state established in
the French royal household in the latter half of the eleventh century.

[8] 46 **performed them well** . . . *tresbien le firent*: Karlsruhe adds fourteen lines on the
men's situation exciting envy, especially in the seneschal.

[9] 74 **my dear friend** *beau compaignun*: manuscript L adds two lines: *En bone foy
saunz tresoun / A nostre seignur seruy auom* (in good faith without treason we have served
our lord).

[10] 49–75 **no other heir** . . . **ask you a favour** *n'out autre eir. . .merci vus cri*: Karlsruhe
substitutes 105 lines expanding the scenes between Charles and Amilun, and Amilun
and Amis, with Amilun asking Amis to accompany him home to Lombardy.

[11] 77–8 **seneschal . . . treacherous** *seneschal . . . desleal*: the seneschal, or *dapifer*, was
another of these officers of state, who at first had no more than catering duties but after
1070 rapidly rose to become director-general of the French palace and commander-in-
chief of the army. In England the office of *dapifer* also became important, in the reign of
Henry I. See L. W. Vernon Harcourt, *His Grace the Steward* (London: Longmans, Green,
1907), 3–5, 21–23. There arc wicked and treacherous stewards in other insular romances,
as in the early part of Thomas's *Tristan* and in *Gui de Warewic*. In *Horn*, however, the sen-
eschals Herland and Hardré are both virtuous.

all the more feared for that. He never cared for you, sought your harm with all his might, but could find no occasion to do you any injury. But when I have gone, then he will be your active enemy.[12] Beware his wickedness, and don't have anything to do with him, for whoever keeps a scoundrel company finds nothing but evil. For nothing can be worse than one friend betraying the other. Make fair answer to everyone and you will gain great honour and profit! Avoid pride and envy, and refrain from gluttony. Cherish your lord and don't let him be dishonoured! We owe him much love and loyalty, for he has held you and me very dear!"[13] Then they embraced and wept for sorrow. No man on earth, had he been there, would not have pitied their grief. They fell fainting to the ground. No one would believe me if I told half the sorrow they displayed.[14] The one departed to his country; the other remained behind, sad and downcast. (47–110)

When he saw he could do no other,[15] he returned to court.[16] As soon as he entered the door, the seneschal met him, with an appearance of love, but in his heart he cared nothing for him. "My lord Amis," he said, "welcome! I was thinking of you just now, and of my lord Amilun, who was such a loyal friend to you. You never cared for anyone else nor showed anyone affection. But now that he's gone, I ask you to be my friend—my friend and well-wisher." And lord Amis then replied: "My lord seneschal, your friendship is not so exclusively devoted to me that I cannot love another when I care and want to do so. Amilun may have gone away, but he has entirely surrendered his heart to me, and I love him, now and in future, and won't desert him for another. A man would be a fool to leave a proven thing for a promise with no security. But this much you may believe of me: if you need my help, I'll do it most cordially, providing it's to the honour of us both!" Then the seneschal held his tongue and went pale with rage; he thought he would take revenge as soon as he saw his opportunity. Amis let time go by, and went and did his office, serving the count as usual, and the count cherished him dearly and truly considered him a closer friend than anyone else in his household. (111–50)

---

[12] 79–86 **powerful kin . . . active enemy** *grant parente . . . fort enemi*: Karlsruhe substitutes nine lines naming the seneschal as Haidre and giving his wicked lineage.

[13] 97–100 **Cherish . . . very dear** *Amez . . . ame vus e mei*: though I have given three different translations of it, the word *amer* (in its different forms) is used three times here. On its use in feudal relations, see G. F. Jones, *The Ethos of the Song of Roland* (Baltimore: Johns Hopkins University Press, 1963), 36–45. Karlsruhe substitutes six lines for vv. 93–100 which omit Amilun's advice.

[14] 108 **displayed** *ont mene*: Karlsruhe adds two lines which repeat and vary the next two (the one . . . the other).

[15] 111 **When he saw he could do no other** *Kant vit ke el faire ne pout*: manuscript L: *Quant Amis de palmoison levoit* (when Amis came round from swooning).

[16] 112 **returned to court** *se retornout*: Karlsruhe adds eight lines on Amis's distress at Amilun's departure.

Now I shall tell you about Amilun. When he arrived in his lands, the people there received him with great splendour. They all did him homage:[17] now he had many barons to rule! There was not one of his intimate friends who did not have ten knights to his retinue. Amilun made himself so beloved, by his household and by others, through his many gifts—he gave horses, he gave money and robes to his knights—and he himself was so handsome that the whole land said if God Himself had fashioned him, he could not be better or more finely made.[18] His men, who loved him dearly, advised him to take a wife. Through their advice he married; he wedded a high-born lady, a count's daughter, who had lost her mother and father. Through inheritance half the earldom fell to her. She was prized for her beauty over every other woman in the land. They were well matched in beauty and rank. (151–78)

Now I will leave the subject of them, and tell you about lord Amis,[19] who had stayed with his lord and served him better from day to day, and the better he served him the more the seneschal hated him. He resented his good deeds, but Amis did not realise it. (179–86)

The count had a wife, whom he loved as his life. He had a daughter from the lady, whom he loved as his soul. The maiden was very beautiful; there was none fairer in the realm. Dukes and counts desired her, wishing to take her to wife. But she replied to them all that she did not yet want a husband. Her father cherished her most tenderly, and her mother also loved her dearly. The maiden was well looked after. She had many companions from amongst the girls of the land, nine or ten in her chamber, who all did her wishes with no talk of contradiction. One day it happened by chance that the count held a feast, on Ascension Day, where many barons assembled. There was the chief cupbearer, Amis, who knew his office well. He was clad in flowered silk and held the cup before the count. He was handsome and well-proportioned, much esteemed by the knights. They said publicly amongst themselves that they did not know a finer knight in the land,[20] and the count said the same, that he had never seen such a handsome knight. All those in the hall had his beauty as their one theme. And the news about the cupbearer came travelling—you can imagine!—to the maiden's chamber: how

---

[17] 145–55 **Amis let time go by . . . did him homage** *Amis lessa le tens passer. . .feseient homage*: Karlsruhe substitutes eleven lines, anticipating misfortune for Amis.

[18] 159–66 **Amilun made himself . . . finely made** *Tant se fist . . . ne serreit fet*: Karlsruhe omits these lines.

[19] 171–80 **a count's daughter . . . about lord Amis** *Ke fille d'un counte . . . voudrai dire*: Karlsruhe substitutes fourteen lines giving us the name (Ozille) of Amilun's wife, her birth (she is the daughter of the duke of Pavia), and her wicked nature. The duke of Pavia is the villain in *Gui de Warewic* and Ozille is the woman he forcibly marries.

[20] 216 **did not know a finer knight in the land** *Ke en le pais si bel ne saueient*: this is manuscript C's original line, which Kölbing replaces with a not obviously better line from Karlsruhe.

handsome he was, such a noble young man, and such a good knight he had not his equal at court. The maiden conceived a weakness for him, so that she fell in love with him. She began to be so badly infatuated she could neither eat nor drink. The girls with her asked her why this was so, and she said she was ill, she did not know how. She ordered them to keep quiet and say nothing about her illness. But she remained languishing in this way until, one day, the count went hunting in the forest with all his knights. Not one of the knights stayed behind in their lodgings except lord Amis, and that was because of illness. The maiden did not hesitate, but asked leave of her mother, who at once granted it her.[21] I should tell you the maiden's name: it was really Mirabele, but she was called Florie by those in her retinue.[22] (187–250)

When Florie was given leave, she made as much haste as she could. With her mother's permission, and a solitary lady-in-waiting, she went to talk to Amis, whom she loved. She talked so much, she stayed so long, that she quite revealed her heart to him, and said that she would die for love of him unless he took pity on her and loved her. For if she did not have his love, she said, she would never love another. When Amis heard her, he thought she was out of her mind[23] and, as someone who did not want to harm his lord, he considered how to reply. Whereupon Florie angrily insulted him,[24] saying: "What? does it distress you that I've given you my love? I'll never feel pleasure at heart in my life, after this day, if I'm not avenged on you! Now indeed I'm truly humiliated, when you don't deign to have me as your mistress: so many noble men have begged me, and I've refused them all. Indeed, you're not a knight but a faint-hearted coward. I'll make it really difficult for you and tell my father you have wronged both me and him, and you will be torn to pieces by horses. Then I shall be thoroughly revenged on you!" Then Florie turned away. Amis thought hard: he feared both the one and the other evil very much.[25] Courteously he answered her: "Pardon, my

---

[21] 244–46 **The maiden . . . granted it her** *La damoisele . . . tantost done*: Karlsruhe substitutes seven lines on the unwisdom of a cupbearer's absence from court and regrets Amis's imminent misfortune.

[22] 250 **by those in her retinue** *De ceus ke furent de sa meisne*: Karlsruhe substitutes *Au muster ou fut baptise*, then adds thirty-six lines of dialogue between Florie and her mother. The bestowal of two "nicknames" on both Mirabele and Amiraunt (see v. 889) is unique to the Anglo-Norman romance. In other narratives, Mirabele/Florie is called Belissant/Beliardis/Belixenda. In the Auchinleck manuscript of *Amis and Amiloun*, Amorant is called Owain until he is twelve.

[23] 264 **she was out of her mind** *ke ele fud devee*: manuscript L adds: *Qe ele pout pur hounte descoverir / Sa volunté e son desir* (That she could shamefully reveal her will and her desire).

[24] 268–69 **angrily insulted him** *par grant irrur / Le rampona*: manuscript L has *par grant errour / Ele li respondi* (making a big mistake, she replied to him).

[25] 288 **feared . . . very much** *l'autre mult dota*: Karlsruhe adds eighteen lines of interior monologue.

lady, for God's sake. I am and shall be your friend[26] and your servant as long as
I live. But I shall not do you wrong, to bring you discourtesy or bodily shame, as
God is my witness. If it were noticed that you had made me your lover, wouldn't
you be eventually disgraced?" "No, no!" said Florie, "we shall carry out all our
pleasures and desires so secretly it will be hidden from any man born." She said
and spoke so much to him that they were agreed on the matter and devised how
and when they could meet. Alas, they would be denounced, because a henchman
from the seneschal's household had heard it all. As soon as he could manage it,
he went to recount it to his master. (251–312)

The seneschal was delighted; now he intended to be well and truly revenged
on this courteous cupbearer. He had all their doings spied upon. When the day
which they had agreed arrived, they came together with great pleasure, exchang-
ing kisses of desire, indulging in the words and the sport of love. I shall say no
more, but I think there was no harm in it. When the seneschal knew the situation between Amis and the girl, he went early the next day to the count and told
him what they were about. Now, unless God were to take pity and have mercy,
the two lovers were betrayed. The count was so distended with anger he could
not speak for a long while. Then he said: "God have mercy! If this traitor, whom
I loved and held so dear, has shamed me thus, in whom can I trust? This is a terrible disgrace: my daughter has become a whore. She's shamed and I'm betrayed:
would I had never seen that wicked traitor! If I can't be revenged on him, I'll be
disgraced forever. Is this true, seneschal? I think you've said it out of malice!"
"My lord," replied the seneschal, "by the Creator of the whole world, if Amis
denies it to me, I will prove it like a faithful knight, and may whoever of us is
defeated be drawn and then hanged!" And the count said: "Now this is damaging; this is an ugly and shameful affair!" Then he entered his chambers and found
his lady on a bed. "My lady," he said, "you don't know what sort of daughter you
have! Now she's a strumpet, and our cupbearer has done that. He repays our
kindness with dishonour; he has wickedly played false with us, for he has raped
our daughter. God send him a bad end! Such he will have, if I live long enough.
He won't escape death: he'll be drawn and then hanged, and the whore will be
burnt at the stake!" The lady did not know what to say. The count turned blacker
than coal with anger and fury. He rushed out of the house and met his cupbearer, to whom he was used to speak courteously. He looked at him with wild
eyes, and Amis was most surprised. "Wretch,"[27] he said, "God curse you! You've
caused my daughter's shame. But you won't get out of it laughing: your death is
fast approaching." "My lord," said Amis, "you are wrong: I am your loyal knight.

---

[26] 291 **your friend** *Vostre ami*: ami can mean both friend and lover; I think Amis's
reactions here suggest the former. Later (v. 754) the double meaning of the word is again
fruitfully exploited.

[27] 373 **Wretch** *Fel*: Kölbing inserts *Hee* (hey) before *fel*, taken from Karlsruhe, although neither manuscript C nor L contains it.

If anyone has told you anything about me except what is loyal and true, I will vigorously defend myself in your presence, if I have to!"

Then the seneschal came up and tendered the glove he held in his fist as sign of a pledge, like a man of great valour, and said he would fight with him and prove the truth. Hereupon the court assembled, the knights and the household. Each antagonist tendered his glove to the other, and the count then received them both. Thereupon all the barons decided they were to find sureties, or else hostages. The seneschal found so many that the count was well satisfied. People were so afraid of the seneschal that Amis could not find a single one, whether from fear or love of him, and everyone saw that their lord mortally hated Amis, whether rightly or wrongly, and they did not dare plead for him. For the count wanted to condemn him.[28] When no surety could be found, he and the girl were as good as dead.[29] Amis was at once perplexed and taken aback. He did not know which to choose, life or death; he did not know what to say. Many pitied him, but his lord was so angry, there was no man so bold as to dare speak a word in his favour. Whatever might happen, his lady could not restrain herself, but knelt down before the count and made a request for the knight: she would be a hostage for him and become his surety.[30] "Indeed," said the count, "do you want it that way? I tell you truly, should he lose the battle, you will have, without fail, the sentence destined for your daughter!"[31] The lady wept for sorrow, yet stood bail for Amis; the girl was heartbroken. Amis thought hard, as he certainly needed to, and he remembered his brother. At once he came to the countess and asked her for leave, so he might speak to his brother; he wanted to tell him his trouble. And the lady, very fearful,[32] answered him: "My good lord Amis, I think you will betray me! If you don't come at the appointed day, don't you know my lord has sworn I shall die for you?" "My lady," he said, "on my honour, you shall not die through my

---

[28] 404 **condemn him** *le vult jugier*: manuscript L: *li velt venger* (take revenge on him).

[29] 408 **were as good as dead** *Mort estoit il e la meschine*: manuscript L: *Pausmé chei la meischine* (the girl fainted).

[30] 395–420 **The seneschal . . . his surety** *Le seneschal . . . sun plegge devendreit*: Karlsruhe substitutes eighty-four lines on Amis's laments and Florie's appeal to her mother, queen Eleyne.

[31] 425 **the sentence destined for your daughter** *La jugement . . . K'a vostre fille est destine*: by the thirteenth century, sureties had to give amercement if the man they stood bail for defaulted, but earlier there was a much more rigorous form of suretyship in England, Normandy, and France, in which the surety was liable to suffer the punishment proposed for the accused. On this, and on the whole subject of judicial combats, see F. Pollock and F. W. Maitland, *The History of English Law before the Time of Edward I*, 2 vols. (Cambridge: Cambridge University Press, 1898), 2: 589–602.

[32] 426–36 **wept for sorrow . . . very fearful** *lermeit de pite . . . mult se dout*: Karlsruhe substitutes fifty-nine lines on the much more active part played by the queen.

fault, so long as I live!" Then she gave him leave and he mounted his palfrey,[33] with neither groom nor squire, for he was travelling not like a knight but like a pilgrim. He stopped neither morning nor evening, ate little and drank less, and slept not a wink. He travelled thus the whole week, never resting at night, till one evening he entered a great wood.[34] Of necessity he had to sleep, or else he thought he might die. He lay down beneath a tree, reined in his horse there, and slept, for he was very weary and his horse suffering.[35] (383–462)

Amilun lay in his bed, next to his wife, and slept. He had a dream that his friend, lord Amis, was attacked by a lion, bent on his destruction. The dream terrified him and he jumped up as if out of his mind. Quickly he called his knights, squires, and men-at-arms and quickly he made them saddle up, giving them no other details except that he wished to visit his brother, whom he had so much reason to love. They had to pack at midnight, which they did not enjoy. They travelled far enough that night that they passed through the wood where Amis was sleeping. Lord Amilun was the first to see him. He quickly turned his steps towards him and gently woke him. His men passed on ahead while he waited; he wanted to know about his situation, and Amis told him everything. There was such joy, and sorrow, as the one found out about the other![36] Then Amilun said very sensibly to him: "My dear brother, since you have done wrong, and will have to swear on oath, I'm afraid that, from sin, that oath will get you into trouble. But I shall undertake the fight for you and safely swear an oath[37] that I never did her any wrong, and they will think I am Amis. I hope by God's grace we shall be avenged on that wretch who thinks to dishonour us. My knights, who are here now, will stay with you henceforward and go with you to my court. For when we have changed clothes, they will truly think you are their lord. Moreover, I entreat you, in all affection, to do the same to my wife, in appearance and in actuality, as if I myself were here, so that she has no reason to think she has anybody except me. For I tell you truly, she has very sharp eyes!" Amis was in complete agreement with his plan. Then they changed clothes, and Amilun departed; he went

---

[33] 442–46 **My lady . . . mounted his palfrey** *par ma leaute . . . son palefrei munta*: Karlsruhe substitutes twenty-one lines extending the dialogue between Amis and the queen.

[34] 456 **a great wood** *En un grand bois est entre*: Karlsruhe adds two lines on Amis being so sleepy he almost fell off his horse.

[35] 462 **his horse suffering** *fuist meseise*: Karlsruhe adds two lines exhorting the audience to listen.

[36] 488–90 **told him everything . . . about the other** *trestut li diseit . . . est aqueinte*: Karlsruhe substitutes thirty-three lines, with Amis's misgivings—*Jurer ne voil ne contredire* (I don't want to swear or deny)—and request for advice.

[37] 498 **safely swear an oath** *Le serment sauvement jurrai*: Amilun does not, in fact, swear any such oath, whereas he does in Raoul le Tourtier's Latin epistle and in the *chanson de geste* (see Introduction, 26, 28).

off quite alone, without company. Now God help him and grant he do well: he undertakes a great matter for his brother! Amis remained with the retinue, like its lord and master; and they all thought, without a doubt, he was their rightful lord. And the lady, once she had seen him, certainly thought he was Amilun. The two were so alike that no one, however observant, would have been able to distinguish the one from the other if he had not heard them named—neither by body nor face, by nothing, unless by dress. When night fell, Amis lay down next to the lady. He placed his naked sword between them, at which she was much astonished. He would not talk to her until morning, when he rose. Every night he behaved in this way until Amilun returned home. (463–544)

Now we will leave him and speak of Amilun. The day fixed between Amis and the seneschal arrived. The seneschal had himself armed and then asked for the cupbearer, and when he could not be found, the lady was taken and tightly bound, and the maiden too. People pitied them very much: they wept and mourned for their beauty. The count, who was very angry, was all for expediting the sentence and swore a great oath that he himself would see them burn. Then they saw a knight coming towards them at great speed, spurring his horse well beyond walking pace. He was dismayed at the sight of the fire and felt great pity for the ladies. "My lord count," he said, "here I am! What is this fire for? To put ladies on the spit is a wicked piece of roasting! Quick, give me weapons to deliver these ladies! I want to defend our rights." When the count saw the knight, he was convinced he was Amis: he was like him in face and body. He asked for good weapons and armed the knight himself. At heart he was very pleased to see him so well equipped. Then he whispered in his ear that if he could win the fight, he would give him his daughter to wife and make him heir to all his land. Lo and behold, the contestants were met; now battle would erupt. Each challenged the other, for there was no love lost between them. (545–96)

Now the warriors, both proud and brave, charged each other.[38] Neither deigned to flee the other, each prepared to strike. Amilun, with a great hilted lance, hit the seneschal through the middle of his azure shield, but the hauberk was tough and strong, quite protecting him from harm. The seneschal struck him in return. Reconciliation served no purpose: each mortally hated the other. They shattered their lances with the blows, and did without them. In this encounter they did so well that neither lost anything. Amilun approached angrily, drawing his steel sword in fury. He struck at the seneschal, giving him a great blow on the helm, but the helmet was so strong that it protected him from death, while the blow came down upon the saddlebow. It completely severed both leather and wood as if by a razor-cut, and the sword glided through the horse's shoulder and down into the ground by more than a foot and a half. Then the seneschal fell

---

[38] 587–88 **both proud and brave, charged each other** *Or s'en ferent . . . corajus e fiers*: manuscript L adds: *Ne avera mester de acord: L'un hiet l'autre desq'a la mort* (reconciliation served no purpose: each mortally hated the other), lines occurring in C at vv. 597–98.

down; [how could he otherwise, when his horse failed him? There was much talk of the stroke, and the one said to the other that the knight was adept at bearing arms, but his blow was too severe.][39] Then the seneschal got up; he wanted to fight upright[40] and was mortified and angry that he had to fight on foot. He would, if he could, quickly take revenge and force Amilun to dismount. But he quickly noticed his conduct and at once withdrew. At once he dismounted from his horse: he wanted to fight on equal terms and so did not need it. So much he did out of courtesy; but he would rather endure the fight on foot than let his horse die. The seneschal, with no love for him, gave him a great blow on the helmet painted with flowers, soon knocking out its colours. The stroke came down on the left side, cutting off more than a hundred links of mail. It passed very close to his side but did not touch the bare flesh. Amilun, full of energy, gave him many blows that day. (597–640)

The battle lasted a long while, past noon; the seneschal did very well, and Amilun was fearless. No one could judge which was the better warrior on the field. Amilun was very vexed that the battle had lasted so long; he wanted to give him a blow to cause him downright harm. But the seneschal struck him first, with a blow only too plain to see. It staved his helmet in, and quite stunned Amilun. Now delay could be fatal. If he did not know how to return the blow, the other would depart jeering. So lord Amilun then struck him with such violence that the sparks flew. He cleft the helmet quite in two, covering his sword with brains and making ears and face fly to the ground. He severed the arm with all the flesh; the sword slipped down into the hip. With this blow his revenge was complete: he would never accuse him any more. It was not surprising if he fell. Now the fight was over; some rejoiced, others wept. The knights all ran up, but the count arrived first and at once had him disarmed. He asked if he were wounded; Amilun replied he was unharmed, sounder than a fish in the sea. Then everyone went to embrace him. Above all, the lady greeted him, and the maiden all the while made signs to him, as much as she dared, for she was very frightened of her father. Then the count called to his daughter: "Tell me, my lovely daughter," he said, "Amis has fought for you and defeated his enemy; he has acquitted you and him of the deed of which you were accused. If he wants to marry you, could you readily love him?" She replied very simply: "At your command, my lord! If you wish to give me in marriage, I have no right to complain." Then all the barons were ordered to be at the marriage. (641–96)

---

[39] 616 **Then the seneschal fell down** *Le seneschal aitant chai*: manuscript L adds the five bracketed lines here.

[40] 618 **he wanted to fight upright** *Combatre voleit en estaunt*: omitted in manuscript L.

The next day, on the stroke of nine,[41] everyone, great and small, came, barons and knights, citizens, men-at-arms and squires.[42] When they were gathered, the maiden was brought, and they came to the gate of the abbey.[43] The priest began his office, saying his psalms and prayers, and then he asked for their names: this must be done in this circumstance. When Amilun had to give his name, he was plunged into thought, and lo and behold, a voice, which nobody heard but he, said to him: "My lord Amilun, don't do it![44] I tell you for certain, if you take the maiden, before three years have passed, you'll be a leper for all to see. Henceforward, there will be no man so ugly!" Amilun heard it well enough, but nevertheless would not stop, and received her as his wife. He did not want it observed how his brother had deceived them. The maiden was well satisfied to have the husband she wanted.[45] The count held a splendid feast for a whole week; there were many gifts of robes, which were supplied to the minstrels. The count gave palfreys and war-horses to the knights.[46] But now I should tell you what happened at bedtime: the lady embraced her lover and often gave him loving kisses. She thought for sure that he was Amis. But the preoccupied Amilun had at heart every intention of not dishonouring her or betraying his brother the while. He uttered a deep sigh and, with the sigh, a heartfelt groan. The lady embraced him tenderly and asked him what he was thinking and why he uttered such a sigh. Then Amilun replied, no longer wanting to hide his name: "I am not the man you think: you are disappointed in your hopes. I can tell it all to you: I hope you will conceal it." He told her all their situation and then took his leave, saying he would return to his land and send her lover[47] to her. The lady was well content; there was no more talk between them. In the morning, when Amilun rose, he

---

[41] 697 **on the stroke of nine** *a tierce sonant*: *tertia hora*, 9 a.m., was one of the "canonical" hours ordering divine services.

[42] 700 **squires** *esquiers*: the combat scene is not in Karlsruhe, owing to a missing leaf, but the manuscript has fifty-eight lines on ensuing events: Charles summons his barons to announce his daughter's marriage, performed by the archbishop of Reims.

[43] 703 **gate of the abbey** *l'us del muster*: marriage outside the church door (*in facie ecclesiae*) was first recorded in Normandy in the early twelfth century. See *A Dictionary of Liturgy and Worship*, ed. J. G. Davies (London: S. C. M. Press, 1972), and G. Duby, *The Knight, the Lady and the Priest*, trans. B. Bray (Harmondsworth: Penguin, 1983), 179.

[44] 709–12 **plunged into thought . . . don't do it** *se purpensa mult estreit . . . sire Amilun*: Karlsruhe substitutes thirty-three lines in which Amilun agonises over whether to give his actual name or not.

[45] 716–24 **a leper for all to see . . . she wanted** *Apert leprus vus serriez . . . a volente*: Karlsruhe substitutes ninety-seven lines: in his anguish, Amilun asks for respite and prays lengthily to God, then returns to the church and declares himself to be Amis.

[46] 730 **and war-horses to the knights** *as chevalers . . . e les destrers*: Karlsruhe then adds twelve lines in which the poet deplores "bragging" about the splendours of feasts, which he will omit.

[47] 754 **her lover** *sun ami*: her lover, his friend. See note to v. 250.

came to take leave of the count and said he would go and tell his brother of his situation. On leave-taking, he took up to ten servants with him and departed into his land. He told Amis everything, how he had concluded the battle and how he had performed the wedding.[48] Then they entered a room and there changed their clothes. Thus no one at all noticed what they were about. (697–770)

As soon as he could, Amis took leave and went back to his country and mistress, whom he loved as his life. Now he had risen to a high rank, for through marriage he accrued great power and great estates; he was lord of many lands, of three and a half counties, once the count died. Now he was beloved and held dear; no longer was he cupbearer[49] but councillor and lord. Whatever he wanted lawfully to utter was observed throughout the land, so great had his position become. His wife loved him most tenderly and did everything he wished. At last the count fell ill and, when he had sickened a long while, died and rendered his soul up to God; and soon after his lady died too. When father and mother were dead, there was neither brother nor sister, but only the lady whom Amis had, so he received the lands.[50] (771–96)

Now I shall leave Amis, who has enough, everything he needs, and I shall tell you of lord Amilun, who was such a true friend. As he lay in his bed, his lovely lady said to him: "Tell me, for love of me, for I love you most truly, why, my lord, did you put your naked sword between us?" "My lady, I shan't tell you; I won't confess it." Amilun knew by this that Amis was a true friend. For a long while he lived together with his wife, until all his skin grew rough; he became so ill and so repulsive that everyone believed him a leper. The lady held him in great contempt and would not enter his bed, nor talk to him, nor eat or drink with him. She said she would rather die than be in any place where he was. Thus he was left alone, that year, in great pain and distress; his knights all departed, his servants all abandoned him. He could find neither squire nor servant to give him cold water.[51] All his men had left him, except for a boy he had raised, a count's son, his relative. He stayed firmly with him and insisted that, come life, come death, he

---

[48] 747–66 **not the man you think . . . performed the wedding** *pas celi ke quidez . . . fet out l'espousaill*e: Karlsruhe substitutes 115 lines of dialogue between Amilun and Florie, and with Charles, when Amilun invents a dream about his "brother" in order to get away.

[49] 771–82 **as soon as he could . . . was he cupbearer** *al plus tost qu'il poeit . . . estre boteler*: Karlsruhe substitutes nineteen lines on Amis's and Amilun's distress at their leave-taking.

[50] 783–96 **and lord . . . received the lands** *e sire . . . les terres recevoit*: Karlsruhe substitutes twelve lines on Amis's heightened standing and love for his wife.

[51] 826 **cold water** *freide ewe li vout doner*: on medieval descriptions of the rough skin and burning heat of lepers, see P. Rémy, "La lèpre, thème littéraire au moyen âge," *Le Moyen Âge* 42 (1946): 195–242, at 203–4, 209 (the ardor of lepers was also sexual desire); and S. N. Brody, *The Disease of the Soul* (Ithaca and London: Cornell University Press, 1974), 41, 51; L. Demaitre, *Leprosy in Premodern Medicine* (Baltimore: Johns Hopkins University Press, 2007).

would never leave him. The lady, very vexed, threw them both out, master and servant, lord Amis and his boy.[52] At the top end of the town was a little hut[53] and there she made them take up lodging.[54] (797–838)

Now my lord Amilun was in a most wretched state. Once he had been lord and master: his grief was not surprising. He longed for death, rather than life, for he had neither comfort nor company, nor anyone to talk to, to whom he could reveal his misery, except the boy alone, who served him and would not abandon him on any account. The longer Amilun lived, the more repulsive he became, so that in court not even menials or old crones would once look after him. The lady issued orders to everyone that no one should be so bold as to care for him or give him anything to eat. When the boy heard this command, he did not know where next to find their food. He quickly went to tell his master, who said: "Here is a bad abode if we have neither food nor drink; we can stay here no longer. Jesus, son of Mary, how long must I live like this? I used to have great treasures, to be served food off silver and gold dishes. Now I am so afflicted, my life is pitiable. If I have to die of hunger, I for one shan't care!" Then he called the boy to him and entreated him, for God's sake, to let him die there and to return to his own land. The boy gently replied: "If you please, my dear lord,[55] I would rather, I swear, suffer with you[56] than be an emperor without you."[57] When they looked at each other, they made great lamentation: they wept and tore their clothes, often called themselves miserable wretches, and mourned the knights, the domains, and the lordship that had once belonged to lord Amilun and now had come to nothing. I will tell you the child's name: people called him Amiraunt, but Owein was his real name. (839–89)

---

[52] 812–36 **skin grew rough . . . and his boy** *la peel li heriça . . . e sun enfant*: Karlsruhe substitutes forty-seven lines, describing Amilun as undeservedly tested and banished to a room in a garden, later called a *bordel* (see below).

[53] 837 **little hut** *bordel*: *bordel* means both hut and whorehouse; the latter meaning is suggested when the lady is later banished there with only a harlot to look after her. Lepers are strongly linked with sexual promiscuity in the Middle Ages. See Brody, *Disease*, 52–56, 129, 143–45.

[54] 838 **lodging** *ostel*: Karlsruhe adds four lines on the lady assigning Amilun a boy who carted dung.

[55] 848–76 **on any account . . . my dear lord** *nel voleit . . . cher seignur*: Karlsruhe substitutes 145 lines, introducing Amilun's son Florentyn, who is beaten by his mother for consorting with his leprous father and dies of the beating.

[56] 877 **suffer with you** *od vus suffrir dolur*: Karlsruhe adds *& totes maneres meschefs auer* (and have all manner of harm).

[57] 878 **an emperor without you** *estre empereur*: Karlsruhe adds four lines expanding on the boy's loyalty.

Then lord Amilun said to him: "Owein, go to the lady: we shall take our
leave of her! We shall quit this land as fast as we can.[58] But I cannot travel on
foot. Ask her, for charity's sake, to provide me with a donkey which I can ride."
The boy went to the lady and told her his message. She gave him the donkey, and
then made him swear by all that was holy that, once he had arrived, he would
never return to the land.[59] They left the country, thinking they would never return. The boy Owein was most faithful, seeking their bread in God's name. But
they came across such a dearth of bread, wine, and corn that they could find nobody willing to give them anything. They could wait no longer but had to sell
their donkey for five or ten sous and a halfpenny,[60] and with this they bought
their food. Besides this, Owein made a litter, on two wheels, which he could
trundle along by hand. He had Amilun lie in it, made him as comfortable as he
could, and took him from place to place. (890–922)

They had so many travels through the land[61] that they met hunger and hard-
ship, until they came to the country where count Amis dwelt, holding a noble
court and doing great good in God's name. All the poor people round about
flocked there as if in procession. The two arrived there, amongst the others. Nobody seeing them knew who they were. Had they been recognised at court, they
would have been received with great honour.[62] They placed themselves near the
door, and the boy, who dearly loved his lord and was well skilled in this, went all
around asking the poor about the condition, manners, and customs of the land.
The nobility, who went by amusing themselves, often looking at the poor, noticed
the boy, handsome and fully-grown, and saw he would look like a nobleman were
he to have the clothes. One of them called him and asked him if he would like to
enter service. And the boy sighed and said that he had a master, whom he would
not leave, not even for the emperor himself. They asked him who that was; but
as soon as they had seen the man he called master, they all thought it folly. But
they pitied the boy, and told count Amis about him; and he, once at his meal,
sent them his first course by one of his chief cupbearers, a most courteous young
man. He sent them half of each course brought to him. Amis had a cup he loved
dearly, for Amilun, so dear to him, had given him it. Amilun himself had its

[58] 885–94 **to lord Amilun . . . fast as we can** *Amilun aveit eu . . . ke nus porrums*:
Karlsruhe substitutes ten lines in which Amilun sends a message to his wife.
[59] 899–904 **went to the lady . . . to the land** *a la dame ala . . . issi serreit*: Karlsruhe
substitutes thirty-four lines repeating the message to the lady, who is delighted.
[60] 915 **five or ten sous and a halfpenny** *cink souz ou dis e maaille*: manuscript L: *cink
souz diz e maille*; Karlsruhe: *VII ou VIII souz* (rationalisation!).
[61] 923–24 **through the land** *tant alerent*: Karlsruhe expands into four lines.
[62] 927–34 **holding a noble court . . . great honour** *court illek teneit . . . honur fussent
receu*: Karlsruhe substitutes thirty-two lines: Amilun and Owein are directed to go to the
court but don't know it's Amis's.

companion, which he would not sell or give away.[63] The two goblets were so alike that if they were held in the same hand, nobody, however much he knew of the workmanship, would be able to tell one from the other. The sick man had his cup, which he would never give up. When the count had had a bite to eat,[64] he called his cupbearer: "Take my cup, with all the wine in it, and carry it to that beggar, the poor man in so much distress, but look after the goblet! Pour the wine into his bowl and bring me back my cup." He obeyed his order and came and brought the gift. The poor man, wasted with hunger, took his cup out of his bosom,[65] and the other poured the wine into it.[66] He looked hard at it and thought: "How can that be? These two goblets are the work of a single man!" At once he returned and told the count about the goblet and how it resembled his. (923–93)

The count was amazed. Then he remembered Amilun and said: "I'm sure I know where it comes from: he's stolen it from my brother. He'll pay dearly for it!"[67] Then he jumped over the table and came running up to the poor man and kicked him so hard that he fell into the mud. The knights came with him, following him closely and trying to restrain him, but nothing they could do would moderate his desire to kill him then and there. When he had beaten and trampled on him until he himself was exhausted, he ordered him to be bound and thrown into his prison. After that, he said, he would send for Amilun and ask him the truth of how he had lost his goblet and how it reached this man. When Amilun heard his name,[68] his heart felt ready to burst with grief. "My lord," he said, "by the faith you owe Amilun, whom you love so, don't put me in prison, but

---

[63] 954–68 **thought it folly . . . give away** *tenoient a folur . . . vendre ne doner*: Karlsruhe substitutes forty-five lines: when Amis is told about the boy and the leper, he sends them money and invites them to his court every day. We are also told that he had the two identical goblets made at the time he served Charles as cupbearer. After v. 968, manuscript L adds two lines: *Mes le hanap tant ameyt / Q'en tot son anguisse guerpir ne voleit* (But he loved the goblet so much that in the midst of his suffering he would not abandon it).

[64] 975 **bite to eat** *poy mange*: in place of this line, Karlsruhe expands for ten lines on the goblets.

[65] 983–86 **his order. . .out of his bosom** *le commandement. . .de sun sein*: Karlsruhe substitutes fourteen lines on Amis's words to his servant and on inciting the audience's pity.

[66] 987 **wine into it** *vin i getta*: manuscript L: *E l'autre la vist, si s'esmerveilla* (and the other saw it and marvelled).

[67] 991–98 **he returned . . . dearly for it** *tantost repaira . . . cher achate*: Karlsruhe substitutes forty-four lines expanding on the cupbearer's suspicions of Amilun and Amis's anger.

[68] 1017 **heard his name** *s'oit nomer*: Karlsruhe expands on Amilun's emotions for five lines. Then the text in this manuscript breaks off at v. 1748: *Qe de fyn doel le quer ne le sent*. Its editor, John Ford, believes from the quiring that K's redactor accepted this as the ending but was using an imperfect exemplar with an ending of some 260 lines missing. (Personal communication: J. Ford, "From *Poésie* to Poetry: *Remaniement* and Medieval

cut off my head at once, for indeed I have lived too long and only too well deserve death!" "Indeed!" he said, "you shall have it. Your request will be granted!" He at once asked for his sword, saying he would do it himself. When his sword was in his hands, he raised it angrily on high, and Amilun stretched out his neck, but the boy, Owein, who could not bear his lord to die, jumped forward and cried out: "Mercy, mercy, by that God who never lied and suffered passion on the cross! For this is lord Amilun himself. Remember, my lord count Amis, how you once loved him! Great need has driven him here: if you kill him, you're committing a sin!" (994–1042)

And when the count heard this, he fell prostrate to the ground. He beat his breast, he tore his hair, he rejected life, and he longed for death. He cursed the hour he was born, when sin had so ensnared him that he did not recognise his brother, who had done everything for him. Everyone wept for pity, and Amis then stood up and embraced Amilun with more than a hundred kisses, soiled though he was. He carried him away in his arms and put him to bed in his room, had him bathed and bled and taken care of like his own person, and given plenty of servants. He had him given the food of his choice, clothes likewise, and he himself went to him every day, six or seven times, and comforted him as best he could. The lady, who loved him most sincerely, often visited him. Had she been twenty times his sister,[69] she could not have showed him more friendship. (1043–69)

In this way he spent three years; his wishes were satisfied in abundance, but he grew more repulsive every day.[70] The servants who waited on him felt great pity for him. The time passed thus until one night, when the count was asleep, he heard a voice, saying he could easily cure Amilun if he tried. He had fathered two sons: if he killed the children and bathed Amilun in their blood, he would become as sound as a fish. When he had seen the vision and woken from the dream: "Oh God," he said, "who has never lied, grant my dream be true. But whether it's true or false, at least I want to test the voice, not ignore it on account of my children. I'll have done a very good day's work if he is healed by their blood!" One day he got up in the morning and went to church. He begged God, for the sake of his holy name, to cure his brother. The lady came there to do the same and often entreated God on his behalf. Then the count returned home and entered a room where the two children were lying and sweetly sleeping. The children's father had no pity, but cut the heads off them both, steeped the sheets in the blood, and wrapped Amilun in them. As soon as he felt the blood, he was cured of his

Techniques of French-to-English Translation of Verse Romance" [Ph.D. diss., Glasgow University, 2000]). I am grateful to Dr. Ford for letting me use this information.

[69] 1068 **Had she been twenty times his sister** *S'ele fust vint fez sa sue*r: I have restored manuscript C's reading here. Kölbing prefers manuscript L: *Commes qe ele fust sa soer*, emended by Fukui to *Comme si ele fust sa soer* (as if she were his sister).

[70] 1072 **grew more repulsive** *plus laid deveneit*: manuscript L: *Tant com il memes desiroit* (just as he desired).

great malady, so that not a trace of the disease appeared in his body or face. Amis felt nothing but rejoicing; he had a new robe brought for him and then led him to church. As soon as the lady saw him, she almost fainted for joy. She ran to her husband and asked if it was lord Amilun, and how he had been cured. "My lady," he said, "I shall tell you indeed, but it will grieve you terribly: know that I have killed your two children to heal him!" The lady stretched her hands up to God and gave Him thanks. Then she said, so as to be clearly heard:[71] "Jesus, son of Mary, can certainly give us children, if He pleases, by His power. If you had lost Amilun, you would never have another like him. Let us think no more of the children; God willing, we shall have some more!" Then she stopped speaking and listened to the service. After mass they went home, joyful and happy for Amilun, and Amis led the lady into the room where he had left the children dead and bleeding. Lo and behold, they found them alive! They were playing together in their bed with a sunbeam.[72] When their father and mother saw this, they thanked God heartily. (1070–1144)

Lord Amilun, healthy and healed of his great malady, took leave of them as soon as he could, and went to his own land. When the lady heard that her lord was cured and was returning to the land with his powerful brother, count Amis, no woman ever felt greater misery and fear at heart than she did. As a result, in the end she felt herself disgraced. She had thought he was no longer alive and had thus got all ready to be married again. But now she called herself wretched and unfortunate, much distressed she was still alive. She did not know what in the world she could do. If she left the country, she had no idea how she would manage. Then she began to think she would become a nun and never see her lord again. But that was not her fate, for one morning the two counts arrived and dismounted at the door. Nobody, great or small, noticed their arrival. The household was asleep and did not know they had come. When the lady heard tell of it, she went to hide in her room. She would rather be hanged than that her lord should see her. Lord Amilun behaved nobly: he gathered all his people, citizens and knights, servants, squires, and men-at-arms. All those who had once held him in scorn wished to beg his pardon. For their sake he renounced his anger, kept them with him, and loved them. Then he sent for his wife, for on her he wanted to have his revenge. They searched till they found her where she had hidden herself for fear. As soon as she saw her lord, she fainted with terror. Her husband raised her and began strongly to upbraid her: "My lady," he said, "let be! You shouldn't show such grief when I return safe and well! By Jesus and our

---

[71] 1125 **so as to be clearly heard** *ke ele fust oye*: manuscript L: *Donqe comence pur fere joie* (then began to rejoice).

[72] 1142 **a sunbeam** *rai del soleil*: the sun was a symbol of Christ. See George Ferguson, *Signs and Symbols in Christian Art* (New York: Oxford University Press, 1966), 45. In the *chanson de geste*, they play with a golden apple; in Raoul le Tourtier's Epistle, red apples.

heavenly Father, had you been the woman you should, you would have profited from it. I shall be held in great dishonour if I don't take revenge on you. If I was ill and disfigured, I had done no wrong, and was entitled to live off my property. My lady, you ought to remember clearly what you brought me to eat and how you drove me from the land. Then you made my servant swear I should never in my life return here, whatever happened. You must remember the hut you gave me as lodging: you shall have it, as long as you live, and keep it as a token of dowry." Then he had a watch-tower made by it, small, but strong and handsome and extremely tall, for all the people throughout the city could see it. The lady was shut inside it. She could never get out and stayed there till she died. Other ladies can take a lesson from it on how to look after their lords. A harlot served her and passed her rations to her through a window every day, as the count had ordered. She lived thus a year and a day, then died of grief. (1145–1232)

Lord Amilun was much praised for not having her punished in other ways. He never wanted a wife again. Having no heir, he richly endowed the boy Owein and made him inherit all his land, for he had well deserved it. He lived a good life for a long time, spending his days charitably, and when he died, went to God, and so did Amis, his brother. Their love was great and true and their companionship good. At Mortara they lie, in Lombardy,[73] where God performs great miracles through them: the blind see, the mute speak. Thus ends the story of Amilun and of lord Amis his friend.[74]

---

[73] 1246 **At Mortara they lie**, **in Lombardy** *A morters gisent en Lombardie*: Kölbing replaced this line by the reading of manuscript L, *lor corps gisent en Lombardie*, but manuscript C correctly retains the tradition that the bodies of Amis and Amilun were venerated at the abbey of St. Albin outside Mortara for many centuries. See J. Bédier, *Les Légendes Epiques*, 4 vols. (Paris: Champion, 1908–1913), 2: 170–81.

[74] 1249–50 **Thus ends the story of Amilun and of lord Amis his friend** *Ici finist de Amilon / E de sire Amis sun compaignon*: Kölbing replaces manuscript C's reading with a corrected reading of manuscript L: *Tot ensi finist le sermoun / De sire Amis e d'Amilun* (So ends the homily [or discourse] of lord Amis and of Amilun).

Appendix of Extracts

Le *Roman de Horn*, La *Folie Tristan d'Oxford*, Le *Lai d'Haveloc, Amis e Amilun*

Le *Roman de Horn*

1.

53. A la chambre s'en vont   main a main dreitement
U la fille le rei,   bele Rigmel, atent,
E l'uissier lur ovri,   il entrent belement:
De la beauté de Horn   la mesun en resplent.
Tuit quident que çoe seit   angelin avenement.

54. Rigmel, quant l'ad vëu,   tut chaunga sun pensé,
Quida ke fust angele,   ki i fust enveié
Del seignur ki sus maint   en haute maiesté,
Si cum el l'esgarde: taunt bel li ad semblé.
Nepurquant lieve sus, si l'ad bel apelé:
'Bien viengez, seneschal!   de mei aiez bon gré
Quant estes si leal; vus iert guerredoné,
Ke le fiz Aäluf   ça m'avez amené.
E bien viengez, sire Horn!   mut vus ai desiré
A vëeir, çoe sacez,   mut ad grant tens passé . . .'

56. Apres se va sëeir   as puceles Herland,
De quei il i parla   nul corteis ne.l demand,
Kar bien le poet savoir,   pur nent l'iert enquerant.
Mes Rigmel prist vers sei   par la main cel enfant;
Sur sun lit se séent   amdous tut joiant—
La coilte en iert mut chiere   d'un paile escarimant.
Ne s'atendi Rigmel,   einz ad parlé avant
Tut issi faitement   cum joe vus ierc disant:
'De vus est mut bien veir   çoe que tuit sunt cuntant,

Ke taunt bel home n'ad en cest siecle vivant.
Joe vus otrei m'amur,   si l'estes otreiant;
Par cest anel que tienc   vus en sui seisissant.
Unkes mes a nul hom   del munde ne dis taunt,
N'a autre nel dirrai   par le mien escïant:
Mez vodreie estre arse   en un feu ardant.'
'Bele,' çoe li dit Horn, 'li sires tut pussant
Vus en rende merciz!   mes ne sui si vaillant
Ke me devez offrir   de vus chose taunt grant.
Povre sui orphanin,   n'ai de terre plein gant;
Ici vinc par werec   cum chaitif esgarant;
Vostre perre m'ad fait   nurrir par sun comant.'

1050–1114

2.

137. Lors pren la harpe a sei,   qu'il la veut atemprer.
Deus! ki dunc l'esgardast   cum la sout manïer,
Cum ces cordes tuchout,   cum les feseit trembler,
Asquantes feiz chanter,   asquantes organer,
De l'armonie del ciel   li poüst remembrer!
Sur tuz homes k'i sunt   fet cist a merveiller.
Quant ses notes ot fait   si la prent a munter
E tut par autres tuns   les cordes fait soner:
Mut se merveillent tuit   qu'il la sout si bailler.
E quant il out issi fait,   si cummence a noter
Le lai dunt or ains dis,   de Baltof, haut e cler,
Si cum sunt cil bretun   d'itiel fait costumier.
Apres en l'estrument   fet les cordes suner,
Tut issi cum en voiz   l'aveit dit tut premier:
Tut le lai lur ad fait,   n'i vout rien retailler.
E deus! cum li oianz   le porent dunc amer!

2830–45

3.

167. Gudmod vint dreit el champ   u sis sires l'atent,
Ki iert plaié al vis   del paien mortelment,
Encore le troeve vif   e devant li descent.
Or li ad demandé   e cel mut bonement:
'Sire, purrez garir?   cumment vus est kovent?'
Çoe li respunt Egfer: 'Amis, mut malement;
Mes d'içoe sui gari   quant ai le vengement,
Quant vus avez paëns   issi mis a turment,
Or murrai plus suëf: çoe m'est vis, mal ne sent.'

168. Gudmod descent a pié   par devant sun seignur.
Si l'ad mut cunforté   ducement par amur:
'Sire, purrez garir   d'iceste grant dolur?
Si joe vus perc si tost,   j'en serrai de peür.
Vostre perë en iert   mis en mut grant cremur,
Jamais jor nen iert lez,   tut perdra sa valur.
Ke fera vostre mere?   ja vivra en langor,
Sa beauté desirra,   chaungera sa colur
Quant si fiz erent mort,   li gentil doneür,
Ki plus ne tindrent plai   d'un destrier milsoudur
Ke d'un malvais runcin,   dunt l'en fait le labur.
Ki ert apres voz jorz   ja mais meinteneör
De gentilz chevaliers?   a ki ert lur retur?'
'Amis,' çoe dit Egfer,   'ke vaut ore vostre plur?
Ne vus aiderai mais   en cembel n'en estur,
Kar ui sui avenu   a mun deerein jor,
Mes merci vus en rende   li haut creator
Ke m'avez si vengé   del felun traïtur
Ki m'ad mort. De saunté   n'i ad mes nul retur.'

                                              3488–515

La *Folie Tristan d'Oxford*

1.

Li fol entre enz par le wiket.
Encuntre lui current li valet,
le escrïent cum hom fet lu:
'Vëez le fol! Hu, hu, hu, hu!'
Li valet e li esquïer
de buis le cuilent arocher.
Par la curt le vunt cunvaiant
li fol valet ki vunt swïant.
Il lur tresturne mult suvent:
est vus ki li gatte a talent!
Si nus l'asalt devers le destre,
il turne e fert devers senestre.
Vers l'us de la sale aprochat,
le pel el col dedenz entrat.

Senés s'en aparçout li rais
la u il sist al mestre dais.
Il dit: 'Ore vai un bon sergant!

Fetes le mai venir avant!'
Plusurs sailent, cuntre lui vunt,
en sa guisse salüét le unt,
puis si amenerent le fol
devant le rai, le pel el col.
Marke dit: 'Ben vengez, amis!
Dunt estes vus? Ke avés si quis?'
Li fols respunt: 'Ben vus dirrai
dunt sui e ke je si quis ai.
Ma mere fu une baleine,
en mer hantat cume sereine,
mes je ne sai u je nasqui.
Mult sai ben ki me nurri:
une grant tigre me aleitat
en une roche u ele me truvat;
ele me truvat suz un perun,
quidat ke fusse sun föun
si me nurri de sa mamele.
Mais une sor ai je mult bel':
cele vus durai, si volez,
pur Ysolt ki tant amez.'

                                        247–84

2.

Tristran vit ke ele l'eschivat;
huntus fu si se vergundat
si s'est un poi tret ensus
vers le parei dejuste le us.

Puis dit aukes de sun voleir:
'Certes, unkes ne quidai ço veir
de vus, franche raïne,
ne de Brengain, vostre meschine!
Allas! Ki tant ai vesquu
quant je cest de vus ai vëu
ke vus en desdein me tenez
e pur si vil ore me avez!
En ki me purreie mes fïer
quant Ysolt ne me deing' amer,
quant Ysolt a si vil me tient
ke ore de mai ne li suvent?
Ohi! Ysolt, ohi! amie,
hom ki ben aime tart ublie.
Mult valt funteine ki ben surt,

dunt li reuz est bon e ben curt,
e de l'ure ke ele secchist,
ke ewe n'i surt ne ewe ne ist,
si ne fet gueres a praiser:
ne fait amur quant voit boiser.'
685–708

Le *Lai d'Haveloc*

1.

       La nuit ke primes li parla
       Tel joie en ot e tant l'ama
       K'il s'endormi e oblia,
       Envers se jut ne se garda
       E la meschine s'en dormi,
       Sun braz jeta sur sun ami.
       Ço li vint en avisïun
       K'ele ert alée od sun barun
       Ultre la mer en un boscage.
       La troverent un urs salvage,
       Gopilz aveit en sa cumpaigne,
       Tote coverte la champaigne.
       Cuaran voilent asaillir
       Quant d'altre part virent venir
       Porz e senglers kil defendirent
       E des gopilz le garantirent.
       Quant li gopil furent vencu,
       Un des senglers par grant vertu
       Vers l'urs ala si l'envaï,
       Iluec l'oscist e l'abati.
       Li gopil, ki od lui se tindrent,
       Vers Cuaran ensemble vindrent,
       Devant lui se mistrent a terre,
       Semblant firent de merci quere,
       E Cuaran les fist lïer.
       Pus volt a la mer repeirer.
       Mes li arbre, ki el bois erent,
       De totes parz li enclinerent.
       La mer crut e li floz munta
       Desi k'a lui—grant pour a.
       Dous liuns vit de grant ferté
       Vers lui vindrent tut effreié,
       Les bestes del bois devorerent,

Celes k'en lur veie troverent.
Cuaran fu en grant effrei,
Tant pur s'amie cum pur sei,
Sur un halt arbre andui munterent
Pur les liuns k'il reduterent.
Mes li liun avant aloent,
Desuz l'arbre s'agenuilloent,
Semblant li feseient d'amur,
E le teneient a seignur.
Par tut le bois ot si grant cri
K'Argentille s'en esperi.
Mult ot del sunge grant pour
E pus ot plus de sun seignur
Pur la flambe k'ele choisi,
Ki de la buche li issi.
En sus se trest e si cria
Si durement ke l'esveilla.
'Sire,' fet ele, 'vus ardez.
Alas! tut estes alumez.'
                                    395–446

2

Savez ke li vallez cremeit
Pur les homes k'il ot oscis
Ke co fust l'us de cel païs
K'um le deust ainsi servir,
Baigner, laver e revestir
E pus juger pur le mesfet
E avant amener al plet.
N'est merveille s'il se dota.
Une grant hache recovra —
El paleis pendeit a un croc —
As dous poinz la tint Aveloc.
Vivement se voldra defendre
S'il le voilent juger a pendre.
Li sensechals le regarda,
Vers lui se trest si l'acolla.
'Sire,' fet il, 'n'aiez effrei,
Cele hache rendez a mei,
N'en aiez garde, jol vus di,
Ma lealté vus en afi.'
Cil li ad la hache rendue
E il la rad al croc pendue.
A une part seeir le fist,
Sa feme juste lui s'asist.

Sun chamberlenc ad apellé,
Le cor le rei ad demandé,
De sun tresor fet aporter
Le cor ke nuls ne poet soner.
Co dit cil k'il l'assaierunt
Saveir si soner le porunt.
Cil ki pora soner le cor
Il li dora sun anel d'or.
N'ot en la sale chevaler,
Sergant, vallet në esquier,
Ki a sa buche nel mesist:
Unques nuls d'els soner nel fist.

                    856–90

Amis e Amilun

1.

Tant parla, tant i demora,
Ke tot sun corage descovri
E diht ke pur l'amur de li
Morreit, s'il n'euht de li pite
E k'ele fuht de li amee;
Kar si de li l'amur n'aveit,
Ja mes, ce dyst, home n'amereit.
Amis, kant l'ad escoute,
Quidout ke ele fud devee;
De respondre se purpenseit,
Com celi ke talent n'aveit
Ke mespreiht vers son seignur.
Est vus, Florie par grant irrur
Le rampona e dist: 'Coment?
Este vus de ceo en marrement
Ke jeo vus ai done m'amur?
Ja en ma vie apres ceo jor
Ne serrai en mon quer haite
Si jeo ne seie de vus venge!
Certes, or sui jeo bien honie,
Kant nem deignez aver amie:
Tant gentils hommes m'unt preie,
E jeo les ai tuz refuse.
Certes, n'estes pas chevaler,
Recreant estes e lanier.
Un plai bien dur vus bastirai

E a mon piere le conterai,
Ke vers li estes de moi forfet,
E serrez a chivals detrait.
Dunc serrai de vus bien vengie!'

256–85

2

Le conte mult s'enmerveilloit;
D'Amilun donke li sovint
E diht: 'Bien sai, dont il vint:
A mon frere l'ad emble,
Ja l'averad cher achate!'
Outre la table saut atant,
A cel poure homme vint corant,
Si fort l'en ad feru del pie
Ke en la bowe est il verse.
Les chivalers vindrent ades,
Ke li siwerent de mout pres
E ke retenir le voleient;
Mes pur chose k'il unc feseient,
Nel porreient assuagier,
K'il nel voleit illucs tuer.
Kant batu l'out e defole,
Tant k'il meimes fu allassez,
Dunc commanda k'um le liast
E en sa prison le getast;
A Amilun dunc mandereit
E la verite enquerreit,
Si son hanap eust perdu,
E com cestui fust avenu.
Kant Amilun s'oit nomer,
De dolur pout son quer crever:
'Sire,' dist il, 'fei ke devez
A Amilun, ke tant amez,
Ne me fetes enprisoner,
Mes le chief fetes tost trencher;
Car certes ai jeo trop vesqui:
Trop bien ai la mort deservi!'
'Voire!' dist il, 'e vus l'avrez,
Vostre demande ne faudrez!'
Tantost s'espeie demanda,
Il meimes dist k'il tuera.
Kant l'espee li fu baille,
Par ire l'ad en haut leve,
E Amilun le col tendi,

Mes li vadlet avant sailli,
Owein, ke ne poeit suffrir
Ke sun seignur deust morir,
En haut cria: 'Merci, merci,
Pur cel deu, k'unkes ne menti
E k'en croiz suffri passion!
Kar c'est memes sire Amilun.
Remembrez vus, sire coens Amis,
Com le soliez amer jadis!
Grant bosoign l'ad ici chacie:
Si l'occiez, vus friez pecche!'

E quant le conte ceo oi,
Tot a terre estendu chei,
Bat le coupe, ses chevus tire,
Sa vie het, sa mort desire.
L'eure maudist, ke il fud ne,
Kant pecche l'out si encombre
Ke son frere desconuisseit,
Ke touz biens fet li aveit.
E Amis atant s'est drescie,
E Amilon ad acole;
Plus de cent fez li ad baise,
Tut si com il fud enboe.
              994–1055

Index of Personal and Place Names
in *The Romance of Horn*

The numbers given below refer to lines in the Anglo-Norman text.

INDEX OF PERSONAL AND PLACE NAMES IN *LA FOLIE TRISTAN D'OXFORD*

INDEX OF PERSONAL AND PLACE-NAMES IN THE *LAI D'HAVELOC*

INDEX OF PERSONAL AND PLACE NAMES
IN *AMIS AND AMILUN*